Praise for
The Fox in the Henhouse

"For the most part, people are unaware and uninformed about the tremendous impact privatization can have on our daily lives and its effect on our democracy. *The Fox in the Henhouse* provides an eye-opening look at this issue. It requires us to become more informed, to deliberate strategies, and to consider what action should be taken."

—Congressman Melvin L. Watt

"This book has some fancy long words in it, but it also has some great stories and songs. You'll learn what some of the long words really mean—the long words used by high and mighty people in this land of the free. Remember, Ben Franklin was 81 when the U.S. Constitution was finally put together 218 years ago. A woman asked him, 'Mr. Franklin, what kind of a government do we have now?' He replied, 'A republic. If you can keep it.'"

—Pete Seeger, Musician

". . . a wake-up call for all who care about our democracy and the assault on public services. While prisons-for-profit is the most alarming aspect of this trend, what the book reveals are the ideological underpinnings of privatization driven by the same greed that produced WorldCom and Enron."

—Larry Cohen, Executive Vice President,
Communications Workers of America (CWA)

"In this impassioned, intellectually exhilarating, and genre-bending book, philosopher Elizabeth Minnich and artist-activist Si Kahn deconstruct the arguments for privatization and identify the cultural traditions, institutions, and social forces that are at work to counter its destructive impact. Every socially concerned American is in their debt."

—Esther Kingston-Mann, author of *The Romance of Privatization* and *In Search of the True West*

". . . one of the most important political books of the year. . . . No one can talk authoritatively about the moral climate of America without taking into account the issues this book brings to light."

—Danny Goldberg, CEO, Air America Radio

"For the last thirty years, a critical part of the conservative assault on government has been their claim that the private sector always works better. It is time to unpack and dismantle each of the components of this myth. Kahn and Minnich have done just that on the issue of privatization. It is a book that every state legislator and editorial writer needs to read and absorb."

—Miles Rapoport, President, Demos, and former
Secretary of the State of Connecticut

"The complexities and dangers of privatization are splayed out in a manner that is reasonable, resonant, and worrisome. The argument for both the public and the independent (non-profit) sector is eloquent. The alarm has been sounded and 'we the people' have been warned. I pray we do not simply roll over and hit the snooze button!"

—Donna Red Wing, Senior Advisor, The Interfaith Alliance

"*The Fox in the Henhouse* is a fitting metaphor for privatization, the transfer to the corporation of government's functions to defend citizens and protect their welfare. . . . With style, stories, and wit, Kahn and Minnich show how to keep the fox out of henhouse America and offer an alternative vision of one nation, unprivatized. Best of all, they prove to be engaging and engaged leaders and role models."

—Peter D. Kinder, Founder and President, KLD Research
& Analytics, Inc., and coauthor of *Investing for Good*
and *The Social Investment Almanac*

"*The Fox in the Henhouse* centers itself in the struggle to right injustice, from Jim Crow and the convict lease system in the past century to the for-profit private prisons that help create the outrageous mass incarceration so many suffer from today. Minnich and Kahn are determined to bring these abominations to light and unrelenting in their insistence that justice for all must prevail."

—Van Jones, Founding Director, Ella Baker Center for Human Rights

"The relentless corporate campaign to turn public goods—such as education, criminal justice and public health—into private commodities is one of the great unreported scandals of our time. *The Fox in the Henhouse* exposes this threat to democracy and community in a narrative that is clear, convincing and, yes, inspiring. If you care about America's future, read this book."

—Jeff Faux, Founder, Economic Policy Institute

"... With incisive analysis and passionate protest, in prose and in song, Kahn and Minnich link ... the corporate assaults on our personal lives and our public institutions. ... An ever more greedy private sector has launched a full-scale assault against the democracy to which we owe all our hard-won protections, and they are winning. Unless we organize and fight back in ways and on issues that are outlined here, we will lose the America we cherish."
—Ruth Messinger, Executive Director, American Jewish World Service

"... Elizabeth Minnich and Si Kahn, living up to their reputations for committed and ethical commentary, have produced a well-researched and clearly presented case against the corporate takeover of the public sector, including higher education. Those of us who struggle to keep our institutions focused on the idea of public service, social responsibility, and a just world now have a companion reader to advise us as we do our work. ..."
—Joseph Jordan, Director, Sonja Haynes Stone Center for Black Culture and History, University of North Carolina at Chapel Hill

"... It is both naïve and dangerous to turn over essential functions of civic life to a private sector whose driving force and end goal is economic profit. The Fox in the Henhouse is a solemn, comprehensive, and well-documented warning that if we succumb to the growing movement to privatize ... core government functions, we put at risk both the moral values and the democratic process which lie at the heart of our national self-understanding."
—Vernon S. Broyles, III, Office of Corporate Witness, Presbyterian Church (U.S.A.)

"The Fox in the Henhouse could not have come at a better time. ... The threats of privatization go far beyond the future of Social Security or outsourcing jobs overseas ... [A] must-read if we're serious about achieving equal opportunity for all Americans—equal opportunity for education, employment opportunity, and home ownership."
—Wade Henderson, Executive Director, Leadership Conference on Civil Rights

"Kahn and Minnich ... present a frighteningly clear exploration of the corporate takeover of the public sphere that is rapidly eroding fundamental rights and freedoms ... and eviscerating democracy itself. Theirs, however, is a prophetic call to action, not despair. 'We the People' must reassert the primacy of the public good over private profit for the sake of us all and before it is too late."
—Sara M. Evans, author of Tidal Wave: How Women Changed America at Century's End, and Regents Professor of History, University of Minnesota

"This important book will equip Americans to stand up to the right-wing drive to put everything, even our criminal justice system, under the control of unaccountable corporations."
—Roger Hickey and Robert Borosage, Campaign for America's Future

"It is way past time that the destructive move toward privatization is exposed for how it can undermine democracy and economic opportunity. The 'ownership society' really means you are just on your own. Kahn and Minnich do us a great service, providing both the exposé and ways in which we can fight back."
—Heather Booth, President, Midwest Academy

"If you ask people who provide vital services to the public every day—educators, health care professionals, public safety workers—they'll tell you they want the resources, training, and staffing to provide a service they can be proud of. But if you ask global corporations, all they see when they look at public services is dollar signs. The promise of America is supposed to be that if you work hard and contribute to your community, you can expect reliable, fair, and accountable public services for your family. *The Fox in the Henhouse* explains how that promise is being taken away, and what it will take to restore it."
—Andy Stern, President, Service Employees International Union (SEIU)

". . . Our private lives are not safe without publicly protected, equal civil rights. *The Fox in the Henhouse* was obviously written to wake us up to the real threats of privatization. It's urgent: read it!"
—Congresswoman Tammy Baldwin

"In accessible and understandable language, this book deals with critical issues soberly and with the right touch of song, poetry, and history."
—David Cohen, cofounder, Advocacy Institute, and past President, Common Cause

"Elizabeth Minnich and Si Kahn are longtime crusaders for the common good, which is threatened by the growing substitution of marketplace values for public ones. This book sounds the alarm and gives us ways to answer it."
—Gara LaMarche, Vice President and Director of U.S. Programs, Open Society Institute

"*The Fox in the Henhouse* is clearly meant to remind us that corporate power and great concentrations of wealth threaten democracy. Neither our public rights nor our private and community lives are the driving causes of globalizing corporations. Profit, not democracy, is their bottom line. It is urgent that we keep all our public goods from being sold off to the private sector."
—Nan Grogan Orrock, Georgia State Representative, and President, Women Legislators' Lobby

"In this engaging and disturbing book, Kahn and Minnich raise and confront critical ethical and moral questions about the nature of privatized power and corporatized politics in our society today. If you care about the future of our public democracy, please read *The Fox in the Henhouse*."
—Rabbi David Saperstein, Director, Religious Action Center of Reform Judaism

"The aggressive movement to undermine public institutions and privatize public resources threatens the very possibility of democratic action on behalf of the public good. Kahn and Minnich document the breathtaking scope of privatization threats—to the values of community and accountability, and to the future of an America governed of, by, and for the people."
—Ralph G. Neas, President, People For the American Way Foundation

". . . We cannot afford to ignore this call to action from two lifelong activists, organizers, and moral leaders. While their stories are disturbing, they also offer us hope by showing how we can organize, build our power, and fight for the future of our democracy."
—Simon Greer, Executive Director and CEO, Jewish Fund for Justice

". . . Kahn and Minnich give us a lucid, readable, and compelling picture of privatization and consolidation of corporate influence that would make Tom Paine proud. With Kahn's trademark plainspoken language and Minnich's probing insight we are given tales, terminology, and tools to take back our democracy. *The Fox in the Henhouse* should be required reading for every patriotic American."
—John McCutcheon, President, Local 1000, American Federation of Musicians

". . . a desperately important book. With poetry, stories, and hard analysis, it demolishes the privatization myth that threatens everything decent and human in our society—and shows the way back to a way of life that is not for sale."
—Charles Derber, author of *People Before Profit* and *Hidden Power*

". . . a roadmap for activists as we fight for and win an America and a world where the values of a caring community, responsibility for each other, and a government that protects the public interest triumph over leaving everyone—no matter how vulnerable—on their own."
—Jeff Blum, Executive Director, USAction

"This book explores the most important issue that we face. The need to understand privatization eclipses even the nuclear power industry and the war, because the corporations' agenda underlies and explains what is otherwise senseless."
—Scott Ainslie, CEO, Cattailmusic.com

"Every working person in this country, whether they are represented by a union or wish they were, needs to read this book. It tells us not just what we have lost, but how and why we must organize, fight back, and win."
—John Sweeney, President, AFL-CIO

"Kahn and Minnich . . . draw the connections between predatory profits and the constant, relentless deterioration of the public good. Only through public service, as well as community building jobs, where dedication and sacrifice are matters of principle, not worn out and archaic beliefs, can democracy grow and survive. This book documents the struggle from the headlines and frontlines down to the grassroots, where every person counts, and every voice must be heard."
—Wade Rathke, Chief Organizer, ACORN

"Kahn and Minnich have written a highly readable treatment of a subject that is usually addressed with impenetrable academic prose or wonkish policy-speak. The result is both a compelling discussion of the consequences of unbridled corporate power and a thoughtful essay on the human condition."
—Philip Mattera, Director, Corporate Research Project of Good Jobs First, and author of *Inside U.S. Business*

". . . an immensely readable and profound book. It uncovers corporate privatization from the ground up and shows how it is being imposed from the top down. Read this book if you want to understand the problems and find out about joining together to reclaim common space."
—Neil Tudiver, Assistant Executive Director, Canadian Association of University Teachers, and author of *Universities for Sale: Resisting Corporate Control over Canadian Higher Education*

". . . a fun, soulful, and inspiring read. An essential guide for anyone concerned that corporate robber barons are looting our common wealth and public services."
—Chuck Collins, United for a Fair Economy and coauthor of *Economic Apartheid in America*

THE FOX IN THE HENHOUSE

"We are moving toward an oligarchic society where a relatively small handful of the rich decide, with their money, who will run, who will win, and how they will govern. The defenders of the present system will fight hard to hold on to their privilege, and they write the rules. Nothing less than our democracy is at stake."
BILL MOYERS

The Fox in the Henhouse

How Privatization Threatens Democracy

by Si Kahn and
Elizabeth Minnich

BK

BERRETT-KOEHLER PUBLISHERS, INC.
San Francisco
a BK Currents book

Berrett-Koehler Publishers, Inc.
235 Montgomery Street, Suite 650
San Francisco, CA 94104-2916
Tel: (415) 288-0260   Fax: (415) 362-2512   www.bkconnection.com

Ordering Information
Quantity sales. Special discounts are available on quantity purchases by nonprofit organ-
izations, corporations, associations, and others. For details, contact the "Special Sales
Department" at the Berrett-Koehler address above.
Individual sales. Berrett-Koehler publications are available through most bookstores. They
can also be ordered directly from Berrett-Koehler: Tel: (800) 929-2929; Fax: (802) 864-7626;
www.bkconnection.com
Orders for college textbook/course adoption use. Please contact Berrett-Koehler:
Tel: (800) 929-2929; Fax: (802) 864-7626.
Orders by U.S. trade bookstores and wholesalers. Please contact Publishers Group West,
1700 Fourth Street, Berkeley, CA 94710. Tel: (510) 528-1444; Fax (510) 528-3444.

Berrett-Koehler and the BK logo are registered trademarks of Berrett-Koehler Publishers,
Inc.

Printed in the United States of America
Berrett-Koehler books are printed on long-lasting acid-free paper. When it is available, we
choose paper that has been manufactured by environmentally responsible processes. These
may include using trees grown in sustainable forests, incorporating recycled paper, mini-
mizing chlorine in bleaching, or recycling the energy produced at the paper mill.

Library of Congress Cataloging-in-Publication Data
Kahn, Si
        The fox in the henhouse : how privatization threatens democracy / by Si Kahn
and Elizabeth Minnich
                p. cm.
        Includes bibliographical references and index.
        ISBN-10: 1-57675-337-9; ISBN-13: 978-1-57675-337-8
        1. Privatization—United States. 2. Democracy—United States. I. Minnich,
Elizabeth Kamarck. II. Title.
HD3888.K34 2005
338.973—dc22   2005047830

First Edition
10 09 08 07 06 05   10 9 8 7 6 5 4 3 2 1

Interior Design: Gopa&Ted2, Inc.   Proofreader: Lunaea Weatherstone
Copy Editor: Sandra Beris   Indexer: Medea Minnich
Production: Linda Jupiter, Jupiter Production

For our grandparents and parents, whose lives and work have inspired us and more others than they ever knew; and for the next generation, Simon P. Kahn, Jesse M. Kahn, David Fernandes, and Gabe Kahn. Each in his own original way, they help us to believe that the future we work for is worth it all.

Table of Contents

Foreword by Troy Duster

THE COVER STORY of *Fortune* magazine on June 13, 2005, shows a picture of Michael Douglas in his signature role as Gordon Gekko, the merciless mercenary from Wall Street. While the movie *Wall Street* was based on fictional characters, the *Fortune* story of late spring 2005 talks about very real persons. Their orientation to the world of finance is captured in the title of the story: "Is Greed Still Good? The Hedge Funds Sure Think So!" Inside, the article's author, Andy Serwer, reports: "I once asked a trader why so many top dogs keep going after they become billionaires. 'If I ever made $100 million, I'd call it quits,' I told him. 'That,' he said, 'is why you'll never make $100 million.'"

No more explicit celebration of human greed for its own sake can be satirized, caricatured, or even conjured by the fiercest critics of this way of thinking and being in the world. The narrow set of marketplace values that has come to dominate our political discourse grows out of a strategic vision that has been carefully nurtured and ceaselessly hawked over the last three decades. Which individuals are at the vanguard of this celebration of personal greed as the highest expression of the collective good? They are the nation's political leaders—or, at least, they are the Richelieus of this administration who whisper into the ears of the president and his cabinet. Karl Rove and Grover Norquist are the two most important among them, so it is worthwhile visiting what these well-positioned political thinkers say they are up to.

Karl Rove, universally acknowledged as the chief political strategist at the White House, has an intellectual hero that should shock those familiar with late-nineteenth-century U.S. history. It is Mark Hanna, the brains behind the disastrous presidency of William McKinley. Hanna was a key architect of a plan that orchestrated and celebrated a certain set of ideas—that the robber barons of that age could and should control the government, that private money could and should influence the choice and voting of members of the Congress, and that any regulatory mechanisms to check the power of the corporate titans should be vigorously opposed. That is Karl Rove's hero.

Grover Norquist is the other major brain behind the presidency of George W. Bush. He was dubbed the "Lenin of the Republican Party" by the *Wall Street Journal*. In an infamous interview with the Spanish newspaper *El Mundo* in early September 2004, this is what he said about the upcoming 2004 election:

Question: Who is going to win on November 2?

Norquist: It doesn't matter. We will control the House of Representatives, and probably the Senate. If Kerry wins, he will not be able to do anything that we do not want him to do. We will not give him money to spend. He will not be able to raise taxes. He will not steal our firearms. Even though we lose the White House, it will not be the end of the world.

Question: And if Bush wins?

Norquist: The Democratic Party will be forever doomed. If we take control of the legislature and the executive branch, we will reinforce our control of the judicial branch to direct it against the Democrats. We will bring about a modest limit of the ability of the people to initiate lawsuits against corporations, which will damage the lawyers who specialize in these cases, which is one of the props of the Democratic Party. We will accelerate the decline of the unions. We will cut funding to groups of public employees, like teachers, who are one of the great sources of Democratic votes. And we will begin to move the welfare state toward a private system, in pensions and health care.

Norquist's frank divulging of the Republican agenda is testimony to how free market values have achieved such legitimacy that such an all-out assault on the public sector hardly raises eyebrows. Milton Friedman, one of the premier intellectual defenders of free market fundamentalism, has argued that the interests of the majority are best realized by an economic system unfettered by government controls. Yet as Kahn and Minnich point out, even Friedman has conceded that there are things that "the market cannot do for itself, namely, to determine, arbitrate, and enforce the rules of the game." *The Fox in the Henhouse* is a remarkably readable and systematic account of why this is the case and how the greatest danger to democracy lies in the privatizing trend that corrodes and erodes the public sphere. The fox not only siphons off resources from the public domain, thereby undermining the common wealth, but is now a dominant player shaping public policy designed to further its own interests.

Kahn and Minnich cut through the rhetoric of privatization, exposing the fallacies of efficiency and expertise that putatively only "unregulated markets" can offer. They show how, on the contrary, big business has actually cost the public more in tax dollars, subsidies to big business, loss of vital public services, and a dramatic weakening and shrinking of those public spheres in which ordinary citizens have traditionally exercised their rights in a democracy.

The power of large corporations has become such that even partnerships between government and business are inevitably imbalanced, promoting trade-offs that further sacrifice the public welfare for corporate welfare. Kahn and Minnich raise critical questions about who is truly served by this privatization trend— then searingly probe the consequences for us as ordinary citizens, taxpayers, workers, and consumers. They dismantle and reexamine taken-for-granted assumptions among Wall Street ideologues, and remind us of what is meant by the public good—when the common wealth is rooted in a democratic tradition in which there is no single dominant player. With this book, they hope to mobilize citizens to restore and reinvigorate this democracy.

C. S. Lewis once said, "Man's control over nature is really best understood as some men's control over others, with nature as the instrument." This book has a parallel message: corporate control over private citizens is really best understood as corporate control over government, with privatization as its method. The privatizing foxes are the greatest danger to democracy, voraciously feeding off the public sector while deploying the rhetoric of what is best for the hens.

TROY DUSTER
Chancellor's Professor, University of California, Berkeley;
Director, Institute for the History of the Production
of Knowledge, New York University

Foreword by Amy Goodman

ON JULY 7, 2005, four bombs exploded in London, killing scores of morning commuters, injuring hundreds of others. It was the biggest attack on London since World War II. In the midst of the wall-to-wall media coverage in the United States, Brit Hume, managing editor of Fox News Channel, shared his personal reaction: "My first thought when I heard—just on a personal basis—when I heard there had been this attack, and I saw the futures this morning, which were really in the tank, I thought, 'Hmmm, time to buy.' Others may have thought that as well."

Maybe how to profit from the killing was the first thought in the Fox newsroom. But for many around the globe, the response was horror and . . . familiarity. That point was underscored when CNN's chief international correspondent Christiane Amanpour's live broadcast from the streets of London was interrupted by an uninvited guest, who shouted: "Tell the truth about why this war happened! Don't touch my bike! Tell the truth about what happened here! We're in Iraq. That's why. That's why it happened. . . . There were fifty killed in Iraq."

The interloper's last point is key: at the time of the London bombings, the same number of people were being killed daily in Iraq. Multiply this body count week after week and you begin to get a sense of the reality of Iraq. This is not to minimize in any way the London tragedy. The global media coverage of the London attacks should be the model for the coverage of the daily violence in Iraq: the naming of names of those lost, the interviews with their families, the stories of heroism of those who tried to save the lives of the victims.

Instead, the bloody images of invasion and occupation are covered up by what has become one of the Pentagon's most effective weapons: the U.S. media. The corporate newspapers and networks spread the lies of the "oilygarchy" in Washington—President George Bush, a failed oilman; Vice President Dick Cheney, former CEO of Halliburton, the largest oil services company in the world; Secretary of State Condoleezza Rice, longtime member of the Chevron board of directors (the company named an oil tanker after her); and Andrew Card, White House chief of staff, former chief lobbyist for General Motors.

This is the "ownership society" created by privatization, and the corporate media that serves it provides a crucial example of what Si Kahn and Elizabeth Minnich write about in *The Fox in the Henhouse: How Privatization Threatens Democracy*. The carefully choreographed marketing of the Iraq war could only have occurred with the massive media consolidation in for-profit corporate hands that now exists in the United States.

I call privatization and consolidation of the public airwaves the Clear Channeling of America. Clear Channel Communications went from owning one radio station in San Antonio, Texas, in 1972, to owning twelve hundred radio stations, thirty-six television stations, and 776,000 advertising displays in sixty-six countries. The company's explosive expansion occurred in the wake of the Telecommunications Act of 1996, a Clinton/Gore–sponsored giveaway of our airwaves that removed long-standing restrictions on how many stations a single company could own in one listening area. Privatizers hate barriers to monopoly.

Shortly after 9/11, filmmaker Michael Moore received a confidential memo forwarded to him by a radio station manager in Michigan. It came from Clear Channel, the radio conglomerate that owns that manager's station. "The company," Moore wrote, "has ordered its stations not to play a list of 150 songs during this 'national emergency.' The list, incredibly, includes 'Bridge Over Troubled Water,' 'Peace Train,' and John Lennon's 'Imagine.'"

Privatizing corporate moguls want ever more monopolizing control over what we hear, think, and talk about. While then–Secretary of State Colin Powell helped lead the war on Iraq, his son Michael Powell, chair of the Federal Communications Commission (FCC), tried to hand over the airwaves and newspapers to still fewer tycoons by further loosening restrictions on how many media outlets a single company could own. This would have enabled Rupert Murdoch, the man who brings us the flag-waving, Bush-friendly Fox News Channel, to control the airwaves of entire cities.

For the sake of the public good, for democracy, we must keep the media a public commons, open to the free and vibrant exchange of ideas. Pacifica Radio and the independent media outlets that the Pacifica model has inspired are part of a countertradition about which Kahn and Minnich also write.

Pacifica founder Lew Hill welcomed people to the airwaves of its first station, KPFA, on April 15, 1949. It sought funding from its listeners, not the corporations "that have nothing to tell and everything to sell, that are raising our children today," as journalism professor George Gerbner puts it. Today, the Pacifica network is part of a vigorous independent global media movement.

I see the media as a huge kitchen table stretching across the globe that we all sit around to discuss the most important issues of the day. If the wholesale privatization of our media and the public good as a whole is to be stopped, each of us must make a commitment to speak out, educate, and organize. In *The Fox in the Henhouse*, Elizabeth Minnich and Si Kahn set out critical food for thought for this public discourse. Your voice, too, is needed.

AMY GOODMAN
"Democracy Now!"

Preface:
Who We Are, Why We Care

Late in the evening as light fades away
In silence we gather together
Searching the faces of those who are here
For those who have left us forever

Where are the ones who caught flame in the night
Fired up by the heat of devotion
Measuring their lives by the light of the truth
They burned like a lamp on the ocean

Who will remember the words of the brave
That lifted us higher and higher
Who will remember the price that they paid
For lives lived too close to the fire

Hearts of the ones who inherit your lives
Will rest in the truth you have spoken
Memory will echo the trust that you kept
Like you, it will never be broken

> *What will I leave*
> *What will I leave*
> *What will I leave behind*
> *When I am gone*
> *Who'll carry on*
> *What will I leave behind*[1]

PHILOSOPHER AND ACTIVIST, educator and songwriter, we have been friends since we were fifteen and sixteen, have made a life together and raised three children—and yes, we're still friends and partners after writing a book together, a process that alternately fascinated and worried our friends and family, not to mention us.

This project started about ten years ago when we discovered that we had both come to the same recognition: Privatization—the corporate takeover of everything public—was a looming issue that must not be ignored if we wanted to serve the causes we had long made our work in the world.

Si started his life work as an activist and organizer in 1965 when he went south to join the Student Nonviolent Coordinating Committee, fondly referred to by its acronym SNCC (pronounced *snick*), the dynamic student wing of the southern civil rights movement. He has been organizing for political, social, and economic justice at the grassroots level ever since. For him, privatization is also a movement, but this time by the most powerful and privileged, whose goal is to undo all that civil rights, labor, feminists, and other progressive movements have struggled so hard to achieve. In this book, he tells several stories from his experiences and his work to show why he sees privatization this way, and what he has been doing about it.

Twenty-five years ago Si founded Grassroots Leadership,[2] a multiracial team of activists who do civil rights, labor, and community organizing throughout the South, building on and continuing the history of progressive southern movements for justice. When Si and his co-workers realized the threat of privatization, they reoriented their whole organization to take it on. As organizers do, they looked for a key issue on which to work. You may want to take on the whole world at once, but to win you have to pick your issue, find a focus that speaks powerfully to people who are ready to act.

Grassroots Leadership chose as their issue prison privatization, the takeover of public prisons, jails, and detention centers by newly established private prison corporations, because it so directly connects with the enduring issues of racial and class inequalities that still poison the quest for justice. We write about for-profit private prisons in this book as both a prime example and a worst case scenario of privatization.

Elizabeth realized that the threat of privatization had to be named, understood, and taken on while she was doing her work as a philosopher, feminist, and educator. Both the need for and resistance to the great movements of our times—movements for full and equal rights for all of us, for peace, to protect the environment—revealed, she believed, a massive failure of the dominant Western tradition that had to be set right if these movements were to change minds and hearts as well as actions and laws. It is hard to undo prejudices when trusted authorities like teachers and famous books keep them alive, and all too respectable.

So, for over thirty years Elizabeth had been working to change what is taught in colleges and universities to make it genuinely inclusive. Studying the real lives of women, of racial minorities, people with disabilities, poor people, sex/gender minorities, exploited ethnic groups, formerly colonized peoples in order to help educators change and enrich their courses, it dawned on her that all these people and groups had been privatized. They had all been shut out of public life, denied rights and responsibilities. They were owned, bought and sold, hired and fired, forced to labor as no more than resources for those who used them.

The great movements of our and earlier times had challenged all that. More and more people and groups had "come out," taken their rights, won some freedom—they had become effective public players. The powers that be wanted that stopped. How to stop it? Attack and discredit the movements, take over or at least limit the government that had responded by extending rights and powers to those so long denied them—and shut those troublesome people back into privatized lives.

From the Grassroots

Ten years ago, Elizabeth joined a small gathering of Grassroots Leadership staff, board members, and allies[3] that Si had convened to talk about privatization. Much of the understanding that informs this book came from such talk with people, as well as from the many books and studies we have read, and found invaluable, since then. It is among people who have been privatized, denied public rights and protections, that what privatization means for real lives, for all-too-real experiences, may be clearest.

Picture that group of women and men, African Americans and white people. We are sitting in a living room looking out on the street. It's the spring of 1995 in our hometown of Charlotte, North Carolina; the trees and flowers are in bloom everywhere. Elizabeth asked what *private*, *public*, and *privatization* meant. Here are some of the comments, taken from the narrative notes of that meeting.

"Given my people's history here in America, the only safe space is the public space. Without the government, people like me are up the creek without a paddle. The government recognizes this, and is moving toward the private place, where I am once again excluded."

"I see it as being more about control, having a handle to shut out. I think of privatization as a gate to come into the city. They can say who comes into that city and who can't come into that city. Just like this home, it becomes private when you can dictate who comes into that home, and public when you can't dictate. On the level of how we're going to run America, keeping out refugees, shutting our doors—because it's public, because America is under the system it's under, it has to allow a certain proportion to enter."

"The political right, when they use the term 'less government,' I deem that as saying to me that, with less government, it would remove accountability and responsibility from the ways in which the country has to respond to me."

"Public and private schools are a clear way of showing the difference. There have been cases where, because a school is public, they had to provide for handicapped, for everybody, race, class, and gender. In a private school, you had to pass a test, you had to go by their rules, they set the agenda. We have one private school that flies the Confederate flag—and there are some black kids that attend there."

"In my head, the distinction between public and private is a trust issue. In my adult life, I've felt more trust in the public, in government, as slow and imperfect as it is, to eventually come around and give me rights. The more people have input, the safer I've felt. I trusted federal more than state more than local. The closer to the individual, the less safe I felt. We lived in a town of four hundred in eastern North Carolina where the chief of police had a 'Wallace for President' bumper sticker [George Wallace ran successfully for governor of Alabama as a rabid segregationist]. He found a black man walking down the street with a goatee and pulled it out with a pliers."

"The only thing we have to wage a struggle is that this is a semblance of democracy. When slaves, women, black people had no rights, there was a struggle, but they had no rights, they were struggling in a vacuum. It's only in the public sphere that you can wage a struggle."

"That's the problem we have, when we allow people we don't have any negotiations with to make decisions for us. If they're of us, they have to include what we say. But if they're not of us, they don't have to."

So, you see, we didn't start our study of privatization as a dry and wonky matter of public policy. We didn't start by thinking about it as just a matter of government contracting out some of its work to for-profit corporations, or an increase in the number and kind of "partnerships" between the public and private sectors.

We don't focus on, although we mention briefly, the takeover of public functions and goods by religious institutions and other nonprofit organizations, which deserves a book of its own. We do discuss the separation of church and state as basic to preserving the integrity of both religion and democracy. These kinds of privatization can pose threats to democracy too. But the greatest danger comes from the privatizing corporations that make use of both religious and secular nonprofit organizations.

We didn't start with the idea that government is the enemy, either. We started with the on-the-ground realization that privatization was being put forward by people and powers that had consistently opposed struggles for equality, for a democracy that could be true to its own claimed ideals and a government that backed those ideals with real actions.

The Fox in the Henhouse begins, then, with our sense of alarm, of threat, to provisions for democracy that we and so many others have turned to in our work for justice, freedom, equality.

We have drawn on our own ways of thinking and expressing ourselves. Elizabeth, who became a philosopher because she so needed to try to understand the world whole, its injustices and cruelties as well as its truths and beauties, cannot help but ask moral as well as political questions, and she loves to analyze those of other people. Si, a civil rights, labor, and grassroots community organizer who also does his work through the songs he writes and sings, cannot keep from remembering his formative experiences in the southern civil rights movement, and never has been able to keep from singing. So there are also songs here. And there is passion, fed both by love of the dream of democracy and the people it should serve, and by fear-fueled anger at the powers that are threatening what we love.

"But don't you think *sometimes* privatization works and is a good solution? I mean, do you want us to believe it is *never* good? Isn't that too extreme?"

It is not extreme to believe that a democratic government must ensure that the people retain control of provisions and protections for the public good. The profit-hungry fox should not be set to guard our henhouse.

"Well, but it's really too late for all that. So much is already privatized; it can't be turned back. What we need to do is figure out how to make it work for the public good, don't you think?"

It is not too late. And there is work to be done.

Some Clarifications

In this book, we focus on the aspects of privatization that worry us most, those that involve the largest and most powerful corporations. We call them the *privatizing corporations*—although, for economy, we sometimes just say *corporations*.

So when we use the word "corporation" in this book, we're not referring to so-called mom-and-pop stores that have incorporated (that is, gone through the legal process of becoming corporations) for tax purposes. We're not thinking about nonprofit organizations that incorporate and seek tax-deductible status so that people who give them charitable contributions can deduct those donations from their taxes.

The corporate privatizers are also not the same as the progressive, socially committed entrepreneurs who are trying to make business a force for social responsibility. So when we talk about the threat of privatization to democracy, we are not referring to corporations that are trying to walk the walk of socially responsible practices, and not just talking the talk for public relations reasons.

We also distinguish between the privatizing corporations and the individuals who are their employees. Systems surpass individuals in power, so they are our focus. Nevertheless, each individual—each of us—is responsible for how we act in relation to the institutions and systems we are part of, that affect our lives and those of others. We are vastly different with regard to the freedom we have to make choices, the power we have and the risks we take if we act, but still we do make choices. To deny that is to deny that there is any freedom left.

We believe that we *are* free, and that we—all of us—are responsible for the choices we make.

Acknowledgments

Writing is supposed to be one of the loneliest professions. As co-authors, we have been much less alone than most. But the truth is that almost no one really writes a book alone, any more than someone alone develops a system of philosophic thought, or teaches a class, or organizes a textile mill or a campaign to abolish private prisons. We are who we are, we become who we become, we do what we do, in relation to other people.

The two of us, Elizabeth Minnich and Si Kahn, have been remarkably fortunate in the many friends and allies who have helped us think through and write about the issues in *The Fox in the Henhouse*. They have given us inspiration, guidance, information, critique.

We are particularly grateful to those who read and commented on various drafts of the manuscript: Dave Beckwith, Heather Booth, Stephanie Bosch, Nova Brown, David Cohen, Josh Dunson, Troy Duster, Alex Friedmann, Colin Greer, Chris Kromm, Gerda Lerner, Susan Seefelt Lesieutre, Ann Matranga, Phil Mattera, Stephen Nathan, Father Brian O'Donnell, Steve Piersanti, Amelie Ratliffe, Jack Schultzius, Joe Uehlein, Matt Witt, and Amy Yu.

For conversation, information, and inspiration over years, and for supporting both this project and our work on privatization in many different but always important ways, we thank Scott Ainslie, Harriet Barlow, Nancy Barnes, Margaret Blanchard, Paul Booth, Lisa Codispoti, Larry Cohen, Bruce Colburn, Chuck Collins, Nidia Cordova-Vasquez, Ernie Cortés, Torri Estrada, Betsy Fairbanks, Marjorie Fine, Helena Huang, William Johnston, Donna Katzin, Peter Kinder, Scott Klinger, Kerry Korpi, Larry Kressley, Jill Kriesky, Raquiba LaBrie, Gara LaMarche, Don Lane, Greg LeRoy, Lance Lindblom, Michael Lipsky, Josh Mailman, John McCutcheon, Joshua Miller, David Morris, Caryn McTeague Musil, Bob Nicklas, Andy Norman, Lincoln Pain, Donna Parsons, Jean Pogge, Miles Rapaport, Donna Red Wing, Rabbi David Saperstein, Carol Geary Schneider, Steve Snow, Alan Solomont,

Andy Stern, Brooks Sunkett, Urvashi Vaid, Steve Viederman, and Harmon Wray. We also thank Laurie Clement, University of Iowa Labor Center, for the great phrase, "Public, it's ours; private, it's theirs."

We want to sound a particular note of appreciation for our researcher, Debbie Alicen, for tracking down so many references with speed and grace; please contact her at debgaryalicen@alumni. unc.edu if you're looking for professional research assistance.

Si Kahn wishes to acknowledge and thank the members of the Grassroots Leadership staff and board who are, except for Elizabeth Minnich, his closest working and thinking companions: current board members Sara Evans, Anton Gunn, Leslie Hill, James Melvin Holloway, Dan Horowitz de Garcia, Joseph Jordan, Mafruza Khan, Easter Maynard, Chandra Talpade Mohanty, Mitty Owens, Mary Priniski, June Rostan, Pete Tepley, and Tawana Wilson-Allen; past board members Stewart Acuff, James Andrews, Yolanda Banks, Julia Beatty, Katie Foster, Jereanne King, Brad Lander, Carolyn Mints, Lenora Bush Reese, Kate Rhee, and Robert West; current staff members Alfreda Barringer, Marianna Dorta, Bob Libal, Kamau Marcharia, Pam Pompey, Tonyia Rawls, Les Schmidt, Silky Shah, Naomi Swinton, and Gail Tyree; and past staff members and consultants Marilyn Baird, Xochitl Bervera, Margaret Chambers, Michael Cooper, Ali Fischer, Michelle Handler, Cathy Howell, May Va Lor, Michelle McNeil, Stella Nkomo, Tema Okun, Kevin Pranis, Megan Quattlebaum, Pam Rogers, Marguerite D. Rosenthal, James Williams, and Precious Williams.

Si also wishes to thank Josh Dunson at Real People's Music, his representative for concerts and lectures for almost thirty years, as well as his close friend and adviser (www.realpeoples music.com).

Working with the extraordinary team at Berrett-Koehler has been part of the pleasure of writing this book. Publisher Steve Piersanti is not only a wise and enthusiastic editor. He has created a socially responsible corporation that reminds us of what is possible. We would particularly like to acknowledge the members of the B-K team with whom we have worked most closely: Sandra Beris,

Michael Crowley, Molly Fenn, Kristen Frantz, Linda Jupiter, Ken Lupoff, Dianne Platner, Jeevan Sivasubramaniam, Jenny Williams, and Rick Wilson.

Finally, we wish to acknowledge how much the women's movement, the labor movement, and the southern civil rights movement have meant to us. If we were to list all of the wonderful people we met in and through these movements, who have helped give meaning and direction to our lives, it would take a book of its own. We remember and thank them for their work in this world.

Charlotte, North Carolina	Si Kahn
July 2005	Elizabeth Minnich

Introduction:
A Road Map

PRIVATIZATION MAY NOT SOUND to you like a threat to democracy. It's not a familiar word, and it isn't often used by people who are struggling for democracy, for freedom, for justice. People haven't usually stood up at rallies and made rousing speeches either for or against privatization.

That's because *privatization* is the kind of word economists and policymakers use. What it means in practice, its purposes and effects both internationally and in the United States, are hidden by such dry language.

We believe not only that privatization is a threat but that it is *the* threat to democratic commitments to the public good. It is a threat to the commonwealth that sustains us all, in the United States and around the globe.

We believe that we fail at our peril to see that the possibility of public provision for our basic human needs, safety and security, our basic human rights, and our high aspirations to liberty, justice, and equality are under concerted attack by corporate privatizers and the officials who do their bidding from inside government. We believe that efficiency in pursuit of profits is not at all the same thing as effectiveness in providing for and protecting democratic values and dreams of liberty, equality, and a decent life for all.

So, then, what is privatization?

Privatization as an agenda for the United States has been described by the *Wall Street Journal*, a generally reliable reflector of corporate thinking, as the "effort to bring the power of private markets to bear on traditional government benefits and services."[1]

Translation: Privatization is letting corporations take over and run for profit what the public sector has traditionally done.

Privatization as an international agenda is usually described this way: "The privatization of state-controlled industries in countries that have had heavily nationalized economies is a necessary step in their progress toward a free market economy."[2]

Translation: Same as above, only more so.

Neither definition makes privatization sound like a threat to democracy. There's that powerful word *free*, the familiar, friendly-sounding *market*, the use of *private* that evokes the Western value of *private property*. Such language makes privatization sound like an economic policy that is true to the democratic way, the road everyone should take to become free and prosperous like the United States.

But this familiar rhetoric hides too many realities. For one, it slides right over the awkward fact that income and wealth inequalities and poverty rates in the United States are actually among the most dramatic of the more developed nations.[3] On a larger scale, it avoids entirely the important questions of just how free today's capitalist economies actually are, whether they really do serve political freedom, and whether it is always progress to join, or be forced to participate, in them.

These dry, common definitions just don't reveal that "privatization of state-controlled industries" means selling off a nation's natural resources—oil, coal, natural gas—for exploitation by privatizing corporations. In many countries, state development of natural resources has provided the funds for essential social services, such as public health care and education. The usual definitions of privatization don't make it clear that those services will not be provided or financed by the corporations that under privatization schemes pocket profits from the natural resources and national industries they take over. Financially weakened national governments cannot afford to provide for the common good. Nor can they stand up to and regulate the huge corporations that are strengthened by privatization, or the individuals who become enormously wealthy by buying and reselling that nation's resources.

The usual descriptions of privatization don't say outright that the possibilities of such enormous new sources of wealth readily lead to national and international corruption and lawlessness. But, by the record, they do. For one example, in a scenario that is strikingly reminiscent of recent corporate scandals in America, the U.S.–based "accounting firm of PricewaterhouseCoopers repeatedly signed off on the books of the Russian central bank, even though auditors knew that the bank was sending its dollars abroad to FIMACO, a shell company in the British Channel Islands with no employees."[4]

Did this make any difference to the Bush administration? You can bet your stock options it didn't. In fact, U.S. officials turned to one of the powerful overseers of Russia's privatization, Boris Yeltsin's Minister of Finance Yegor Gaidar, to advise them as they set out to privatize Iraq's state-owned resources and enterprises. Gaidar has been called an economic shock therapist for his advocacy of "instantaneous, nonevolutionary transformations, wholly indifferent to the human cost of the policies they imposed."[5]

The transfer of wealth and power from nations and their governments to private corporations is not a benign step on the road to freedom and progress. It doesn't just happen as economies and governments and people "mature," as societies "evolve" and "develop." Privatization is an agenda more or less forcibly imposed on governments that lessens their powers in favor of the largest corporations.

It needs to be said: This transfer of wealth and power from governments to corporations, and from the commonwealth of the people to the global oligarchy against which commentator Bill Moyers warns us, is precisely *not* the triumph and spread of democracy. It is the triumph and spread of dominance by privatizing corporations for which national boundaries, along with provisions and protections for the people, are nothing but barriers to their pursuit of profits.

A Definition of Privatization

Here, then, is our take on privatization:

> *Privatization is a concerted, purposeful effort by national, multinational, and supranational corporations (and the individuals, families, officeholders, nonprofit and religious organizations they have made or promise to make enormously wealthy) to undercut, limit, shrink, or outright take over any government and any part of the public sector that (1) stands in the way of corporate pursuit of ever larger profits, and (2) could be run for profit.*

We think this definition of privatization is more accurate and truthful than the less explicit, common, dry ones. Insofar as we are right—and of course you will judge that for yourself—there are realities of privatization about which we believe it is wrong to remain neutral and disengaged.

Descriptions, explanations, and analyses have political and moral significance just as actions do. For example, it is true that the United States has growing inequalities of wealth, that the gap between the rich and the poor has been widening—but it is not right. And if it is not right, then we are called to act—and the sooner, the better. There is always time to stand up for what is right, but it's obviously a lot harder when the systems have become fully entrenched.

So we write about privatization—what it is, what it means, what it does, what it threatens—to sound a political and moral alarm, not just to prove our point by piling up facts and logical arguments. We do that too, and are beyond grateful to all the superb scholars, analysts, and reporters whose books and papers now fill virtually every corner of our house (well, our offices were already bursting, but we used to have a dining room table we could actually eat at, and we really didn't have books under as well as on top of chairs). But we also write in many senses from where and how we live, as who we are, because we got caught up in this research for personal, political, and moral reasons, not just as disinterested researchers.

This is why we use examples from our own and other people's experiences as well as facts and figures, and tell stories as well as make arguments. Because Si has spent the last six years working to abolish for-profit private prisons, jails, and detention centers, and because private prisons are such a prime example of privatization run completely amok, we devote a special section to them as a worst-case scenario.

We also came to some conclusions, some generalizations that emerged to make sense of all those stories and facts and experiences and analyses. Here they are:

✦ Selling essential protections and provisions for the public good to private profit-making corporations puts democracy itself on the auction block.

✦ Privatization is not just an economic policy. It doesn't just happen as economies and nations develop. It is a purposeful, planned, global, political agenda with dramatic consequences for the lives of people in the United States and around the globe.

✦ The difference between the values and goals of privatizers and the values and goals of those committed to the public good is *the* great divide of our times.

✦ Privatization empowers and enriches supranational corporations that have no loyalty or obligations to any nation, any state, any community.

✦ The free market is not the same as political freedom. Privatization shrinks the spheres in which citizens have political rights that are legally established, protected, and backed up by good governments.

✦ The free market is neither free nor equal economically. Corporations dominate it and set the rules in their favor.

✦ Privatization has already cut deeply into the public control and accountability of crucial functions such as the military, public security, health and safety, education, and the environment.

+ Privatization radically increases the gap between the wealthy and powerful and the poor and vulnerable. The rising tide that supposedly lifts all boats actually sends many more to the bottom. Wealth does not trickle down; it sucks ever more up from the many on the bottom to the few on the top.

+ Corporate privatizers seek to control governments, to break unions, and to discredit and disempower people's movements that challenge their dominance.

+ The takeover of public goods by for-profit corporations does not lead to greater efficiency and does not save public money.

+ Governments that hand their proper functions over to corporations to run become dependent on those corporations. Corporations then become ever more powerful; conflicts of interest and corruption increase.

+ It is essential that corporate economic power be checked and balanced by governments, just as it is essential that governmental power be checked and balanced by independent legislative, judicial, and executive branches that are held accountable to constitutions and to constituencies.

+ Rule by corporate powers is just as threatening and frightening as rule by any other power that is not balanced and checked. Economic, political, military, and religious monopolies are all enemies of democracy.

+ Democracy requires the healthy functioning of separate spheres, of many differing centers of power, of multiple interest groups. By limiting, checking, and balancing powers, democracies increase their responsiveness, their openness, to the differing people on whose consent their legitimacy rests.

These are our conclusions—the way privatization looks from the grassroots, from the ground up.

The view looking up from the grassroots is very different from the view looking down from above. The lawn mower looks quite different to the grass than it does to those who want the grass cut down, cut back, kept neatly under control. No single blade of grass matters to the owner of a private lawn. Wildflowers and independent plants sprung from roots and seeds that spread themselves and grow where the soil and sunlight and rainfall are right for them are nothing but weeds to those who have a plan for their fenced-in garden, their one-crop field. Fine; we've pulled out some plants to protect others; sometimes we even mow our lawn. And we live on foods grown by other people who have to tend and protect them.

But what will happen when the whole earth—land, plants, animals, water, and all that lies under them, and the air, the sky above them—is owned by just a few who can and will use those gifts, and use them up, without giving a thought to anything but profits? What would it *really* mean for the whole world to become "an ownership society?" That's the question that kept us going—that, and why on earth so many people find that proclaimed goal of President George W. Bush to be appealing rather than appalling.

More Conversations

Back when we started talking about privatization, some people just looked at us blankly. We would then say something like this: "You know, it's when things are turned over to private corporations—like federal lands turned over to be logged, and public health care, public education, public prisons, or welfare being run for profit rather than by the public sector."

A pretty basic, not at all analytical statement, but most people would nod when we mentioned at least one of these examples. "It's not just one thing," we'd say. "It's lots of things. It's happening more and more."

Some people knew entirely too much about the privatizers. If they were union members whose jobs had been targeted for privatization, they knew about the dangers firsthand, and most had fought back. Some had lost their jobs to the privatizers; others had succeeded in fighting off the attempt and were now waiting for the privatizers to come back and try again. If they were students at one of the more than five hundred U.S. colleges and universities where the foodservice contractor was Sodexho-Marriott, they probably knew that the French-based parent corporation, Sodexho Alliance, was the major shareholder in the largest for-profit private prison corporation in the world, Corrections Corporation of America (CCA). On many of these campuses, students participated in a hard-hitting international campaign led by Grassroots Leadership and the Prison Moratorium Project that eventually forced Sodexho to divest its shareholding and withdraw its representative from the CCA board of directors.

But through all of this, what too often went unasked was why there were growing numbers of stories about privatization, growing numbers of "dots" on the economic map. Even when some political analysts and activists became concerned about privatization, they tended to focus on a tree or two rather than the whole forest—or on the forest but not on what had made it grow so fast and spread so far into the public sector, into our government itself.

Studies of privatization in particular areas—say, privatization of welfare services—are invaluable. They go into depth as no overview, no attempt to analyze the whole picture, possibly can. Our bibliography at the back of this volume contains many of these excellent studies, and we hope you will make use of it.

Still, it seemed evident that we needed to keep talking, listening, watching, analyzing, following the breaking news, because the privatizing that had been going on for some time was both escalating and reaching a critical level. The changes to our democratic republic were threatening to become much harder to stop, much harder to reverse.

A Privatization Field Guide

Because privatization is both a national and an international agenda, and because that agenda is at work in so many different areas, it can look quite different at differing times and in differing situations. Nevertheless, when you have been immersed in tracking it down for a while, some identifying markers begin to emerge. Privatizers have a consistent rhetoric, a view of history, a political and economic position, and an ethics that is used to justify all of these.

Rhetoric

The spokespeople for privatization frequently use the following words, and pairs of opposed concepts, to shape discussion and debate.

Dependence versus independence. Privatizers use the term *dependence* to characterize people's relation to government. In particular, they call people "dependent on the state," or even "wards of the state," when there are programs designed to serve and protect the public good, such as Social Security retirement and disability benefits, unemployment insurance, and welfare. Privatizers contrast this supposed dependence with what they call *independence,* by which they mean having no rights to public goods and services and no governmental programs through which people spread among themselves the kinds of risks that can impoverish us, such as long-term illness, disability in a society that does not provide essential access, job loss, and economic depression.

Self-reliance. Privatizers praise *self-reliance* as an opposite to *dependence.* Conservative spokesperson Dinesh D'Souza summed up what this means in practice by saying, "When I'm old I'll rely on my family or rely on charity, or frankly, if I don't have the resources, that's my own tough luck."[6] So, in this view, reliance on family, charity, and luck is self-reliance; paying your own hard-earned money into Social Security is dependence.

Freedom. In the language of privatization, we do not need and should not want government, laws, or rights to establish and protect our freedom. In his second inaugural address, in 2005, President George W. Bush told us that he would work to give us freedom *from* government. In the rest of the world, though, he said he would work for freedom of government. Since we have a democratic form of government, and he said it is his cause to spread democracy around the world, this is a bit odd. But it makes sense to privatizers, because for them freedom does not refer to political freedom.

The free market. When privatizers use the term *freedom*, whether from or of governments, they are actually referring to the free market. And by free market they mean capitalism with no constraints—no antimonopoly laws, no environment-protecting regulations, no unions, no consumer organizations, no constraints on entering other countries' markets, no health and safety regulations at home or abroad. Most of all, "free" capitalist markets means no strong governments that can check and balance the global power of profit-seeking corporations. It doesn't mean that you and I are free from the dominance of those corporations.

The welfare state versus the free market. The "welfare state" is scorned as a too-powerful, centralized government that turns citizens into its dependents. Conservatives attack it as a failed system that destroys the potential for economic productivity and growth that has made America the richest and most powerful nation on earth. The "free market" is presented as the engine of that wealth and power, and history's obvious winner. Corporations are thereby cast as the fittest economic beasts around, the ones that outcompeted all others and came out on top.

To hear the privatizers talk, you'd think that in a welfare state everyone is on welfare. But this is not what the term means. In a true welfare state—unlike in the free market—government is responsible for the welfare of all the people who live there. It's the job of government, for example, to guarantee that everyone has access to schools, that no one dies for lack of affordable health care. These provisions do not make us dependent. Quite the contrary.

Competition. Since winning economically is taken to justify everything, to prove historical superiority, economic competition is touted as the engine of all progress and achievement. Cooperation, care for others, collective provisions for safety nets that protect people from complete devastation are seen as brakes on progress rather than a way of making progress more equitable and just.

Failed systems, social problems. Privatizers characterize the public governmental programs of the welfare state that they want to run for profit as failed systems. They present themselves as the only ones capable of running effective systems. Does that sound reasonable? Think again. It wasn't corporations that defeated the Nazis in World War II. That was done by a highly effective, well-organized, dynamically led *public* military, commonly known as the armed forces of the United States of America, together with our allies.

Efficiency and the bottom line. Privatizers link the efficiency they claim as their defining virtue with their responsibility to the bottom line. People, agencies, and programs working for the public good rather than profits are dismissed as inefficient at best—whether or not the evidence supports that judgment.

Thus, privatizers equate democracy with unregulated capitalism and equate freedom with corporate license. They equate having rights to government services with being dependent, and having no recourse except charity with independence. They glorify efficiency in all-out competition to make the biggest profits, and claim it as their prime virtue. They want us to believe that no-holds-barred competition is the only reliable motivation for those who deliver—or in their case, sell—public services.

A VIEW OF HISTORY

Obviously, a view of history shapes this rhetoric. This view takes history to be the story of humankind's economic progress toward achieving global capitalism. Since global capitalism is equated with democracy, the history is often told as if it were political rather than economic—the story of a triumphal march toward democracy and freedom. Thus spreading democracy (that is, the free market) around the globe can be cast as a crusade justified by history. And what about states that are already democracies? In the terms of this historical story, those states need to be shrunk, limited, beaten back so that the free market can continue taking over everything.

POLITICS AND ECONOMICS

In the worldview of privatization, politics is only important or real in relation to the engine of progress and power: economics. States, nations, governments—these are either irrelevant or outdated barriers that must be made to yield to and do no more than serve the imperatives of the serious players, the supranational corporations competing for global markets.

ETHICS

The ethics of privatizers are those of "winners." If you are rich, if you are powerful, they assure you that you have done good by doing well, an evaluation that is applied to the United States as a whole as well as to individuals. By this ethic, the United States is to be judged a morally good nation because it is the richest and most powerful. This coldly competitive creed is also often accompanied by invocations of Christian values that are used to suggest that it is part of God's plan to divide the world into the saved and the damned, the good and the evil. God is then said to be on the side of the saved, good, economic "winners" in their struggle against the evil, damned, economic "losers."

Tactics for Privatizer Wannabes

All this serves the cause—which is to say, the profits—of privatizers very well. But there is also a practical set of steps that they tend to follow, and it is helpful to be familiar with those. We end our introduction, then, with a shorthand guide to the strategies and tactics we have seen over and over as we have studied and organized against privatization.

As you read our book, it will be useful to keep in mind these preparation and action steps that we have distilled. Sometimes, as in the case study of the effort to privatize Social Security (see chapter 12), virtually every step we list is quite evident. Sometimes, when we tell much less of the story of a particular effort to privatize, fewer will show. Nevertheless, whether visible or invisible, the steps the privatizers take in the process of preparing the public (that's us) to go along with their takeover of public goods and services follow these lines. There need not, we should say, be a conspiracy for there to be an evident pattern that shows when you stand back and look at a whole picture as it unfolds over time.

PREPARATION

First, you must undercut the people's respect for and trust in their government and public employees, in unions, in movements for social justice. Do so whenever and however you can. Glorify corporate executives.

Say that the public goods, services, protections that you want to run for your own profit are "failed systems," "broken," "in crisis." Repeat as often, as unambiguously, as publicly as possible. You want people to believe that providing adequate funding, effective job training, and more incentives for public employees to do better work can't possibly succeed. You want people to believe that the reason provisions and protections for the public good have problems, any problems at all, is that they are run by *public* agencies, staffed by *public* employees.

ACTION

Meanwhile, go ahead and break those public systems. (Yes, it's an interesting way to be a truth-teller—sort of like telling someone who's about to hire a mover, "Don't hire her; she hasn't got a single truck that runs," and then having your friend the mechanic mess up all of that mover's trucks when she brings them in for their required annual inspection. "After-the-fact truth," we might call it.)

Many of the public services you want to take over were underfunded to begin with, so cut their funds even more and they'll barely be able to function. That will make the public get really mad at the people and agencies that provide those services, which is what you want. At the same time, impose costly new requirements on them. Support private, for-profit alternatives, offer to reward people for using these services, and of course, do not make up for the funds this takes away from the public services. In short, starve them of money while requiring more of them.

Offer yourself as the only possible savior of what you have broken. Stress your efficiency and accountability. If problems in your own operation are exposed, put more money into image advertising.

If people still refuse to believe that the public system you want to run for profit needs rescuing by you, tell them that your takeover plan is really just a responsible effort to find a better way to run public services. Float possible fix-it plans that privatize at least some aspects of the system. Back off (but only temporarily) from anything that arouses significant opposition.

Continue creating facts on the ground by privatizing whatever you can. The more little bits you get, the easier it will become to get bigger bits later.

This is the way privatizing is presented to us, and over time, continues and spreads, hiding the reality that the interests of We the People really are not served when provisions for the public good become profit centers for corporations.

Privatizers have a bottom line. Everything they do has as its goal to strengthen that bottom line, to increase profits.

We believe that the majority of people in the United States have a bottom line too. It's called *democracy*. They believe in it, they care about it, they work for it, they try to keep it strong. In this book, *The Fox in the Henhouse*, we show how privatization threatens democracy.

PUBLIC, IT'S OURS;
PRIVATE, IT'S THEIRS

In Memoriam

On December 22, 2004, in Mosul, Iraq, insurgents blew up the U.S. troops' chow hall, killing 22 people. There were the usual efforts to figure out whether it was done by rockets or suicide bombers.

On December 23, Gwen Ifill interviewed retired Lieutenant Colonel Ralph Peters on *The NewsHour with Jim Lehrer*. He raised another question. "What mystified me when I heard about this, Gwen, was that even in maneuvers back in the Cold War days when you were just playing war, you got your chow and you dispersed, because in war, if an artillery shell hit you, you wanted them to kill two or three or four soldiers at most, not forty or fifty or sixty or eighty.

"And what's clearly happened in Iraq is we violated our own rules about troop dispersion in wartime. I suspect it has to do with outsourcing. This mess hall, mess facility, chow hall was run by a contractor.

"Instead of security, what we saw was convenience and efficiency. But it just baffled me that this base and this chow hall, specifically . . . had been attacked before with rocket fire, with mortars. And we were still crowding these troops, not even staggering the schedules. It just astonished me."[1]

Outsourced, contracted out: Feeding the troops had been *privatized*.

CHAPTER 1

"Morning in America"?

We hold these Truths to be self-evident, that all Men are created equal, that they are endowed by their Creator with certain unalienable Rights, that among these are Life, Liberty and the Pursuit of Happiness. —That to secure these Rights, Governments are instituted among Men, deriving their just Powers from the Consent of the Governed, —That whenever any Form of Government becomes destructive of these Ends, it is the Right of the People to alter or to abolish it, and to institute new Government, laying its Foundation on such Principles, and organizing its Powers in such Form, as to them shall seem most likely to effect their Safety and Happiness.
—DECLARATION OF INDEPENDENCE

We, The People of the United States, in Order to form a more perfect Union, establish Justice, insure domestic Tranquility, provide for the common defense, promote the general Welfare, and secure the Blessings of Liberty to ourselves and our Posterity, do ordain and establish this Constitution for the United States of America.
—PREAMBLE TO THE CONSTITUTION OF THE UNITED STATES

Lockheed Martin doesn't run the United States. But it does help run a breathtakingly big part of it. . . . "The fox isn't guarding the henhouse. He lives there."
—"LOCKHEED AND THE FUTURE OF WAFARE," New York Times

DECISIONS MADE by rich and powerful privatizing corporations increasingly affect virtually all aspects of our lives. The leaders of these corporations, many of whom live in the United States and enjoy its benefits, do not seem to care about what is happening to our country, to any country, because their loyalty is first and foremost to making profits for the multinational corporation they serve.

That's not what democracy is or should be about. We want rights that give us the ability to act, the dignity of individual people who matter, a kind of citizenship that lets us know that we can and do have an impact on important decisions that affect us and future generations.

Private Decision Makers, Public Goods

The wonderful woods behind your parents' house where you explored and played and hid, where you saw deer and raccoons and the occasional snake when you managed to sit quietly and watch— gone now, sold to developers who have become rich selling ugly, identical houses. You had no say: No one asks, no one cares, there seems to be nothing you can do.

You had a decent job that gave you enough to take care of your family, to send your children to school. Suddenly it is gone, and there you are with a pink slip, no paycheck, no insurance, little chance of a new job at age fifty-five, after thirty years with one corporation that just shut its doors and moved to where the labor is cheaper. You had no say: No one asks, no one cares, there seems to be nothing you can do.

A war is declared by the president of the United States. He gives reasons that keep changing as each previous one turns out not to be true. Men and women are sent off to fight, to kill, to die, even as it becomes evident that both war and postwar plans are too narrow, too unrealistic. Mistakes are made—and denied—so no one is held accountable. "Holding firm" rather than doing better is presented as a virtue.

Huge sums of our money—income from our tax dollars—are spent. Yet the men and women on the front lines of a war that did not end with the invasion, that did not end when the president declared it over, men and women who risk their lives in support of a decision they did not make, don't even have the equipment that might save their lives.

None of this money comes to your community either. You don't have enough firefighters or police anymore. They were in the National Guard and reserve units that were called up to fight and have not come back home. If they are not among those who have died or been seriously wounded, still they are not coming home. Their terms are being extended, extended, extended.

There is no public money to hire replacements for the good people who did the public work in your community. Families and friends and communities of our military volunteers hold local fundraising events to raise money to buy them the equipment they so desperately need. In San Jose, California, they plan an auction to raise money for body armor for their daughters and sons, sisters and brothers, wives and husbands, fathers and mothers, neighbors and friends.[1] Meanwhile, our tax dollars go to privatizing military corporations that are, as always, pursuing their profits. Some corporations begin to pull their employees out of the war zone because it is too dangerous. No one pulls our volunteer troops out. They stay there, underequipped, under stress, under fire.

Who is in power in our democracy? Who and what are they really serving?

So many times in history
We've watched them march away
Some cry out for victory
Some just stand and pray
For this father's daughter
For this mother's son
What will happen to the rest of us
When the war is done

Some are quick to honor
Some are quick to blame
Few can face the truth
That this all happens in our name
Before the first shot's fired
Our battle has begun
> *What will happen to the rest of us*
> *When the war is done*

Those who fight the battles
Are not those who make the laws
But bravery is still bravery
Even in an unjust cause
From the hand that signs the order
To the hand that fires the gun
> *What will happen to the rest of us*
> *When the war is done*

Some lie solitary
Beneath a hero's stone
Some return to loved ones
But will always be alone
Something sacred will be lost
Even when the war is won
> *What will happen to the rest of us*
> *When the war is done*

> *What will happen to the rest of us*
> *When the war is over*
> *What will happen to the rest of us*
> *When the war is done*[2]

This is a war fought by brave and loyal volunteers: the young man next door our sister coached in Little League, the young woman our brother taught in high school. But this invasion is also carried out by private contractors—that is to say, as it rarely ever is, by mercenaries, people paid to do the work of the U.S. military. Not for honor, not for country, not for freedom—for profit.

Privatizing the U.S. Military

Few people know that the U.S. military is now among the most privatized in the world. During the revolutionary war some of the sharpest anger and harshest criticism was reserved not for the soldiers of the British Crown but for the Hessians, the mercenaries, the soldiers-for-hire King George III paid to keep his colonists from breaking away from England. This time, the mercenaries are on the U.S. payroll, and this time they are working for supranational private military corporations that will send their employees anywhere, anytime, to fight on any side—ours, or theirs.[3]

There is even a new video game that invites people to have fun—and spend money—playing at being mercenaries, people who fight and kill and blow things up for pay, not for patriotism. It is not irrelevant, when killing for money becomes not only acceptable but glorified, that the torture exposed at the U.S.–run Abu Ghraib prison in Iraq also involved "contract workers"—mercenaries, privatized military personnel. In Afghanistan, a former Army Ranger working then as an independent contractor—a mercenary, a private soldier—beat to death a man named Abdul Wali who had surrendered for questioning.[4]

Privatizing the military means that corporations that supply the fighters are also hired to do intelligence work, training, and much of the work of protecting and reconstructing communities that the massive use of violence has just destroyed. In all these roles, their employees—contractors—are far better paid than our military volunteers, our National Guard members and reservists, our friends and children and partners and spouses who are even assigned to protect the mercenaries and other private contractors, a dangerous job not described in the exciting recruiting talks they were given.

Meanwhile, because of all this but also because of tax cuts that benefit mostly the rich, the federal government is in debt—to a staggering, record-breaking extent (as of February 2005, $427 trillion and growing). Because of reductions in federal aid to education, your child's school has its budget cut again, a setup for the privatizers. A private corporation, in the business to make a profit, is hired to come in and run the schools. Your sister, a dedicated third grade teacher for fifteen years, loses her job, as does everyone else working in the school, from the custodian to the principal. They are all encouraged to apply to get their old jobs back with the new corporation, and your sister, a fine teacher by everyone's account, is rehired.

But now her salary is lower, her benefits sliced. Her job security is gone, along with the union that once represented her. She is told what to do by someone hired by the corporation; it doesn't matter that she is one of those teachers who gets letters from former students telling her "Thank you; I will never forget. . . . " She lasts for a year, and the day after her students finish third grade, she turns in her letter of resignation. "If I can't teach with integrity," she writes, "I can't teach." A new teacher with no real experience is hired in her place, for even less money. More seasoned teachers leave: good for the bottom line.

The schools do not get better, and the states' budgets shrink still further because of cuts in federal aid to education that do not stop the federal debt from ballooning further out of control. Our shared public life and goods, the future that depends on them, the future we want for our children, are on a starvation diet, while corporate privatizers' profits get fatter. Further cuts are proposed in student financial aid. George W. Bush even proposes, in the opening days of his second term, to tax that financial aid. He spends trillions, he cuts the taxes of the richest people, and then he tries to get it back by nickel-and-diming our most crucial public goods, the ones for which nickels and dimes matter most.

Ensuring That Public Systems Fail

In those instances where our public systems are failing, they aren't failing all on their own. They are being starved and broken. The fat corporations circle around. They tell us how much more efficient and effective they are, that if they ran those systems, all would be well.

But when you call a corporation to complain that your new telephone doesn't work, it seems as if there are no people left in the world. Recorded directions take you through a maze that gets you nowhere. It hurts the bottom line to pay people to deal with people. The corporations have decided to automate, to do it electronically. Where there is still need for real live people to be sitting there, so that there's an unsynthesized human voice on the phone, they sometimes hire people in Third World countries, or in prison, to do it. No workers come cheaper than those who have no choices.

It's true. For a while, when you called Trans World Airlines to make a reservation, the person on the other end of the line was a prisoner behind bars at a California state prison.

"Good morning, TWA. May I help you?

"Yes, please. I'm thinking of flying to California for a vacation."

"I'm sure you'll have a wonderful time. Would you like to purchase a ticket?"

"Oh, I'm glad you think California is a good choice. We've never been. Do you live there?"

"Yes, sir, you might say that."

"Well, what do you think? Would our family enjoy a vacation there?"

"I can honestly say I haven't seriously planned on leaving in the ten years I've been here."

"That sounds wonderful. Let me have four round-trip tickets."

"Very good. Thank you so much. Now, please give me your name and credit card number, and I'll see what I can do for you."

How do we have our say in the decisions that affect so very many of us when our government is influenced most by the big bucks that buy elections and influence policy? How do we protect our rights when everything we count on from government is privatized—outsourced, contracted out, leased, sold off to the highest (or the lowest, the only, or the most powerful) bidder? What happens to our freedom of conscience and of religion when we must go to religious establishments that get government funds to deliver our public services?

Most of all, what will we do when our government has been so weakened that it cannot work for us, and cannot stand up against the privatizing corporations that now take the whole world as their domain? *What do we do when government itself is privatized?*

Whatever happened to the idea that We the People are the public, to the faith that government was established to serve the public good, not to help increase the profits of privatizing corporations and their control over our lives?

CHAPTER 2

Drawing the Line:
Private Versus Public Goods

Over the last century and a half, the corporation has sought and gained rights to exploit most of the world's natural resources and almost all areas of human endeavor.

—JOEL BAKAN, *The Corporation*

R EAD THAT AGAIN. Corporations have gotten the *rights* to seek profit from "the world's natural resources" and from "almost all areas of human endeavor."[1] This means that our governments have participated: Rights are legal provisions and protections. They are created and enforced by governments—by executive, legislative, judiciary, and law-enforcement provisions.

Did We the People mean for this to happen? Did we vote to give corporations the same rights as individual human beings, in addition to the special protections that only they have? Did we hold a referendum on giving them the protections of the Bill of Rights? Did we agree in a town meeting that the constitutional right to freedom of speech meant corporations could use the money they get from us, as consumers and taxpayers, to influence elections?

The Expansion of Private Control

We could have seen it coming; many did. Almost seventy-five years ago, Adolf Berle and Gardiner Means wrote this in their book, *The Modern Corporation and Private Property:*

> Following the lead of the railroads, in the last part of the nineteenth century and the early years of the twentieth, one aspect of economic life after another has come under corporate sway. . . . In field after field, the corporation has entered, grown, and become wholly or partially dominant. . . . On the basis of its development in the past we may look forward to a time when practically all economic activity will be carried on under the corporate form.[2]

That was 1932. In 2004, Joel Bakan writes, "That time has come. Today practically all economic activity *is* carried out under the corporate form."

But then he says, "One large barrier remains, however, to corporations being in control of everything: the public sphere." That one large barrier is now directly, purposefully, and increasingly effectively under ideological, political, and financial attack.

The main tool of attack: privatization. Public life and public goods, established, enabled, and protected by public laws, regulations, and government, are being undercut, sold off, handed over to profit-seekers. We want to say, "The British are coming, the British are coming"—but of course it isn't the British this time. And the truly weird thing is that quite so many people have let themselves be convinced that it is our government that is attacking us, while the corporations that are tearing off hunks of public life and the public good in their privatization feeding frenzy are portrayed as the good guys.

"Lockheed Martin doesn't run the United States. But it does help run a breathtakingly big part of it." So began the article on the front page of the business section of the Sunday *New York Times* that we quoted earlier (right under the Declaration of Independence and the Constitution). The report quotes Danielle Brian: "The fox isn't guarding the henhouse. He lives there."[3]

Brian, who is with the Project on Government Oversight, isn't just referring to Lockheed Martin's role as the nation's largest military contractor. This corporation does much more than negotiate lucrative contracts to make the expensive and profitable tools of contemporary warfare and welfare. It has "built a formidable infor-mation-technology empire that now stretches from the Pentagon to the post office. It sorts your mail and totals your taxes. It cuts Social Security checks and counts the United States census. It runs space flights and monitors air traffic." And to do all this, it "writes more computer code than Microsoft."[4]

Lockheed Martin—and by no means this corporation alone—is no longer just making a nice profit from, let us remember, our tax dollars. The defense of our country, as well as the other social serv-ices for which this corporation has contracts, is now dependent on "the contractor's expertise," as the New York Times put it. This means that Lockheed Martin is now involved in making, not just benefiting from, public policy and the decisions of our government. Robert J. Stevens, the CEO of Lockheed Martin, said, apparently with no sense at all that this should not be happening, that his com-pany is involved in "thinking through the policy dimensions of national security as well as technological dimensions."[5]

Most of us would call this a conflict of interest: You don't let the people who will profit from a policy set the policy. You don't set the fox to guard the chickens, and you surely don't let it move right in.

The New York Times goes on to report that "nearly 80 percent of [Lockheed Martin's] revenue comes from the United States gov-ernment." And of the remaining 20 percent, most "comes from for-eign military sales, many financed with tax dollars." Oh, great: So you and I are also financing the military strength of other coun-tries. Remember, many of the weapons now being used against our military personnel in Iraq and Afghanistan were originally pur-chased from U.S.–based corporations.

These huge sales of arms and technology profit "private" corpo-rations, doing "private" business, and making huge profits from our tax dollars. At the same time, these corporations are increasingly involved in the thinking and planning that shape our country's policy decisions, which have the potential to lead to ever larger profits—and to a more dangerous world, armed to the teeth with weapons bought from corporations competing to sell ever more arms to whatever country or group anywhere in the world that can get the money to buy them. More wars result—including wars claimed to be needed to control "rogue" countries that bought their deadly arms, or the materials they need for them, on that (more or less legal and open) lucrative international market.

Arms, of course, can be turned against former supporters as well as the enemies they were originally purchased to combat. The U.S. supported Saddam Hussein's Iraq in its war against Iran, you should remember—and guess to whom both of these countries are causing a great deal of trouble now? In the Falkland War between Great Britain and Argentina, the British lost two ships and thirty-four sailors to French-built Exocet missiles the Argentineans had purchased. Did the French corporations that manufactured those missiles send notes to the families of the British sailors who died, expressing their condolences and saying they hoped this wouldn't cause stress in the relationship of two countries that, while rivals for centuries, were now partners in the European Economic Union?

Our military personnel in Iraq must feel a special appreciation to Lockheed Martin for helping arm the forces that are now attacking them.

Lockheed Martin, grown rich on war and its instruments, is also making a profit from the welfare system here at home.

Just in case your reaction to the preceding statement is, "Say what?" here's one bit of what has happened as Lockheed Martin has gone into the welfare business. In 1996, when George W. Bush was governor of Texas, he approved a deal under which that company would take over the entire state welfare system. Lockheed Martin was to pay Texas some astronomical figure, in effect to "purchase" the system, and then get annual payments for running it. There was tremendous organized opposition, not least from all the social workers and other public employees who were going to lose their jobs, to be replaced by minimum-wage workers. In the end, President Clinton vetoed the total takeover, which he was able to do only because there was federal money involved.[6] However, privatizing corporations are still able to pick off parts of the system and are indeed running them for profit.

If the idea of the world's largest military contractor making sure that the children of unemployed single parents get fed doesn't strike you as, say, odd, ask yourself if it's right for a corporation of this size to be making a killer profit from services for which our tax dollars pay? Yes, you may say, as long as that company delivers the services at the same or less cost than government employees would.

But how is that possible, when government is run not to make a profit but, rather, to do various specific jobs and tasks? Of course, it's theoretically possible if the costs of the contracting corporation are held down, below those of a governmental agency. The corporation has to cut its own costs (but not necessarily those to the government) in order to make a profit. Profit, after all, *means* the money above and beyond what it costs to make a product or deliver a service. So the corporation needs to give its employees significantly less in wages and benefits than they would receive if they worked in the public sector—or it needs to pay them the same but increase their "productivity" (read, force them to work harder and faster, whatever that does to them or the people they serve). This also means the corporation needs to fight off unions that would demand that their employees have reasonable work hours and workloads, be paid fairly, have health insurance for themselves and their families, earn pensions, be paid overtime when they work it (even though a certain amount of overtime pay is required by law, it often takes pressure from a union to make sure employees receive it), and otherwise be treated and compensated fairly.

Privatizing thus leads not to decreasing but to increasing the number of lousy jobs in this wealthy, supposedly equality-loving country in which "all people have a chance" to "better themselves."

And remember that for-profit corporations are increasingly involved, as Lockheed Martin is, in making governmental decisions, and that it is our tax money that is to provide profits above and beyond reasonable expenses for those companies.

It does seem ironic, and troubling, does it not?

That's what privatization looks like in the real world. It is not a private matter; it does not mean that we'll have less bother from government, more freedom to enjoy a real private life. It means

that ever more of our private lives will be affected, shaped, dominated by the corporate powers that are no longer stopped by public laws and protections. *If we do not have a public life protected by a
democratic government, we also do not have protections for our private
lives.* Ask "illegal aliens" who are not citizens, who have no right
to the protection of our government, if they have rich and full and
free private lives. Ask women who know what it was like before
women had public rights and the vote what it was like when getting married meant belonging to the male "head of the household."
Ask African Americans what it was like when they were denied
the right to vote, to a free and equal public life protected by law.
Ask sexual minorities what it is like to be denied the protection of
law for private life and loves.

That's what privatization looks like in the real world.

That such reports worry us greatly does not mean that we—or
the *New York Times* business section—are paranoid alarmists. As
someone said, "Just because you're paranoid doesn't mean they
aren't out to get you." Or, from the great African-American baseball pitcher Satchel Paige, "Don't look back—something might be
gaining on you."

Having Lockheed Martin run a large part of our government is
not what the creators of our democratic republic had in mind when
they oh, so carefully crafted the remarkable system of checks and
balances that has well served the people of the United States
through so many other dramatic changes.

As alert as the founders were to differing kinds of overconcen-
trated power, of tyranny, they did not adequately guard against the
kind of concentrated economic power today exercised by privatizing corporations with budgets that exceed those of most whole
countries. They did, though, see and rebel against such power in
their times. James Madison wrote, "There is an evil which ought
to be guarded against. . . . The power of all corporations ought to
be limited. . . . The growing wealth acquired by them never fails to
be a source of abuse."[7] But that warning was not well heeded; it did
not adequately make its way into the U.S. Constitution or system
of governance.

Today, just under half (49 percent) of the one hundred largest economic units in the world are countries. The other 51 percent are corporations.[8]

A note to the nations of the world: "Don't look back—some corporation *is* gaining on you."

Meanwhile, governments are ever more dependent on these corporate giants to do what needs to be done, which makes the corporations ever more able to insist on more privatization as the price of their cooperation.

If the corporation you turn any of these systems over to does a terrible job, or demands much more money than originally agreed on when the contract comes up for renewal, what do you do? The corporation (unlike public safety employees) can, in effect, go on strike. It can unilaterally decide to stop doing the work it agreed to tomorrow. We cannot pick it up the day after; they have us over a barrel.

Schools, prisons, welfare, Social Security, water and sewer systems, buses, trains, subways, highways, waterways, sanitation systems are not exactly the kinds of things you start up overnight. And you can't just build an army, navy, air force, or coast guard when you suddenly discover you need one. Look at the experience in Iraq, where what is arguably one of the best-trained militaries in the world couldn't get the new Iraqi armed forces it desperately wanted and needed off the ground fast enough. So it turned to more "contractors," more employees of those terrifying private military firms that will train people to fight for anyone who will pay them—and like all corporations, can decide to switch sides should there be more profits to be made that way.

To get their first contract, they may come in with what's called a lowball bid, doing the classic bait and switch. In other words, they deliberately bid not only less than it was costing us to do those things through our government with public employees, but less than they know it will cost them to do the job. Once they get the contract, or the first time the contract comes up for renewal, they announce they can't do it for that price. If that's the case now, imagine how much worse it will be if corporations have a monopoly and the public sector no longer has the capacity.

The corporations already have power over our economic life through their bought influence inside government, because they can threaten to leave a community that has become dependent on them, and because, being the major economic players, their troubles really can become ours in all sorts of ways. It's not "What's good for General Motors is good for the USA." It's "What's bad for General Motors is bad for the USA." Or, "When GM sneezes, the economy gets pneumonia."

Take Wal-Mart, the largest retail corporation in the United States. You may assume that it is so successful because its prices are so low that other stores can't compete. That's not all there is to it. Have you also heard that the profits it makes despite such low prices are subsidized by your tax dollars?

"Wal-Mart stores collected well over $1 billion in state and local government subsidies during its decades-long expansion from a regional discount chain to the world's largest retailer," reports the national monitoring organization Good Jobs First.[9] *Subsidies* is an innocent-sounding word for taking our public tax dollars and moving them into the pockets of a profit-making private corporation. This is not unusual in today's corporation-dominated world, nor is it illegal. But it surely does raise questions about what is private anymore.

Here is what the *New York Times* had to say about this corporate boondoggle:

> A survey by Georgia officials found that more than 10,000 children of Wal-Mart employees were in the state's health program for children at an annual cost of nearly $10 million to taxpayers. A North Carolina hospital found that 31 percent of 1,900 patients who described themselves as Wal-Mart employees were on Medicaid, while an additional 16 percent had no insurance at all. And backers of a measure that will be on California's ballot tomorrow, which would force big employers like Wal-Mart to either provide affordable health insurance to their workers or pay into a state insurance pool, say Wal-Mart employees without

company insurance are costing California's state health
care programs an estimated $32 million a year.[10]

Did you hear that? Some $32 million a year is going to subsidize
Wal-Mart's profits by holding down its costs. And that's just the
cost in one state out of fifty.

The article continues: "Although Wal-Mart officials flatly deny
it, some Wal-Mart employees say they are encouraged to turn to
public health care assistance. When Wal-Mart hired Samantha
Caizza, a single mother of three, as a cashier at its Chehalis, Washington, store, she says she was told by a personnel manager 'to get
ahold of the state' for coverage for her children."

Samantha Caizza isn't ripping off the taxpayers: Wal-Mart is.
She's just doing a job and trying to take care of her children. But
she and other single mothers are all too often the ones blamed by
outraged taxpayers and conservatives, who like to rail against
being forced to support "people who won't take care of their own."
How about the world's largest retail store? Shouldn't it take care of
its own employees, rather than expect the rest of us to pick up the
tab for their health care through our taxes?

Again: Are Wal-Mart's profits really private if public money
underwrites them, makes them possible? Is it a private matter when
public health care benefits are exploited by Wal-Mart so that the
children of the corporation's founder—who are ranked numbers
four, five, six, seven, and eight on the *Forbes* list of the four hundred richest Americans, at $18 billion each—don't have to lose a
bit of profit to pay them?

And all this time you thought you were saving money with those
cheaper prices. When you add on the tax bite you didn't vote for,
they're not quite so low.

A Free Ride for Wal-Mart?

Think of it like this. You, like most people in this country, probably think you're paying way too much in taxes. But public taxation
is taking money from all of us to support public services such as

Medicaid. Wal-Mart, by forcing you to subsidize the Medicaid costs of its employees, is really increasing the taxes you pay and decreasing its own costs. Although you may not immediately think of this as a form of privatization, that's exactly what's going on. Your taxes are being funneled through the public structure of government into the private pockets of a corporation.

Did you vote to have your tax dollars support corporations that exploit their employees, drive down wages in their competitors' shops, cause small local businesses to fail and close, add to traffic messes, and otherwise drastically change the communities into which they choose to move, often over the opposition of the people of those communities? Reminds us of one of the bumper sticker slogans that appeared after a horrifying oil spill: "We don't care. We don't have to. We're Exxon." And we worry about nonresponsiveness from the public sector?

Do you want to be supporting corporations that drive employers who care about the people who work for them out of business? "Socially, we're engaged in a race to the bottom," said one such beleaguered employer, Craig Cole, the chief executive of Brown & Cole Stores. Brown & Cole is a supermarket chain that employs some two thousand workers in Washington and adjoining states. Its stores reportedly provide health insurance coverage for about 95 percent of their employees.

"'Do we want to allow competition based on exploitation of the workforce?' Mr. Cole asked."[11] That's a political and a moral question, and it is coming from people inside as well as outside the corporate world.

Some corporate leaders believe that exploiting workers in order to lower costs, and so increase profits, is right and fair—or just the way free competition goes in the free market. They wouldn't call it exploiting their employees, of course; more likely they'd call it paying people market value for their work. They oppose unions because they "force companies to raise wages when they can't afford it," and are pleased that today a lower percentage of the U.S. workforce is unionized than in the past. This is a mindset that takes making the maximum possible profit to be justification for anything that is a means to that one end.

Let's say it was really legal to do *anything* that was considered necessary to make the highest profit possible. What do you think some corporations might do? Sell untested drugs without consumer warnings? Manufacture cars that are "unsafe at any speed"? Hire children to work twelve to fourteen hours a day for below-minimum wages? Send people into conditions from dangerous to deadly in workplaces ranging from coal mines to chemical plants? Cut down every tree a company can sell or use for its products? Strip-mine every mountain that has coal? Pollute streams, rivers, and lakes with heavy metals and PCBs?

> Strip every mountain
> Poison every stream
> Pollute every rainbow
> 'Til you find your dream

Corporations have done every one of these things in the past. In many countries around the world—and more often than you might think in the United States—they're still doing them. Do you think the only reason they don't do them as openly anymore in the United States is because of the goodness of their corporate hearts? No, they don't do them because our government has passed laws limiting these appalling practices or making them illegal, because public law enforcement employees do still sometimes track down violators, and because public courts do still sometimes hold them accountable.

Making the highest profit possible is not, or surely should not be, the most important purpose of our lives. But whatever the other purposes and values held by corporate officers—and there is no doubt that some of them as individuals hold values and wish to serve purposes that any of us would admire—it is their ability to bring in a profit that marks their success or their failure in their own sphere.

Imagine picking up the *Wall Street Journal* and finding a front-page article with this headline: "CEO Cuts Profits to Increase Employee Pay."

> The board of directors of the Wall Street investment bank Swenson, Swenson, Swenson and Swenson today gave a standing ovation to CEO Walter Swenson for achieving his long-held goal of cutting corporate profits by 50 percent in order to double the pay of the firm's janitors, secretaries, and receptionists.
>
> "For God's sake," said Swenson, "all of us corporate officers are already filthy rich. We can buy and sell most small countries. Why do we need more? What are we going to do, purchase Tuvalu? I mean, what's another $100 million in your checking account compared to the chance to make sure hundreds of our employees' children will go to college?"
>
> News of the achievement pushed the investment bank's stock (NYSE: SWE) up 8¾ points to close at 52¼.

Here's what the *Wall Street Journal* actually thinks: "If there is any place where Wal-Mart's labor costs find support, it is Wall Street, where Costco has taken a drubbing from analysts who say its labor costs are too high. Costco's pretax profit margin is only 2.7 percent of revenue, less than half Wal-Mart's margin of 5.5 percent."[12] There we have it: Costco has a lower pretax profit margin than Wal-Mart, so Wal-Mart is rewarded not only by pocketing those larger profits but on Wall Street and by major investors who otherwise have nothing at all to do with the company.

This was not an aberration. Wall Street analysts have also spoken threateningly to Timken, a corporation that makes roller bearings. What was Wall Street's problem? Timken had made a commitment to produce high-quality goods no matter what and to stay in its hometown, which it had done for one hundred years. Wrong decision, apparently. It is quite literally not your business,

Wall Street firmly reminded the good folks at Timken, to do anything other than make profits and grow.

Wal-Mart, we should say, continues to deny what reporters keep telling us. And they are working hard to undo all this bad press. Not by providing their employees with health care insurance, mind you—they say they can't afford to do that. No, they're spending millions of dollars on a public relations campaign to clean up their image. That, apparently, they can afford. The corporation and public relations folks get richer; workers and their children, and taxpayers, lose again. Actually, we've now seen several of the Wal-Mart public relations ads. Very touching.

There are other issues here that are your concern, and all of ours. "The larger issue of whether companies can and should absorb the soaring cost of health care is a national issue," said Susan Chambers, the executive vice president who oversees benefits at Wal-Mart. "You can't solve it for the 1.2 million associates if you can't solve it for the country."[13] "Associates" is what Wal-Mart calls its employees. Maybe it makes them feel better about being on Medicaid instead of a decent corporation-paid health insurance plan.

Chambers is quite clear: Wal-Mart is so big, and it employs so many people, that how it does its business necessarily becomes a national issue. We can probably count on it that she and other corporate officers do not mean by its being a national issue that the federal government should step in and tell Wal-Mart to provide its employees with health insurance instead of passing those costs on to the taxpaying public. However, we can absolutely count on their wanting to step in to tell the federal government what it should do.

There's been a lot of talk about the importance of communities and states and the federal government being "business-friendly" (notice that it is put this way, rather than "corporation-friendly," which probably wouldn't go far as a popular slogan). "Business bashing"—raising questions, investigating, publicizing, acting against business interests, criticizing corporations that destroy the environment—is in disfavor these days. But did you know how often being business-friendly means providing welfare payments for corporations, while welfare payments are slashed for under-trained, undereducated single parents—and profits from administering welfare are made by other corporations?

Which is the real scandal? Paying an unemployed parent a below-minimum monthly supplement so she or he can keep the children fed, clothed, and housed? Or paying gigantic Lockheed Martin (or another corporation that bought its most profitable subsidiary—hard to keep up with these guys and their lucrative deals) billions of dollars in corporate welfare?

The interests and purposes of some corporations may be good purposes in their arenas, and the people who serve those purposes may be good people, individuals with compassion and commitments to justice and equality. Still, however you cut it, corporations' purposes are not the same purposes as those of government, as those of the public sector, as those of We the People. Where they differ, it is their own purposes and interests that the corporations will pursue. As privatization increases, that means that government is rife with conflicts of interest.

President George W. Bush's number two, Dick Cheney, could not have remained head of Halliburton while vice president because, as a public employee (really hard to call Dick Cheney a "public servant," which is what he should be while we're paying his salary), he is not allowed to. Conflict of interest: We know the interest of the public and the interest of corporations are not the same, and the line between them must be held firm. But Halliburton has in fact made out like a bandit from the war against Iraq, which is what happens when privatizing corporations are awarded major contracts without full, fair, open competitive bidding.[14]

At one point, Halliburton was caught red-handed billing the government for $74 million in gasoline that it hadn't delivered. This was in Iraq, mind you, in the middle of a war. Imagine if two *Wall Street Journal* reporters were in an armored vehicle that ran out of gas in the middle of a firefight:

"Wow, I think we just ran out of gas."

"Well, of course. You didn't really think Halliburton would deliver all the gas the government contracted for at the low price they bid, did you? Not with a third-quarter earnings statement coming up."

"All of the other military vehicles are leaving us."

"You can't really expect a major corporation like Halliburton to jump just because some petty government bureaucrat waves the contract they signed at them. They have a responsibility to the bottom line, to their shareholders. If these directors don't manage for a profit, they could be sued for malfeasance. You know that as well as I do."

"I think we're the only Americans left here."

"You have to understand the imperatives of the marketplace. Quite possibly the price of gasoline took a sudden jump on the spot market and Halliburton was flexible enough to divert these shipments somewhere else."

"Is that a shoulder-fired missile that guy is aiming at us?"

CHAPTER 3

Introducing Corporations

The concentration of income at the top is a key reason that the United States, for all its economic achievements, has more poverty and lower life expectancy than any other major advanced nation. Above all, the growing concentration of wealth has reshaped our political system.[1]

—PAUL KRUGMAN, "FOR RICHER," *New York Times Magazine*

PEOPLE ALL OVER the United States share a sense of uneasiness, of loss of control over their jobs, lives, communities. Most of them do not connect this sense to the role of corporations in their lives. They have not realized just how purposeful and far-reaching the corporate takeover already is, or how much privatization is driving it.

But they feel the impact. Many of us feel the anxiety, frustration, anger, and outright fear that comes from being vulnerable to decisions made by people who do not know us or give a damn about us except as consumers or votes to be won using the same slick advertising they use to make us think we're nothing if we don't go out and buy what they're selling. We know we do not exist for these corporations as individuals, as communities. We do not exist for them as people who have lost our jobs and run out of unemployment, who have lost our pensions, our benefits, our unions that fought for rights and protections not just for their members, but for everyone. Corporate leaders and their political supporters talk about our problems, but it seems always to be their own power and profits they're really out for.

A Few Facts About Corporations

Here are some interesting facts about corporations that most folks don't know.

Corporations are treated legally as if they were individual human beings. The word *corporation* itself comes from the Latin word *corpus,* meaning *body.* In 1886, the United States Supreme Court ruled, in *Santa Clara v. Southern Pacific Railroad,* that corporations are considered to be "persons" covered by the U.S. Constitution—including the Bill of Rights.[2] So, for example, corporations are considered to have freedom of speech. This is interpreted to mean that corporations can say what they want in paid advertisements, and can make campaign contributions to people running for office. People say that money talks. In this case, they couldn't be more right. Corporations can't vote, but still they are empowered to participate in affecting the political process as if they were just one of us.

As legal "persons," corporations can exercise a right to trial by jury in criminal cases, and are protected from unreasonable searches and double jeopardy—just like you and me, but, shall we say, more so. Among other things, they have a right to exist indefinitely while we, being mortal, really aren't eligible to share in such a right.

Corporations offer legal protection to their officers and directors. If they make decisions that result in human tragedy, environmental disaster, community destruction, the directors and officers are usually not personally liable (and, in any case, are covered by insurance). It's the corporation's fault, not theirs. So no matter what corporate officers and directors have done, no matter how much death and loss their decisions have caused others, no matter how many lives have been spoiled, their millions of dollars, their mansions, their second, third, and fourth homes, their yachts, their private planes have usually remained safe. Few indeed have been the corporate criminals who go to prison—or who, if they do go, emerge from prison genuinely broke. True, the Sarbanes-Oxley Act of 2002 included provisions for some possible fines and prison sentences, as well as protections for whistle-blowers, but less than three years later the Republican-dominated U.S. Congress was being heavily lobbied to revert to the good old days.

Corporations are legally required to manage for maximum profit. If the officers and directors of a corporation fail to do so, stockholders can sue them for damages. So even if they believe that the corporation they direct should act more humanely, compassionately, generously, even if they think there should be protection for workers, for communities, for the environment, corporate officers and directors are at risk if they act on those beliefs unless what they do is going to make money for the corporation.

Rather surprisingly (if one of the things you knew about Henry Ford's milk-of-human-kindness record was his active and truly nasty anti-Semitism), the founder of the Ford Motor Company tried to do right by his employees and customers. Ford reportedly said, "Sometimes I do not believe that we should make such awful profits on our cars." He cut the price from over $900 to $440 (in 1916 dollars). Just as surprisingly, he paid the people who built Fords more than the going market rate at the time, and by more than just a token amount. In a famous court decision, *Dodge v. Ford*, Henry Ford was set straight. It was established that it was literally not his business to try to be fair to his customers and good to workers.[3]

The purpose of a corporation isn't to do good. The purpose of a corporation is to make money. This is not a secret, or an unfair oversimplification made only by radical anticorporate types. It is a legal, historical, theoretical, and even, in the view of some corporatist theorists, a political and moral imperative.

For example, the influential free market economist Milton Friedman—whose early book *Capitalism and Freedom* is now in its fortieth anniversary edition—writes that the view that corporate officers have a social responsibility shows "a fundamental misconception of the character and nature of a free economy." Why? Because "few trends could so thoroughly undermine the very foundations of our free society as the acceptance by corporate officials of a social responsibility other than to make as much money for their stockholders [he doesn't say 'for themselves,' we note] as possible."[4] This, says Friedman, "is a fundamentally subversive doctrine." Subversive of what? "Our free society." Note that for Friedman and the conservatives who revere him, "our free society" is one and the same as a capitalist system in which corporations have as their sole purpose "to make as much money as possible."

These days, one of the easiest and fastest ways for corporations to fulfill their obligation and moral mission to make even more money is by privatizing public goods and services. It is rather hard to believe that this will elevate the moral standards by which we live individually, or those to which we want our government and the public sector to adhere.

Healthy families and communities work because people make commitments to each other and do their best to keep them. That's what makes a good partnership between two people, for example. It's mutual. It's a two-way street. When two people decide to live together, or to marry (or both), they in effect say to each other: "If I agree to care for you and help you, to put time and effort into this relationship, then I expect you to do the same for me." People in a mutual relationship have the right to expect that their partner won't abandon them, won't just walk out on them. It doesn't always turn out that way, but part of the reason we cry at weddings as well as over breakups is because commitment is important to us. We care about it, it moves us.

Think how different that is from the attitude most corporations have toward the communities in which they're located and the people who work for them.

> Evening hangs like smoke
> On this mill town that I love
> My thoughts they roll and tumble
> Through the years
> My old heart drifts through the haze
> Back to Youngstown's better days
> The mills have gone away
> But we're still here

We're still here
We're still here
The mills have gone away
But we're still here
With our neighbors and our kin
Right here where we've always been
The mills have gone away
But we're still here

Looking down the street
To the days when I was young
I can see my friends and neighbors
Strong and clear
They came from near and far away
Built their lives from day to day
Through the good times and the hard times
We're still here

Dreaming down the days
'Til time circles home
When our children face
The future's hope and fear
Nothing went the way it should
But we did the best we could
When the whistle blows for courage
We're still here[5]

All over the United States, there are communities with boarded-up Main Street stores and "House for Sale" signs in the neighborhoods. But these aren't just houses. These were homes to people—to couples, to families, to friends. It's not just jobs that are being destroyed: it's lives, homes, friendships, marriages, partnerships, neighborhoods, communities.

All over the United States, there are people trying to get by on minimum-wage jobs with next to no benefits, people who used to have good-paying work.

All over the United States, there are families that have broken up under the stress and strain of economic hardship. There are children having a hard time learning in school because times are so tough at home, just as there are broken marriages and troubled children and left-behind older family members and friends because a corporation told the breadwinner to move, and then to move again, and again—or lose her or his job.

The corporations have no loyalty whatsoever to the people who worked for them, came to the job every day, stuck with them through hard times as well as good times, gave their all and their best. They have no loyalty to the communities that courted them, welcomed them, gave them tax breaks and economic incentives.

They do talk a lot about loyalty, though. They take people on retreats, hold company parties, and give people psychological tests to help them work better together. But when there is a decision based on consideration of the bottom line, who are the corporations loyal to? Not to the people who work for them. Not to the rural crossroads communities, towns, cities, counties, states, or countries in which they're located.

The corporations speak a lot these days about "managing for excellence," about "spiritual leadership," about "servant leadership." They bring in high-priced consultants to help them make the workplace a friendly, even inspiring, place. Why? Whose interests are served if we come to find all the meaning in our life in working for them? It might break their hearts to cut our unit when they downsize—but they'll still do it.

Of which country are corporations loyal, responsible citizens? Not this one, not any one. What they're about these days is getting into as many markets in as many countries as they can. They want, and get, all kinds of subsidies and protections and tariffs from one government—the one they have the most influence with—but they'll take what they can get elsewhere, too. They fight tooth and nail to keep other potentially competing corporations from getting the same breaks, to keep countries from erecting any trade barriers that might stop them from going wherever they want, whenever they want, on whatever terms they want.

Meanwhile, they praise competition. Right: as long as they're winning, and only until they have won. The prize is to have no competition at all, not from other corporations, not from governments, not from unions, not from grassroots organizations and movements.

The (Corporate) Benefits of One-Way Sharing

Corporations also love privatization because it leads to a redistribution of wealth—not from the rich to the poor, that old nightmare of the wealthiest, but from middle and bottom up to the top.

This doesn't happen directly, of course. Ken Lay, the Enron CEO under whose leadership the corporation went massively, disastrously wrong and then bust, didn't have to write personal checks to the thousands of workers who lost their jobs and pensions, some of whom committed suicide—although it's nice to think about a system of justice in which that would happen. No: Lay stays rich, the former employees find themselves much poorer.

The United States instituted a system that was supposed to redistribute the other way, to ensure that lives would not be destroyed because people did not have enough even to obtain minimal levels of housing, food, clothing, medical care, education, and to fulfill other basic human needs. The progressive tax system was developed to ensure that wealthy individuals and corporations contributed their fair share to sustaining the common goods on which they too depended. That system, and that notion of fairness, have been pretty much cut to pieces by procorporate, prowealth elected officials who've radically reduced taxes on corporations and the rich while not reducing spending on corporation-fattening contracts, government-funded subsidies that underwrite their profits, corporate bailouts. As corporations take over the public sector, they get more of our money and pay back less.

In the public sector, most employees make at least a fair living wage. Not everyone, of course, but the great majority. They tend to have decent pay, medical insurance, and pension plans that supplement Social Security. Particularly if they're unionized, as many public employees are, they're likely to be doing reasonably well. Even if they're not represented by a union, public employees tend to have better wages and working conditions than lower-level employees in the private sector. It's pretty rare to hear of a public employee who makes only the minimum wage. These jobs have been very important in building a strong middle class and a sturdy economy in the United States, one in which people have found good, steady work that allows them to help the next generations of their family—their children, nieces and nephews, and grandchildren—have a good start and a fair chance in life.

Some people think that the reasonable salaries and benefits paid to public employees cause problems for government budgets. In fact, most of the people whose income comes from our tax dollars today work not directly for government but for private corporations that contract with government. For example, of the 6.75 million people who worked directly or indirectly for the federal government in 2003, only 1.75 million were public employees. The remaining 5 million worked for corporations with federal contracts.

How many of us tell stories like this: "My grandmother came here as an immigrant, not speaking the language, without education, without the skills a modern industrial job required. But she was lucky. She got a job working in the laundry at the city hospital and joined the union. The work was hard, the hours were long, the wages were only so high. But she had good medical insurance, so the little money she was saving didn't get wiped out when she or her family got sick. And she knew she had her city pension coming, plus her Social Security, so she was able to make ends meet and even put something aside for my parents. She gave them a good start so that, when the time came, she and my mother were able to send me to college. It was a public university where tuition was low, and I had to keep living at home. But there was money for books, and subway fare, and a used typewriter. That's why today I'm a schoolteacher [a nurse, a social worker, a small business owner, a lawyer, a physical therapist]. I am the granddaughter of an immigrant woman who came here with no education and no skills that American employers wanted. But she learned new ones, she worked hard, she kept her pride and her hopes—and look at all of us today."

Some people rise through the ranks of public service to become high-level managers—and some, of course, come in at that level to start with. But even the highest-paid public employees make salaries that are in the same ballpark as those who make the least. It's rare for public employees, whether they work for a city, county, state, or the federal government, to make less than $25,000 or more than $150,000 a year. This is very different from the private sector, where many people earn the minimum wage and a handful of executives are paid millions and millions of dollars a year just in salaries, not even counting their bonuses and stock options.

Apparently, such "incentives" are considered necessary to persuade these executives to do their jobs well. After all, it would hardly be fair to expect CEOs making a lousy $3 million a year to go the extra mile unless there was something in it for them. Guess they don't have the work ethic and respect for what they do that our grandparents did; these CEOs seem to need to be outrageously bribed—and even then they're not loyal. A bigger bribe, and off they go.

So here we have a setup for destroying the public sector jobs that our grandparents and parents gave their working lives to—as have many of us. Corporations face a problem when they privatize public services. To get the contract at all, they usually have to promise to do it for at least 10 percent less than the public sector. Then, to get the money to pay their shareholders (including other large corporations and investment banks) and those million-dollar executives, they need to turn a very hefty before-tax profit.

Where is all that extra money going to come from?

Well, it's not going to come from the mythical modern management methods that corporations like to brag about. They love to talk about how they're going to modernize and streamline archaic government bureaucracies. Cut the fat, go lean and mean. Teach those lazy, out-for-themselves public employees to be efficient and accountable, as corporations are.

Yeah, right. Anyone who's even vaguely aware of the corporate scandals of recent years (Enron, WorldCom, Halliburton) knows that slimming down the oversized salaries and bonuses they give their top people is not exactly what corporations specialize in. If they were Executive Weight Watchers, they'd be out of business. Nor are they reliably accountable. Accounting firms have gone down with them, sleazy financial scams have been exposed after years of secrecy. And no matter what, it costs a lot to manage their huge operations. Large public bureaucracies are a problem; large corporate bureaucracies are even more of a problem, and they cost us a lot more. When was the last time you heard of a scandal involving public employees that even approached the scale of WorldCom, HealthSouth, and Enron?

What they do cut and trim is the wages and benefits of the once-public employees who do the same basic work to keep these systems going.

When Governor Mark Sanford of South Carolina was asked how privatizing prison medical services was going to save money for the state, he explained that the private corporation wouldn't have to pay into the state retirement fund for its employees, whereas the state was legally required to do so—and that would be a savings of 10 percent of personnel costs a year.

That's really clever. Just cut out the pension plans for hundreds of dedicated nurses, pharmacists, physical therapists, counselors, so that out-of-state corporate executives can make more millions.

This is one of the classic ways in which privatization works: Robin Hood robbing from the poor to give to the rich. And it does *not* save the state money in the long run. No pension means less money for people who retire. That means less paid in taxes to government at all levels. Not exactly good for small local businesses either, which depend on real people coming in and buying, not on the long-term government contracts that keep privatizing corporations rolling in dough.

To illustrate, here's our fox and chicken story again, with a twist. Every schoolchild knows that the U.S. economic model is based on competition. This is true, in a sense. We see this in nature. Whether in the wild (to the extent that there are wild chickens) or in the henhouse, the fox and the chickens are in competition to meet their goals. However, they have very different goals. They both need to eat to live. But while the fox can, and truly desires to, eat the chickens, the chickens can't eat the fox, and they must spend a lot of energy to avoid becoming fox food. The chickens' goal is to stay alive, which involves staying as far away from the fox as possible. The fox's goal is, quite literally, to swallow the competition.

Farmers who raise chickens for eggs and meat build henhouses to keep them close to hand—and to protect them from those foxes. But then the foxes get smart. They hire marketers and public relations people. They contribute to the animals who are running for those offices that decide how the chickens will be kept secure and protected from outside invaders seeking to destroy the happy farmyard way of life. Reinvented as guardians of the farm and its system, the foxes get themselves a contract to guard the chicken coop. And then, promising to provide the best and cheapest care for those chickens, they move on inside.

The rest, as they say, is history. The foxes get fat—until there are so few chickens left, they get hungry all over again and start fighting each other. The farmer goes broke, the bank forecloses, and the farmer goes to work at Wal-Mart. Pretty soon, the foxes have to travel on to new lands, new farms and farmers, new henhouses—wherever in the world they might be.

The Soup Song, written by Detroit labor lawyer Maurice Sugar, is a great parody from some seventy years ago—before all the regulations and "safety net" provisions we now take for granted were established because we saw what a Great Depression can do. The song captures the lessons learned about loyalty when it is required only of workers. In a nice piece of musical irony in this age of corporate global colonization, it's sung to the tune of My Bonnie Lies Over the Ocean:

I'm spending my nights at the flophouse
I'm spending my days on the street
I'm looking for work and I find none
I wish I had something to eat

> Soo-oup, soo-oup,
> They give me a bowl of soo-oup
> Soo-oup, soo-oup,
> They give me a bowl of soo-oup

I spent twenty years in the factory
I did everything I was told
They said I was loyal and faithful
Now even before I get old

I saved fifteen bucks with my banker
To buy me a car and a yacht
I went down to draw out my fortune
And this is the answer I got

I fought in the war for my country
I went out to bleed and to die
I thought that my country would help me
But this was my country's reply

I went on my knees to my Maker
I prayed every night to the Lord
I vowed I'd be meek and submissive
And now I've received my reward[6]

The Soup Song was written in the early 1930s, before President Franklin Delano Roosevelt created the New Deal, which put the government more squarely on the side of the majority of this country's people and against the corporations. Still, now as then, people complain about government telling them what to do. They rail against government. They make cynical jokes about it.

Right attitude, wrong target—except from the point of view of the privatizing corporations and right-wing think tanks, which have been working hard to direct our legitimate anger towards the governments that are increasingly in their service, rather than at them. It's interesting that we have words for many forms of government, but not (yet) for what happens, as David Korten put it in his book title, *When Corporations Rule the World*—although Mussolini, taking power at the same time as Hitler and Stalin, said that the form of government that he invented should be called "corporative" as well as fascist because it merged the powers of the corporation, labor, and the state. *Fascist* remains a label of insult; *corporative* never caught on.

What we are facing today is a merger of the powers of the corporation and the state. Privatization is both its method and its purpose.

CHAPTER 4

Forms of Privatization

The private sector has been increasingly focused on the potential market that a huge public sector provides in countless service areas.
—M. BRYNA SANGER, *The Welfare Marketplace*[1]

Common Practices

THE PUBLIC SECTOR is already very lucrative for the corporations that have found ways to privatize parts of it. Following are the more obvious ways the transfer of our tax money from our government and public agencies into private pockets is already taking place.

OUTSOURCING, CONTRACTING OUT

A contract to do public work is given to a nongovernmental entity, with its nonpublic employees. Public money is used to pay for the work done under this contract. Corporations benefit greatly, but there are also nonprofit organizations, including religious ones, that get their pieces of public funds—and profit from them (meaning that they make more money than it should cost to do the work, as evidenced, for one thing, by the corporate CEO–scale salaries some pay).

Nonprofits, religious and secular, also enter into contracts with for-profits. Sometimes corporations set up nonprofits to get their tax breaks, and then get contracts from them. It's a cozy world of blurry boundaries, all fueled by public money.[2]

Contracting out government work has a long history in the United States and has supported many small businesses that do responsible work. But it is quite another thing when public work is contracted out specifically in order to "shrink government," using privatization as a method to do so. These decisions are not made on the basis of careful assessment of real need, actual costs, and the availability of a corporation that is truly qualified in the area of work to be contracted out. The older forms of the practice were designed to support our government in doing its job of serving us. Today, privatizers seek to limit and weaken government—to make it dependent on corporations.

No matter what, though, contractors often lack knowledge in accomplishing military or other government jobs long done by public employees who have built up specialized expertise over their own years of work, and have had the benefit of a work culture that spreads and facilitates the transmission of that expertise. The death of twenty-two U.S. servicepeople in the Mosul, Iraq, bombing described at the beginning of this book is a tragic example of failure to bring to a job the essential, specific expertise it requires. Feeding troops in a war zone just isn't the same as setting up tents to feed guests at a big party.

Contracting can also become so habitual as a way to do business that it shades into the idea that government can pay a non-public person or group for *anything* an administration wants, including control of the news. In 2005, the conservative newspaper columnist and commentator Armstrong Williams was exposed as having accepted $240,000 passed to him by the Department of Education and a private public relations firm— $240,000 of taxpayers' money—not to report on but *to promote* the Bush administration's agenda. This secret bribing, and perversion, of a news source has been called "checkbook journalism": You want it, you buy it—with the public's money.[3] No matter that this, shall we say, informal "contracting" is unethical, a conflict of interest, and that it is illegal to use federal money for "covert propaganda,"[4] as the General Accountability Office has ruled in this and two other such cases during the Bush administration thus far. (Four others have also been exposed, and further instances are beginning to be uncovered.)

Want it done? Don't let governmental laws, rules, and regulations stop you. Pay a nongovernmental person to do it: Make it a contracting matter.

Even the best contractors who have signed on to do honest work must be supervised, of course. You don't hire someone to mind your kids and never check on him. It's not safe for a builder to contract out electrical work and never think about it again. So contracting out, which is usually said to be done to enhance efficiency and save taxpayers money, actually requires more work and more of our money than it might seem. As an expert who has tracked privatizing by contracting out concludes, "The idea that transfer of responsibility from the public to the private sector allows government to withdraw from oversight, reduce staff, and place sole or even primary responsibility for accomplishment of public policy objectives on private service providers is an invitation to trouble."[5]

PARTNERSHIP

Public agencies and nongovernmental entities "partner" to set up quasi-public institutions or projects that are supposed to serve both their purposes.

A good example is the quasi-public Fannie Mae, which was set up to get public money to for-profit banks so they would make more mortgage deals with people who needed loans to buy their houses. This was an elaborate public-private deal that seemed to be good for both sectors and all of us. The pressure to make profits and control against losses to the bottom line that banks claimed kept them from making loans to some people was to be balanced by a government committed to affordable housing, a public good. And both banks and government were to do well financially to boot.

But as Fannie Mae got established and plump, it became far more like a heavily subsidized private corporation. Happens: For-profits are, precisely, for making profits. Furthermore, while the partnership holds, the public party to it is actually not only subsidizing the profits of its partner but getting special low interest rates. Government is handing over public funds, which are supposedly to be spent on public services and goods (that's what we pay taxes for), but it is not getting anything like 100 percent public goods and services for that money. A lot of those public funds are making extraordinary executive packages and corporate profits possible. In short, the "result is a heads-I-win-tails-you-lose proposition for taxpayers. If Fannie . . . prosper[s], benefits go to shareholders; if [it] get[s] in trouble, government would almost certainly rescue [it]."[6]

In the case of Fannie Mae, in 2004 an accounting scandal was uncovered and its top executives were forced to resign. As is common among the rich and powerful, this wasn't your garden-variety firing, where you walk away with virtually nothing from the corporation that let you go (and if it weren't for government unemployment benefits, might be totally without income). The benefits Fannie Mae said it was offering its two officers, who were investigated for responsibility for scandalous accounting practices, "range from a $1.4 million-a-year pension payment for life to former CEO Franklin Raines, 55, to stock options for Raines and former chief financial officer J. Timothy Howard, 56." The CEO of a research firm estimated Mr. Raines' pension plus stock options payout to be all together $2.5 million a year.[7]

Some of these partnerships between government and private-sector businesses are even worse than the historic imbalance in marriage between men and women, itself a kind of contractual partnership. She stayed home and took care of the kids and did some underpaid office work to help put him through medical school. And when the marriage broke up, guess who walked away with more money, and the potential (underwritten by her) to make still more?

If the two authors of this book, Elizabeth Minnich and Si Kahn, entered into a partnership with Donald Trump, we would be pretty foolish to think we had suddenly become his equal in power and wealth. Add our assets to his, and together the three of us are worth billions and billions. But we'd better not count on that partnership for our retirement, or on getting half the money if it breaks up. We feel much safer relying on Social Security.

LEASING

Leasing is making deals that allow profit-seeking businesses to exploit public goods, such as leasing national forests and wilderness areas to a corporation whose business is timber, natural gas, or oil. The argument here is that both the public and profit-making purses will benefit from leasing publicly owned land to a corporation that will "harvest" (read, cut down every tree in sight, a practice known in the timber industry as clear-cutting) and "extract" (read, strip-mine every inch of land) and sell what is on top of or under the land. Letting those national forests and wilderness areas *just sit there doing nothing* seems like such a waste, especially when there's this huge national debt to be reckoned with. Why not let those idle resources—the trees just standing there enjoying the wind, the oil and natural gas lying around underground doing who knows what—pay their way by sacrificing just a portion of their number for the financial good of human society?

Here's how it worked in Appalachia for decades, before the law was changed to a somewhat fairer system.[8] The United States Forest Service owns vast percentages of many mountain counties, over 40 percent of the surface land in fourteen of them. Of course, the Forest Service, being part of the federal government, doesn't pay taxes on this land as a private landowner would.

Bad news for county government? Not at all, the Forest Service said. We make payments in lieu of taxes to every county in which these lands are located.

And how was the amount determined? Well, the Forest Service gave the county 25 percent of the income it received from selling standing timber (that's trees that haven't been cut down yet) to corporations and individuals to harvest. Fine in theory. The problem was that the Forest Service sold the standing timber—a public resource—at prices way below market value. Some counties got payments in lieu of taxes as little as twenty-two cents an acre. The corporations got a steal, and the public, the people of the county, got stolen from.

Like any contract or partnership between government and corporations, leasing can go bad. Big money out to make profits and the public good rarely make for an equal marriage.

SELLING OUTRIGHT

It's obvious: What was public is turned into a resource for profit making. Once privatized, a formerly public good or service is likely to be handled differently to cut costs and increase profits. And should that turn out to make the public need to take it back, there are serious problems. It is too expensive to buy it back or start it up anew, and in any case, government expertise and provisions to run it, provide for it, care for it have been lost.

The public—particularly less wealthy, under- and uninsured people—has depended on public hospitals. Where these have been privatized, sold off to private corporations, costs were cut— and guess where the quick and easy cuts were made? Privatizers may believe in charity, but not from them. Preventive care is also likely to be cut, or cut back: Hospitals that profit from having patients do not have a stake in keeping us well by offering low-ticket wellness services. Even privatized hospitals that want, or are required under the terms of the sale, to keep up preventive and charity services may not be able to afford them.

Furthermore, when a public hospital is sold to a religious organization, that religion's beliefs can be imposed on health care professionals they employ, and on their customers (which is what those in need of care have become, although customers without much choice). Catholic hospitals, for example, will not offer services in support of reproductive choice, particularly abortions and birth control. This might be their own business if the public could go elsewhere. But when public hospitals are sold to Catholic orders, they can become, as they have in Eugene, Oregon, just about the only show around. No religion should decide, on the basis of its own doctrine, what health care all of us can and cannot get.[9]

Selling off a public good or service can, then, significantly lessen fair, inclusive access to it because the need to profit (or to serve other primary values, such as religious ones) can affect quality, scope, and kind of services offered.

DISINVESTMENT

Divestment means pulling out public funds so that public goods and services deteriorate or even fold, and can then be taken over or bought by for-profit corporations without public protest. Or, cutting back a public commitment to fund a service so far that those who are trying to run it are forced to seek money from the private sector. Private money means greater private control. *Disinvestment* (a polite term for breaking your word and going back on a commitment of public funds, much as *disinformation* is a polite term for lying) can also force responsible public officials to make deals with private for-profits even when they do not think it a good idea.

Disinvestment in education, for example, leads to the overcrowded, undersupplied classrooms that allow privatizers to say, "See? Public education is failing," and then further undercut those schools by offering vouchers to parents to send their children to private schools. In public universities, it leads to desperate administrators putting great pressure on faculty to bring in fat grants or to work on projects under university-corporate partnership arrangements. Scholars must then look first for what might get funded, rather than to what we need and want to know.

Disinvestment can also be used against federal funding agencies. In early 2005, the Bush administration pulled back monies promised to the Fund for the Improvement of Post-Secondary Education (FIPSE), which had supported innovative programs. Authors of proposals that had already been approved for funding were suddenly told there would be no money after all. More people who might have improved education were forced to seek private funding—more private-sector control over education.

CREATING AND CONTROLLING MARKETS
THAT REQUIRE PUBLIC FUNDING TO SERVE

One way privatization takes chunks out of public funds for the good of for-profit corporations is literally by creating public need and demand. This takes time and determination, and often, collusion of various more or less open sorts, but indeed it can be and has been done.

Here's a dramatic example. Most major cities in the United States used to have a trolley system that provided relatively efficient, inexpensive, and nonpolluting public transportation. But, one by one, the trolley systems disappeared.

What happened to these sensible trolleys? Were they too slow for fast-moving modern people—lumbering dinosaurs whose time had come and gone? Too expensive to maintain? Obsolete in a world of subways and airplanes? Too cute for serious cities with purposeful, high-powered people?

No, none of the above. The trolleys were doing just fine. The problem was that this public form of transportation competed directly and successfully with the emerging automotive and oil industries. Remember, the trolleys ran on electricity, not on oil or gasoline. So these corporations (including the Rockefeller oil corporations, Ford Motor Company, and Goodyear Tire and Rubber) simply bought up the public trolley systems and closed them down—wherever across the country they could.[10]

The profits made by the oil, car, and associated corporations are by now monstrously huge. Meanwhile, government has to build and maintain all those public roads we drive our cars on, provide traffic cops and all the paraphernalia, like stoplights, we need not to kill each other on the roads—and on and on, all the way to involving our government, including the military, in global struggles to keep the oil flowing.

These days, in Charlotte where we live, we are investing ever more tax money in trying to provide public transportation to get us out of those cars. Part of the plan includes—guess what? A public trolley system.

Now, let's be clear. We think having a public trolley system is totally great (partly, we have to admit, because there's a stop three blocks from our house). The trolley cars—lovingly rebuilt over many years by volunteers who were determined to convince the city to bring its trolleys back—are just beautiful. But because the old trolley system was deliberately undermined and shut down, providing public transportation today is going to cost millions of our tax dollars. If the corporations hadn't worked to destroy the public transportation systems we had in the first place, we wouldn't as a city and as a nation be spending billions to rebuild them now from scratch.

The corporations that consciously worked to destroy this country's trolley systems take no responsibility for helping rebuild them. No surprise there, though. Remedying harms to the public good is not the corporations' business—even when they are the cause of those harms.

SUBSIDIES

Public monies—our tax dollars—are used to lower corporations' costs so they can continue to make, and grow, their profits. These range from so-called tax incentives to government purchases of land that are then offered to corporations that, if given sufficient incentives (that's the polite term for bribes), just might locate where jobs are needed, to tax breaks for the same reason, or to keep a corporation from moving elsewhere, to bailouts of faltering corporate giants—to military presence and actions, and today, ongoing U.S. presence and war in oil-rich regions of the world.

Subsidies are another reason corporations are interested in contracts, leasing, and partnering with the government. Public money or other goods (including credibility) is the dowry the bride brings that goes toward strengthening the groom's economic potential.[11]

The reasons given for these more or less obvious bribes, collectively and politely called subsidies—or, a bit more honestly, corporate welfare—are various. Most of them, though, invoke the need for a now thoroughly corporate-dominated economy to keep growing. That these reasons have some truth to them makes a prime point about the privatizers' agenda. We and our government are being made so dependent on corporations that they call the shots, which is just what they want.

And we are encouraged to think that it is good for us and good for America to subsidize the very corporations that are taking away our public powers and profiting from provisions for the public good. Matter of fact, we're not even supposed to notice that the difference between our country and the corporations is nowhere near as clear as it should be.

ENCLOSURE

The enclosing of what was free, held in common, shared, open to all, so that it becomes private, is a very basic form of privatization. It takes what was public and puts it in private hands. When settlers staked their claims on land the Native Americans had used but not owned, there were fierce conflicts. When ranchers built fences to keep the animals they raised in and other ranchers' animals out, they were turning open territory into private space. When farmers came along and fenced in more of the open territory that the ranchers had used to drive their stock to market, more struggles erupted.

Further back in history, in sixteenth-century England, the growth of the wool trade led to the enclosure—the fencing in—of what had been *commons*, land used in common by groups of people. This was a major change with serious economic, social, legal, and political consequences. The British government was pressed into service by the owners of the privatized land, and its powers were both used and increased on their behalf. For example, between 1688 and 1820, "the number of capital crimes in England increased from 50 to 220; almost all were related to crimes against property. Particularly notable was the imposition of the death penalty as punishment for writing anonymous letters to protest the enclosure of common lands."[12]

Enclosure, then, is obviously related to freedom, and to claims to conflicting kinds of rights.

Freedom has many meanings, but basic to our experience of being free is that we can go where we want, say what we think, act as we will. Obviously there are constraints on these freedoms even when we have public rights that protect our ability to choose to exercise them. We can't go anywhere, say anything, do anything anytime we want to, because we are only human, and we are social, moral creatures. We set limits on ourselves and on each other so that my freedom cannot be used to harm you, or to limit your freedom. But freedom is limited in a more concrete and telling way where private property becomes a right that outweighs almost all others.

Rights to own property are deeply valued in societies that have them. But they are also rights that can be, and have been, extended from land to all sorts of material things—and to other human beings, as with slavery. It's one thing to have a small farm you can own, fence in, post No Trespassing signs on, and use as you will; it's quite another thing to own slaves. Slave owners, we know from U.S. history, will then agitate for laws that enshrine and expand their "property" rights. When concentrated ownership becomes unjust, government can become party to its perversion.

Today, when corporations take over publicly owned lands and water, it's recognized as privatization. But this is connected to the older, more widespread taking over of what was open to all, and that is less often recognized. It should be recognized, because when the right to private ownership takes precedence over other basic rights of freedom, the sphere of our shared freedoms always shrinks.

For example, although our right to freedom of expression is protected against government restrictions by the Constitution, it is not fully protected against private owners. When someone owns property—like an apartment building, a mall, an amusement park, a retirement home—that person, or corporation, can refuse to let people holding views the owner disagrees with speak on the property, or speak about political issues at all.

Simply put, the less public space we have, the less freedom we have to exercise our public rights—and today public space is disappearing, being enclosed, at an accelerating pace.[13] Look around you: How many new gated communities are going up? How many restricted housing developments? How many shopping malls? On the other hand, how many places in your community are still free and open to people who want to pass out leaflets asking people to join a union, work to elect a favorite candidate, carry a picket sign protesting injustice?

The loss of public space also means that the sphere of power of our government is shrinking. Government cannot enforce your right to free speech when you are on the private property of someone whose ownership rights the government protects. The government then serves its citizens as owners, rather than simply as We the People, whoever and wherever we are, whatever we have or do not have.

The decision to protect those who benefit from the enclosure of the commons (from land to air rights, from water to mineral rights, from knowledge and information to images and symbols) has long since been made in many countries. Private property is a deep cultural value, and very much a part of the way we lead our lives. But as privatization of all sorts spreads, a careful, equitable balance between our differing rights threatens to be lost in favor of those who own ever more, and can, where they have taken control, legally shut us out, shut us in, and deny us the expansive freedoms for which democracies were created.

In 1953, the words of the chair of General Motors, Charlie Wilson, made it into public folklore: "What's good for General Motors is good for America." In 2001, right after 9/11, General Motors proudly launched an advertising campaign for its cars based on the same premise. "Keep America rolling," it said.[14]

Ownership and consumerism as patriotism, patriotism as consumerism and ownership—not always an easy sell, but there are politicians as well as corporations working hard to convince us.

There is no such thing as a private democracy.

Who Is Not Served by Privatization?

Si is an organizer. Organizers, like all craftspeople, have a tool kit, a set of physical and intellectual resources they turn to for help when they know what's happening but not why. If organizers or any other people don't understand why something is happening, any effort to change what's going on is likely to lead them and us in many wrong directions.

A key question organizers ask is, "Who does it serve?" Actually, it should be, "*Whom* does it serve," but organizers, like politicians, pride themselves on being plainspoken and tend to avoid certain technically correct grammatical constructions if they think using these forms might make them appear too pretentious. For example, most organizers would never use the preceding sentence in public.

Sometimes, to figure out whom something serves, organizers look around to figure out, first, whom it does *not* serve. Here's a list of those privatization has *not* served.

COMMUNITIES

People tend to be loyal to the community in which they live. Corporations tend to be loyal only to themselves, meaning their executives, board members, and of course, their largest shareholders, many of which are also loyal to other corporations, from which they profit. (Just to thicken the mix as much as possible, some of the largest shareholders *are* other corporations). When people leave a community, they sell their house to someone else. When corporations leave, there's often nothing left but the empty building where people used to work—and a lot of "For Sale" signs in front of the houses of the people who used to have jobs in the now empty building.

TAXPAYERS

The basic argument privatizers use to promote their agenda is that it saves the public money. Those who favor privatization do studies proving that it saves money; those who oppose it do others proving the opposite. What is perfectly clear is that, even if major privatization takes place, and even if the quality of service goes down, taxes usually remain the same. The difference is that more of those public funds go into private corporate pockets.[15]

PUBLIC EMPLOYEES

Corporations have learned an important if obvious lesson: If you pay people less, and if you pay less people, you can keep more of the money for yourself. When public services are privatized, it's common to terminate most if not all of the public employees who worked there. Those who are hired back, and those who are hired to replace those who lose their jobs permanently, almost always have lower wages or salaries and benefits than when those jobs were public. The individual, the family, and the community are all poorer for it, in many senses of the word.

SMALL BUSINESS OWNERS

When people have less money to spend, guess where they spend even less of it? People with a little extra disposable income can afford to support their small neighborhood and community businesses. People living on the financial edge, however they may feel about Wal-Mart, end up shopping there.

COMMUNITY ORGANIZATIONS

Just as people who've lost part of their income are likely to have to transfer their business from small neighborhood stores to the Big Boxes, they're also less able to contribute financially to community organizations. Plus, because they're likely to have to take on a second job to make ends meet, they have less time to volunteer for good causes and organizations—assuming they don't have to leave town to find a new job.

MILITARY PERSONNEL

Privatization of the military has meant that employees of private security corporations working in war zones make as much as or more than $100,000 a year—again, that's our tax dollars—while some of our enlisted women and men on the front lines of battle don't even have the equipment to protect themselves. Their families and friends back home hold fundraising drives to buy body armor so that their loved ones have at least a better chance of getting home alive and in one piece. And family, friends, and neighbors pitch in to help military families too, because the pay is so low that life is otherwise very hard indeed.[16]

PEOPLE IN PRISON

For-profit private prisons have meant higher levels of prison violence, fewer educational and training resources, a higher probability of being incarcerated a long way from home, and so less chance to turn your life around. We all lose when that fails. To people in prisons add people who suffer from the crimes committed by those who have already been incarcerated and came out more hardened, more desperate—or just unemployable in a world where no job means no money, no food, no chance. With over two million people already in prison, and many more millions in their families, the United States can't afford the pressure to expand incarceration created by the private prison industry.

If neither taxpayers, public employees, communities, community organizations, small business owners, military personnel, nor people in prison or the victims of crime benefit from privatization—which is to say, most of the people who live in the United States—why are we doing it? Who/whom does it serve?

Privatization serves corporations.

Now, that's not the official line, of course. To hear some elected officials talk about privatization, you'd think it was the best thing since sliced bread. It's Mom, apple pie, and the Fourth of July all over again. These politicians and their corporate allies present privatization as a sort of miracle ingredient that will cure much of what's wrong with society and government.

Let's take society first. Are the leading advocates for privatization—which is to say, the major political and economic conservatives in this country—really sincere when they claim that privatizing will build a better society by improving services to the poor and needy? Since when have conservatives (compassionate or not) tended to make the spending of money needed to ensure quality public services for the less fortunate the centerpiece of their time in office? Compare the following two lists and think which of these groups benefited most from conservative-led efforts to move

public funds, through privatization and other means, to constituencies they care about:

First group: single working mothers; homeless families; poor and
working people; people with HIV/AIDS; disabled veterans of
World War II, Korea, Vietnam, Afghanistan, and Iraq; inner-city
schoolchildren; rural communities threatened by environmental
disasters; day care workers and the women who can't take or keep
jobs without them; skilled workers unemployed because of changes
in technology; minimum wage workers; below-minimum-wage
workers; workers with disabilities; immigrants fleeing political tur-
moil in their home countries.

Second group: energy corporations, defense corporations, mining
corporations, natural gas corporations, timber corporations,
agribusiness corporations, pharmaceutical corporations, aerospace
corporations, oil corporations, private military corporations.

Also in the second group: individuals and families of wealth. (We
don't want to suggest that conservatives only care about corporations and have no regard for individuals or some families' value).

To think that the reason conservative political leaders want to
privatize is so that the most vulnerable will be empowered by being
treated more equally is to ignore a long, sad, and painful history. If
you believe these leaders want to privatize because of their deep
humanitarian concerns, we have a bridge we'd like to sell you.

Another dubious miracle claim is that privatization will fix
much of what's wrong with the government, which is where we're
supposed to put the blame for any troubles we have.

Organizers, though, also ask where the power is that keeps the
benefits flowing in one direction and not others. Elected officials,
people often say. Okay, but who and what are they using their
power *for?* Most of the elected officials who are working so hard to
promote privatization aren't trying to improve government.
They're not working to make government agencies more accountable, or public employees more responsible.

They're trying to do two things. First, they're trying to move as
high a percentage of public funds (meaning the money from your
taxes) into the pockets of corporations and individual people of

wealth (among whom they are planning to be, if they aren't already).

If the rest of us are judged by the company we keep, these officials should be judged by the companies that keep them.

Here's the second thing privatizers are trying to do. They're aiming to destroy independent, democratic government itself.

Well, let's not exaggerate. Antitax activist and Republican political strategist Grover Norquist said only that he wanted to make government so small he could haul it into the bathroom and drown it in the bathtub.[17]

When people meeting together to figure out what's going on and why they're hurting begin to put the pieces together, they realize that Grover Norquist was not joking. Neither were spokespeople for Governor Mark Sanford when they suggested that administration could run South Carolina with one thousand public employees. Nor was Governor Jeb Bush when he envisioned a Florida in which the buildings that used to house public employees stood empty.

These elected officials are not just indulging in the time-honored American tradition of bashing government and public employees. They are operating in a conscious, very disciplined manner. Their actions speak as loudly, and are every bit as antigovernment, antidemocracy, as their words.

It's actually not hard at all to figure out what they're trying to do. They're *telling* us—but they're also telling us that it is for our own good—that the very government we elected them to is what we should watch them drown in their bathtub.

The rationale for letting the foxes take over? Well, if we have foxes guarding the henhouse, we're told, we'll be safe from all those rogue predators out there in the wicked world. These will be *our* foxes—so forget that foxes, too, are predators. Predator foxes just love chickens, so we'll be safe with them.

And we should feel even more secure when the Guardian Foxes invite some of their kin to go right on into the henhouse. Lovers of chickens that they are, they'll provide for our needs far more efficiently and effectively, we are assured, than that old bungler, that bleeding heart Uncle Sam who thinks he should feed even the scrawniest, even the sickest and smallest chicken in his flock. If the Guardian Foxes have to take some risks, such as culling some of the chickens who are less likely to make it so that the others may flourish, or raiding other henhouses, then we can only admire them for their leadership and willingness to make the really hard decisions.

A terrible thing, that: Uncle Sam forgot that his one and only role as farmer is to plump up chickens to be sold, thereby making the money on which the world runs. He went and fell for those chickens, started caring about them, and refused to leave them unguarded against the foxes. (He had some help from the chickens in this change of heart, of course: Organized chickens had done a lot of squawking.) With his handouts, Farmer Sam has turned his chickens into dependents and cheats. Let the Guardian Foxes stand their watch, let their crony foxes into the henhouse, and the chickens will be liberated.

As Little Red Riding Hood said to the foxes' brother, the Big Bad Wolf, when he clothed himself in her grandmother's nightgown and cap and pulled the covers up to his chin, "My, what big teeth you have, Grandma." "All the better to eat you with, my dear," said the rather more honest wolf.

PART II

PRIVATIZATION AT WORK

IN MEMORIAM

BRIAN TETRAULT WAS FORTY-FOUR when he was led into a dim county jail cell in upstate New York in 2001, charged with taking some skis and other items from his ex-wife's home. A former nuclear scientist who had struggled with Parkinson's disease, he began to die almost immediately, and state investigators would later discover why: the jail's medical director had cut off all but a few of the thirty-two pills he needed each day to quell his tremors.

Over the next ten days, Mr. Tetrault slid into a stupor, soaked in his own sweat and urine. But he never saw the jail doctor again, and the nurses dismissed him as a faker. After his heart finally stopped, investigators said, correction officers at the Schenectady jail doctored records to make it appear he had been released before he died. . . . Investigators concluded [that] the culprit was a for-profit corporation, Prison Health Services, that had moved aggressively into New York State in the last decade, winning jail contracts worth hundreds of millions of dollars with an enticing sales pitch: Take the messy and expensive job of providing medical care from overmatched government officials, and give it to an experienced nationwide outfit. . . . A yearlong examination of Prison Health Services by the *New York Times* reveals repeated instances of medical care that has been flawed and sometimes lethal.[1]

CHAPTER 5

A Worst-Case Scenario:
For-Profit Private Prisons[1]

The issue of private versus public isn't really about privatizing prisons. It's about privatizing prisoners. Prisoners, who have traditionally been the responsibility of state and federal governments, are being contracted out to the lowest corporate bidder. Convicts have become commodities. Private prisons aren't in business for the "public good," nor are they accountable to taxpayers. They're in business to make money and are accountable to their shareholders. Period. To them, it's the only bottom line that matters.

—ALEX FRIEDMANN, WHO WAS INCARCERATED FOR SIX YEARS IN A PRIVATE PRISON[2]

BEGIN YOUR JOURNEY through time in Durham, North Carolina, driving north on Interstate 85 toward Richmond, onetime capital of the Confederacy. Just before the Virginia border, turn east onto U.S. 158. Travel through Littleton, where members of the Lumbee-Tuscarora tribe routed the Ku Klux Klan in the 1950s. Pass through Roanoke Rapids, where in 1974 workers at the town's seven J. P. Stevens cotton mills voted to join the Textile Workers Union of America and started a historic six-year international campaign for a contract. Keep traveling through history until you cross into Hertford County. There, not far from where the Meherrin River flows into the Chowan, you'll come to the old Vann plantation.

Just a few years ago, it didn't look like much, just some cotton fields backed by scrub forest. But in 1850, it was a major plantation with over fifty slaves. In 1860, only 611 plantations in the entire state owned more than fifty slaves, making the Vanns one of the larger slaveholding families in North Carolina.

These days, the old Vann place is back in business with a vengeance. The GEO Group (formerly Wackenhut Corrections Corporation), a multinational corporation that, among other things, constructs and runs private prisons for profit, has built a 1,320-bed prison here. The company operates it under a contract from the Federal Bureau of Prisons, which has shipped the prison twelve hundred young men from the District of Columbia, almost all of them African Americans. So a private for-profit corporation is importing well over one thousand black men from the District of Columbia and imprisoning them on the same plantation where other African Americans, possibly including some of their own ancestors, were held as slaves 150 years ago.

> I was hiding in the brush by the Ohio River
> Sarah by my side, the baby in my arms
> When the slavecatchers found us with our backs against
> the water
> Winter come late and the ice not formed
> > *And they sold me back South to the old Vann plantation*
> > *Two hundred miles from my home and kin*
> > *To be buried in a grave with no marker on it*
> > *Right on the spot where the new prison stands*

> I was walking the streets by the Anacostia River
> But no one was hiring a young black man
> When the District police picked me up for no reason
> Gave me fifteen years for less than ten grams
> > *And they sent me down South to the old Vann plantation*
> > *Two hundred miles from my home and kin*
> > *To be buried in a cell in a for-profit prison*
> > *To make some men rich from the trouble I'm in*

There were four million slaves from the African nation
Now there's two million prisoners in the "land of the free"
It might be right on this spot that my great-great-grandmother
Had done to her what they're doing to me
>   *I can feel her spirit on the old Vann plantation*
>   *Beneath the towers and the razor wire*
>   *All for the profit of some prison corporation*
>   *If you say that's not slavery, you're a goddamn liar*
>   *If you say that's not slavery, you're a goddamn liar*[3]

The for-profit prison that has replaced the old Vann plantation is just one example of the many ways in which the private prison industry is trying to change the nature of the criminal justice system in the United States. The rise of for-profit private prisons raises critical issues for democracy, as well as for the balance of public and private power in an open society.

Lessons from the Nineteenth Century

For-profit private prisons are both a result and a cause of prison expansion, as well as a relatively recent development. The current wave of interest in privatization in general in the United States is less than twenty-five years old. This increase in privatization of all kinds was paralleled by a radical rise in this country's prison population and consequently in new prison construction. As late as 1983, there wasn't a single private prison in the entire United States. In the twenty-one-year period between 1984 and 2005, the number of people incarcerated in private prisons, jails, and detention centers increased from none to over 120,000.

But this isn't the first time we've had a for-profit private prison system in the United States. Following the Civil War, many of the defeated southern states passed restrictive legislative known as "Black Codes," a set of laws that only applied to the newly freed African Americans. The massive arrests that followed filled the South's prisons and jails beyond overflowing, creating a crisis for states impoverished by the war.[4]

The crisis was resolved through the creative entrepreneurship of a Mississippi cotton planter named Edmund Richardson. In 1868, Richardson signed a contract with the federal government of Mississippi (remember, at this point the southern states were under military occupation by the victorious North), which turned over a number of former slaves they held as prisoners to his custody. Richardson got the right to work these ex-slaves on his land as hard as he wanted, as long as he fed, clothed, and guarded them. Best of all, Mississippi paid him to do this. He got paid for their labor; he paid the laborers nothing at all.

This virtual reinvention of slavery was the origin of what became known as the *convict lease system*. Eventually, inspired profit-seekers even more creative than Richardson developed a new twist to the system. Instead of only working the leased prisoners themselves, these entrepreneurs subleased them to the railroads, turpentine camps, coal mines, and sawmills of the industrializing South. Not only adults, but juveniles and children were leased out. According to David M. Oshinsky, author of *Worse Than Slavery: Parchman Farm and the Ordeal of Jim Crow Justice*, 17 percent of Mississippi's leased convicts died during one year (1882), and "not a single leased convict ever lived long enough to serve a sentence of ten years or more."[5]

The convict lease system, deadly to the "ex"-slaves, benefited not only those in power but also citizens who rarely had to face up to their complicity. According to Oshinksy, "Convict leasing made money for the state while keeping taxes down."[6] Another key point about privatization: It is all too easy to avoid seeing the real human cost of keeping public taxes down and private profits up.

Convict leasing eventually spread to most of the states of the old Confederacy, where conditions were as brutal as they had been in Mississippi—and as lucrative. In Alabama, "convict leasing generated about 6 percent of the state's total revenue in these years, giving Alabama the most profitable prison system in the country."[7]

Eventually, the convict leasing system was outlawed everywhere in the United States. But despite the brutality and inhumanity of the system, it took sixty years to abolish it. Alabama was the last state to do so, in 1928.

Not Just There, Not Just Then

Today's privatizers and their political allies rarely consider—let alone publicize and teach—such searing histories. But the convict leasing system *was* a form of privatization. These people—primarily ex-slaves, remember—were prisoners of different southern states and counties. They were prisoners in a public system of incarceration. That public system then leased them to for-profit private corporations and individual entrepreneurs, who in turn subleased them to other for-profit corporations, for which they suffered and died, often literally worked to death. That's a classic if particularly appalling case of privatization.

But it's also critical to remember that, while it took too long, this privatized system of incarceration was eventually outlawed. People of conscience, political reformers, courageous newspaper publishers (several of whom were shot to death in duels for acting on their consciences) agitated and organized to end the convict lease system. Over time, they won.[8]

Privatization is not a system found in nature. It has to be created and maintained. And it *can* be successfully opposed and abolished, even where it has established itself, and come to seem essential to an economy grown dependent on it, for years, even centuries. Slavery—the denial to people of any public standing, any public rights, in order to use them for their owners' profits—*was* ended. So was the convict lease system.

But why, more than fifty years after the convict lease system was finally outlawed everywhere, and despite the terrible experiences the first time it was tried, did prison privatization reappear? In addition to the unscrupulous greed of some people, it was partly a response to economic and political conditions (reasons that regularly trump moral concerns, sad as that is to say). Cities, counties, states, and even the federal government were hard-pressed financially and politically by the "need" for increased prison "beds" (the term preferred, for public relations reasons, to *cells*), and turned to for-profit private corporations to provide them.

Here's why, from the point of view of some elected and appointed officials, prison privatization is worth considering. By contracting with for-profit private prison corporations, elected officials avoid both prison construction costs (although they ultimately pay for those costs through the per diem rates charged by the private prison corporations) and the need to go to the voters with politically risky bond issues for new prison construction. They can also report the costs of these contracts under operating rather than capital expenses, thus *appearing* to cut certain costs—while actually just moving them from one budget line to another. And because the employees in private prisons work for a corporation rather than directly for the public, elected officials can claim that they've put more people in prison without adding any "government jobs." This is technically accurate, but substantially untrue. The government, with our tax money, is still paying for those jobs. It's just doing so through the corporation rather than directly. Of course, the corporation also takes care of its bottom line: less for us, more for them.

To for-profit private prison corporations, the issue is simple: the more people in prison, the more profit. They have a *stake* in more things being criminalized (that is, in more acts being redefined as crimes). They have a *stake* in longer, more standardized prison terms (all that erratic coming and going of the people they need to fill their cells to keep their profits rolling in makes a mess of business planning). They have a *stake* in there being more crime, matter of fact: less crime, less business, less profit.

This partly accounts for the for-profit private prison corporations' aggressiveness in trying to privatize as much as possible as quickly as they can. Like an army on the march, they're working to establish facts on the ground. So they're trying to grab as much territory as they can before the growing resistance to for-profit private prisons, from such sources as the faith community, labor unions, grassroots organizations, students, and the families of people in prison, reaches a critical mass.

Some in the faith community have been roused to action. The Presbyterian Church U.S.A., for example, has passed a resolution calling for the abolition of all for-profit private prisons, jails, and detention centers. So resourceful privatizers are busy offering access to once-taboo government money to other, more cooperative faith-based institutions.[9] President Bush's "faith-based initiative" in effect says to these religious organizations, "You, too, can get in on the spoils of privatization. What was public, and protected as such by one of the most basic American principles of all—the separation of church and state—is now open to you. Make us a proposal, and we may fund it." True, religious organizations are not for profit, but just as true, they can be very lucrative. These are groups that should be consulting their consciences rather than their pocketbooks, but never mind. Like corporations, if they get more of our tax dollars, they can do more of their own work (which they, too, like to think is good for us whether we agree or not).

The private prison corporations have another strategic reason for speed. If they can keep the present trend toward prison privatization going, it will eventually reach a tipping point after which private rather than public prisons will have become the norm. At that point, any possibility of restoring prisons to public control will be gone. Any idea of restorative justice will have even less hope than it does today. It's difficult enough now, when most prisons are publicly held and operated, for all those working to change conditions: people in prison, their friends and families, and all those who believe prisons can and should do far better at rehabilitation.

Imagine how much less likely serious rehabilitation efforts will be if the majority of prisons, jails, and detention facilities are in private corporate hands. If all prisons turn private, their parent corporations will have no more interest in reducing the shameful number of people imprisoned in this country than Marriott does in holding down its number of hotel guests. Through campaign contributions made possible by increased profits, they'll become an even more significant pressure than they are now to imprison the maximum number of people for as long as possible. Profit rather than public safety will increasingly become the measure of all things.

The development and growth of for-profit private prisons has many such negative consequences, including the current interstate commerce in prisoners by for-profit private prison corporations. This is one of the many tragedies of prison privatization. People are incarcerated at great distances from their families, homes, and communities, simply to suit the convenience of profit-seeking corporations. This is not only morally suspect; it has practical consequences. Many studies have shown that the further from home people in prison do time, the more likely they are to be rearrested and returned to prison after they are released.

But it's not just studies that show this. It's common sense. If people are in prison close to home, they're much more likely to see their family and friends, to feel more of a connection to a community in which there are people and institutions ready to help them when they are finally released. The corporate interstate commerce in people who have been imprisoned endangers both those people and the many communities and neighborhoods to which, sooner or later, almost all of them return.

This "export-import" business has a particular impact on the South. The "exporting" states tend to be those with higher costs per day for people in prison, places like Hawaii, Alaska, and Wisconsin. Exporting prisoners is not just about solving prison overcrowding but also about cash-strapped states trying to save money, including the capital costs of building new prisons. The "importing" states tend to be those with lower costs per prisoner per day, often a reflection of their significantly lower labor costs as a result of lack of unionization among correctional officers and other prison employees. Not surprisingly, the importing states tend to be in the South, with its historic low labor costs and lack of unionization.

But as with the convict lease system, resistance to the for-profit private prison corporations' reliance on this shameful human import-export business has sometimes been successful. In Wisconsin, which had the highest percentage of its prisoners incarcerated in for-profit private prisons outside the state, organized public pressure on the governor convinced him to bring the majority of those prisoners home. Similarly, in North Carolina, the state legislature responded to grassroots activism by passing a law making it illegal to bring people into the state to be incarcerated in a for-profit private prison.

There is no guarantee, of course, that even the best organized resistance will always defeat the privatizing corporations. The only absolute guarantee is that if we fail to organize and resist, they will always win.

Absent organized resistance, it's possible to foresee a scenario in which the South, already the site of incarceration for so many of its own people, becomes the holding area for many of the prisoners from the rest of the nation. The great majority of these people will be young African Americans, Latinas and Latinos, and other people of color for whom this "land of opportunity" has turned out to be quite the opposite. The South already has a long history of racialized incarceration, the convict leasing system, chain gangs. This shameful history tends to make prison privatization more familiar and so more acceptable.

And this sad history continues. The majority of people incarcerated in private prisons are in the eleven states of the old Confederacy. This keeps the South imprisoned in its own tragic history of building an economy on the backs of unfree people—people who are owned and exploited for the profit of others. People who are, we might indeed say, privatized.

Escalating Effects of Modern Private Prisons

Another negative consequence of prison privatization is the growth of "speculation" or "spec" prisons. The creation of speculation prisons took almost as much imagination as coming up with the convict lease system. Here's how it works. Let's say Joe, a friend of yours, drops by your place one evening. After the usual pleasantries, he gets to the point. "Say, Ed," he says, "you still got that 160 acres out there by the swamp?"

"Sure do," you reply. "It's sure as hell not going anywhere all by itself."

"You got any plans for it?" Joe asks.

"Nope," you say. "Too snakey to timber, too swampy to farm."

"How'd you feel if I was to lease it from you?"

"I'd say, 'You're crazy, Joe, but not that crazy.'"

"No, no." Joe says, "I've got something going. Look, here's how it works. You and me, we start this partnership. You give me an option to buy that quarter section—just on paper, of course. I take that option to the bank and I borrow money on it. We take that money and we build us a prison."

"Now I know you're crazy. You can't just build a prison all on your own. And where are you going to get the people to put in the prison? You can't just go out and arrest them."

"Believe it or not, Ed, if it's your private property, you can build a prison there if you decide you want to do it. You don't even need a prison permit. I mean, we'll have to work out the water and sewer permits, but you and I both know those boys up at the courthouse. There's no zoning in the county, so otherwise we're home free."

"Okay," you say. "Where are you gonna get the prisoners?"

"That's easy," Joe says. "There are these guys called 'bed brokers.' We call them up and say, 'Look, we've got this new prison coming online down here. We can take three hundred low-security prisoners and we can do it for $30 per prisoner per day.' These bed brokers, they all come out of one prison system or another, so they all know each other. They'll call up one of their buddies who's running a state prison system up North, where it can cost them $50 a day or more. Next thing you know, we're in business, making money hand over foot. Of course, once they get to where they can't do without us, we'll jack it up to $40 or $50 a day."

Now, why didn't you think of that?

Speculation prisons are particularly insidious, not just because they sidestep the intention of responsible state legislators to restrict and control prison privatization, but because they create pressure for more people to be sent to prison. From a management point of view, a prison is like a hotel or motel: You want to fill every bed, every night. If you don't have enough guests, you do whatever you can to get them, including supporting campaigns for mandatory minimums and longer sentences.

Privatized prisons have experienced numerous incidents involving deaths, disturbances, physical and sexual abuse of prisoners, to an extent much higher than in public prisons, which have enough problems of their own. This is not a coincidence. Such incidents are built into the operation of for-profit private prisons, which usually have very high employee turnover rates and consequent lack of experience among prison personnel. Experience at for-profit private prisons in many rural areas has shown a turnover rate considerably higher than that found in public facilities. In the poor rural counties where most private prisons are located, it's not long before the private prison corporation has run though the available workforce and starts recruiting personnel from farther and farther away. Sometimes they do this from the start: It costs them money to train the locals, after all. The long distances some of their new employees need to drive to work further increases the likelihood that they'll quit before long.

All this gives the lie to the corporations' promise to the desperately poor communities in which they purposefully locate that a new, for-profit private prison will mean more jobs for people who truly do need paying work.

Prison privatization frees the corporations from public requirements for open decision making and access to information. Privacy and secrecy are obvious conditions for the breeding of corruption. It's difficult enough to control corruption in prisons under any circumstances. When you also impose the veil of secrecy and some legal protections for privacy that are standard for most major corporations, you are not only inviting additional corruption but are making sure it will be more difficult to root out.

For-profit private prisons are one of the forces driving the increased incarceration of young people of color. Whole inner-city communities—already suffering increased poverty, joblessness, concentrations of drug dealers, poor schools, deteriorating housing, and the flight of people and employers able to leave—are being robbed of their economic and social potential as young

African-American and Latino men, and increasingly, women, are arrested and locked up, a pattern that is repeated in other communities of color. The statistics related to the African-American community are both well-known and discouraging. Of African-American men between ages twenty and twenty-nine, one of three is either in prison, on probation, or on parole. These days, there are more African-American men in prison than in college.

It is common knowledge how devastating this trap of racialized effects has been to communities of color. Prison can feed destructive anger and fail to show that there are other ways to live. It can keep people from pursuing education and training that are crucial to changing lives. And no matter what job training is or is not made available, having a prison record too often bars those who have done their time from future employment. How are they then to find the money to get through the days, let alone turn their lives around? Should we be surprised when communities of color are left behind economically and politically, when they have so many young people that no one is willing to hire because they've been to prison? Or when young people of color say that things today are worse than forty years ago, that the civil rights movement accomplished nothing, that there is no point even in trying to make it into the mainstream?

One of the ironies of the growth of public prisons is that it has created economic opportunity for some people of color. Increasing numbers of correctional officers, not to mention other prison employees, are themselves people of color. Because they are public employees, and because public prisons tend to be unionized, they often enjoy reasonable wages and benefits, along with job security.

But even this troubling kind of economic opportunity changes when prisons are privatized. Some for-profit private prisons pay wages that are barely above the legal minimum, with few or no benefits other than those required by law, such as Social Security, workers' compensation, and unemployment insurance. As already noted, turnover among employees in private prisons is consistently higher, and often significantly so, than in public prisons. Working conditions are both difficult and dangerous.

It is unfortunate that one of the few economic opportunities open to poor and working people, to people of color, in so many poor and rural communities is guarding other poor and working people, other people of color, including often their friends, neighbors, and family members.

I was raised in Mississippi
Down by the Natchez Trace
My best friend's name was Thomas
My momma's name was Grace
We grew up kind of wild
Robbed a store one day
The deputy caught Thomas
But me, I got away

Thomas came from poor folks
No lawyer and no bail
I left home for the Army
Thomas went to jail
Three years in Okinawa
With a company of MPs
In all the years I was away
He never told on me

It's quiet on the tier tonight
No sound to wake the dead
I can hear my old friend breathing
In his narrow iron bed
Though steel bars stand between us
The prisoner and the free
There but for the grace of God
Goes me

When I got home to Momma
The mill was closing down
Storefront windows boarded up
On the main street of our town
But just outside the city line
Some company'd come to stay
Building a brand new prison
In the fields where we used to play

I took my discharge papers
Stood there in that line
The warden took one look at them
Said, Son, you'll do just fine
When the only job is work or don't
You've got to earn your bread
So old friends sleep in narrow bunks
And the living guard the dead

> *It's quiet on the tier tonight*
> *No sound to wake the dead*
> *I can hear my old friend breathing*
> *In his narrow iron bed*
> *Though steel bars stand between us*
> *The prisoner and the free*
> *There but for the grace of God*
> *Goes me*[10]

Troubling, those prison jobs. But as long as these are the few jobs that are available, they need to be good jobs, with decent salaries, good fringe benefits, job security, adequate training, and union protection. Like other work, jobs in prisons need to enable parents, children, and communities to achieve economic levels that help provide for better health, more safety, and—perhaps most of all— better education. It is education, after all, that leads to hopes that might be fulfilled and to more choices that can really be made.

In fact, prisons and education have long had a relation to each other.[11] What that relation is and should be has always divided us. Those who stand with the less powerful have wanted more public monies to go to schools, less to prisons. Those who stand with the powerful have wanted to spend less public money in general, but have been more than willing to keep funding prisons.

This is why "Education, not incarceration!" is a slogan used by anti–private prison activists and prison reformers. It is a slogan that takes on historical resonance when we remember the struggle to desegregate schools—a struggle that has lessons to teach us about privatization, then and now.

CHAPTER 6

Tracking and Backtracking Politicians

I T ISN'T ALWAYS EASY to be an elected official who has signed on to the privatization agenda, for better or for worse, in sickness and in health. When former member of Congress Mark Sanford took office as governor of South Carolina, one of his first proposals was to privatize the state's colleges and universities. You could hear the howling of the alums and football fans all the way up to North Carolina. It was the first time the Tigers of Clemson University and the Gamecocks of the University of South Carolina had agreed on anything since what most people call the Civil War, but what some white people in South Carolina refer to as the War Between the States or the War of Northern Aggression.

It would have been interesting, given corporations' mania for putting their names on everything in sight, to see if the football teams would have been renamed as well. Can't you hear the announcer? "Folks, it's a beautiful November day here at Lockheed Martin Field as the Enron Gamecocks square off against the Wal-Mart Tigers."

Just Say Anything (to Further the Agenda)

Actually, and not surprisingly—since it is really hard to believe an electable candidate would not know that—some smart South Carolinians think Governor Sanford never really intended to privatize the entire state university system. Shrewd observers of the political scene think he just wanted to scare people with a proposal so outrageous that whatever he proposed to privatize next would seem reasonable by comparison (sort of like President George W. Bush going after Social Security).

There's evidence for this argument. Spokespeople for Sanford's administration have reportedly claimed that they can run the state of South Carolina with no more than one thousand public employees. That's somewhere in the neighborhood of fifty-nine thousand fewer public employees than the state has now.

Just to be absolutely clear, they were talking about *only* those public employees who work directly for the state of South Carolina. There are thousands of other public employees living in South Carolina but working for one of the state's cities and towns, or for one agency or another of the federal government.

So, under this new plan, would one thousand public employees, working as hard as they could, presumably using the most modern management techniques and powerful computers, be able all by themselves to operate the state of South Carolina? Think of all the operations and agencies they would have to administer. In some cases, a person might end up being the only direct state employee in the whole place.

Of course, the Sanford administration didn't really intend for one thousand state employees to do the work of sixty thousand. Even the kind of draconian management methods favored by Wal-Mart don't force people to that level of productivity (read, overwork). No, the governor's plan was to privatize virtually everything the state now does. The one thousand public employees who didn't lose their jobs to privatization would no longer, one presumes, spend most of their time directly doing the work of We the People. Instead, they'd be drafting RFPs (that stands for "request for proposal"—it's what you send out to let people know you have a contract you'd like them to bid on), reviewing bids, drafting and reviewing contracts, and then, more or less effectively and determinedly, monitoring the corporations that signed those contracts. At least, that's the work they'd need to be doing, despite having no training for it, and not likely to get it, either. Training public employees to be sure the contracting process really did serve the people would be costly to the cost-cutting governor. Anyhow, it might seem unfriendly to the state's new corporate partners.

Whether Governor Sanford really intended to privatize the state university system at that time (and whether he still hopes to privatize it some day), he wisely decided he'd be better off if his next target was something that didn't have a constituency that would rise up in arms if he tried to privatize it. Something most people would just as soon not think about. Something almost nobody cared about.

How about sick people in prison and the health care personnel who work with them?

Now, let's tell the truth here. Most people could care less about people in prison. It doesn't matter if those people are incarcerated in the prison or if they work there. Unless they're members of your family or a close friend, it just isn't something you think about. The basic attitude is, "Out of sight, out of mind." That's one of the reasons why we lock people up in the first place—so we don't have to deal with them, let alone care for them (or "coddle them," as the conservatives like to say).

Except in those poor rural counties where there are virtually no jobs except at the local prison, and where just about everybody who has any kind of job at all works there, you'd be hard-pressed to find a parent who will tell you, "When my daughter grow ups, my fondest dream is that she'll become a correctional officer." Or, "I'd be so happy if my child became a registered nurse and spent his life working with people with highly contagious diseases who are doing long sentences in a maximum-security prison."

This is not exactly the American Dream, although there are some wonderful people working in prisons, doing everything they can to help the people who are incarcerated there turn their lives around. We know several people who were transformed by such dedicated good souls, who came out of prison committed to help-ing other people. Unfortunately, because there is so little emphasis on rehabilitation in prisons, and so little support for those coming out of prisons and reentering the community, these are quite rare and special cases. So people who work in prisons, no matter how good and how dedicated, find it very hard to do much that can make them really proud of themselves.

Governor Sanford was being more than a little foxy when he chose prison health care services for what he hoped would be his first successful privatization campaign. And there's a key point: Privatization was and is a campaign. This governor, like other political figures who are helping to drive the privatization gravy train, is not just trying to fix some things that are really broken. He's trying to hand the work of the state over to privatizing corporations, which will then not only make their profits but move on with their efforts to take control of more of the public sector with all of its juicy, exploitable human and natural "resources."

Privatizing Can *Be Stopped: An Example*

Luckily for the public good, Governor Sanford didn't succeed in privatizing prison health care anymore than he did college football. It wasn't just luck that made the difference, though. It was an aggressive, six-month campaign led by prison health care personnel and their allies. They had put together the pieces, and they knew both their jobs and the work they really cared about were at risk. So they called meetings to build their base, to get to know and trust each other, to locate allies and pool knowledge and resources. They organized a steering committee, and when they had an organization, they brought in coalitional partners. Together, they did their analysis, set their goals, made plans, held rallies in churches and in the state capitol. They practiced making their case and supporting it, and when they had it down, they lobbied state officials and legislators. (No high-paid lobbyists involved: They went to see their representatives themselves as the people can, and should.) They built relationships with newspaper writers and editorial boards, calling them up, sending them information, keeping them informed, and inviting them personally to cover the campaign.

Because of the effective advocacy by the public prison health care workers and their allies, including peace activists, labor leaders, community organizations, and other public employees, the legislature passed a law requiring the state to conduct a study before any privatization could legally take place and then overrode the governor's veto of that legislation. Finally, the director of corrections announced that none of the bids that had been submitted met the state's needs and that therefore privatization would not take place—a reasonably graceful exit from a situation that had grown increasingly untenable for an appointed official who clearly wanted to run for higher office. When the people, the electorate, shined a bright light on what was really happening, he couldn't just go ahead and sign off on deals corporations offered behind closed doors.

This campaign illustrates how critical good research and information are in fighting privatization efforts. Two special reports were released at press conferences held in front of the governor's office by two of the organizations helping with the fight, South Carolina Fair Share and Grassroots Leadership.

The first report, *Prescription for Disaster: Commercializing Prison Health Care in South Carolina,* documented the dangerous and expensive prison health care services provided by for-profit corporations in South Carolina and elsewhere from 1986 to 2000. The report summarized examples of deplorable health care provided by the three commercial health care companies that had submitted bids for South Carolina's prison health care contract award.[1] The second report, *Prescription for Recovery: Keeping South Carolina's Prison Health Care Public and Making It Better,* showed how both improved service delivery and cost savings could be achieved by keeping the prison health care under public control, rather than contracting it out to a private corporation.[2]

In a letter published in the *New York Times,* Dr. Marguerite G. Rosenthal, author of the two reports, stated:

> Many states and county jails have sold their constitutionally mandated health care responsibilities to companies whose purpose, all too often, is to make money while providing minimal and frequently substandard health care. These companies create barriers to service, employ personnel with dubious credentials, skimp on needed medications, and avoid appropriate monitoring by public authorities. Prison health care is indeed in crisis. Selling

this public health responsibility to private entities has made the problem much worse.[3]

Not long after, the *New York Times* published a scathing front-page exposé of Prison Health Services, one of three corporations that had bid on the South Carolina contract.

Other efforts at public education were also important to the campaign and to the legislature's eventual action. Anton Gunn, executive director of South Carolina Fair Share, debated Jon Ozmint, director of the Department of Corrections, on South Carolina educational TV. In a press release, Gunn told the media:

> There are fundamental services that are the duty of the public sector to provide. Purchasing automobiles and copying machines from commercial dealers is one thing; states do not manufacture and supply themselves with these sorts of items.
>
> Running prisons, on the other hand, is an age-old function of the state. Caring for those in prison is a public obligation stemming from the consequences of prisoners' losing their liberty. Selling this obligation raises the specter of incompetent care, profits to corporate executives and shareholders—most of whom live and spend out of state—paid for by South Carolina taxpayers, and exploitation of prisoner-patients.[4]

When Ozmint tried to contain the spreading public outrage by issuing a gag order preventing corrections employees from talking to the media, nurses in whites passed out leaflets to other state employees that read, "Privatizing public services: Are you next? The job you save today may be your own."

The campaign continued to seek and to receive excellent coverage from South Carolina media, which was particularly important in building support for the campaign among legislators. *The State* in Columbia editorialized, "The state is obligated to provide quality health care to prisoners. It cannot simply subcontract those duties to a private firm and allow the free market to govern how services are delivered."[5] A column in *MetroBeat* in Greenville put it even more graphically:

> There is apparently no human tragedy so grim that some enterprising businessmen won't find a way to use the misfortunes of others to line their own pockets. The good folks at Halliburton have managed to turn the Iraq misery into a profit pipeline by selling food and gasoline to the military—and if they get caught gouging the taxpayers a time or two, well, c'est la guerre.
>
> Closer to home, a contract to provide medical care for 24,000 adults doing time in South Carolina prisons is up for grabs. In its wisdom, the state has decided that private companies can do the job better than the Department of Corrections and still make a tidy profit. If they're wrong, nobody suffers except people who have managed to get themselves locked up in prison.[6]

The *MetroBeat* column concluded, "Maybe we should be asking why our country continues to lock up her citizens at a higher per capita rate than those bastions of freedom Russia and China."[7]

Prison privatization isn't the whole answer to *MetroBeat's* question, but it's a critical and growing part of the problem.

CHAPTER 7

Keep the Paying Guests Coming: Filling Up the Prisons

Just as long as I can remember
Every four years, about November
Folks that wouldn't talk to me on the street
Are coming in my house, wiping their feet
Kissing my wife, kissing my babies
I guess they'd even kiss my old mule
If he hadn't voted for Roosevelt

They shake my hand, they smile and say
I'd like to have your vote, come election day
You don't need to know where I stand
Just vote for me as many times as you can
That'll be ten dollars now
And ten dollars more
Just every time that you vote

I promise you that if I'm elected
I'll raise the dead, have 'em resurrected
I'll fix your road, put a bridge on your creek
And sweep out your cow barn myself twice a week
Now there just might be something to that
'Cause I ain't never seen
Nobody else who could shovel that stuff as fast as a
   politician

Election's come and your road's still muddy
You try to find your old good buddy
He's down at the courthouse, grinding his axes
Only thing won't get cut is your taxes
I've been sliced this way so many times
I'm starting to look like a tomato

The hand you shook behind the plow
That hand is in your pocket now
You look for your mule and find he's missing
Better start hunting that politician
But there's one good thing—weren't for politicians
The rest of us folks wouldn't have nothing else
To laugh at except Nixon[1]

H ERE'S A CAUTIONARY TALE about the motel and the county commissioner.

You own a motel—and it isn't doing very well. Some nights, barely anyone checks in. On your best nights, it's maybe half full. You advertise, you offer special deals, but nothing changes. It's not like the roach motels, where "they check in, but they don't check out." In your motel, they check in, and they don't ever come back. From the front office desk, standing behind the counter, you look out at the highway, night after night, and watch the cars and trucks going by, going by, going by.

Other than the traffic zooming past the neon-lit entrance, the only steady thing is your costs. Every month you have to pay the principal and interest on the mortgage. There are taxes on the property, steep because it's right there on the highway. There's the electric bill, and the water and sewer bill. The only good thing you can say about the water bill is that, since you don't have very many customers, you don't use up a lot of water washing the sheets, pillowcases, towels, and washcloths.

Some days you feel like you only have one friend in the world. Luckily, that friend is the chair of the county commission, the most powerful politician in the county.

"Hey, why don't you come for lunch at the motel on Tuesday?" you invite him over the phone.

"Am I going to have to cook?" he asks. "Didn't you let the chef go two months ago because there weren't any customers to cook for?"

"Well, yes, we've been a little shorthanded around here lately," you say. "But she'll be here Tuesday. I've got a couple of nice T-bones in the freezer locker. One o'clock?"

Over steak and potatoes, you lay out your heart. "Here I am, a loyal, patriotic, red-blooded, tax-paying American citizen, working my fingers to the bone, and I'm going broke."

"Well, I guess if you don't have a lot of customers, it's easier on your fingers," says the commissioner.

"I mean, isn't this the land of the free enterprise zone and the home of the brave? How's it going to look to all those former Communist countries that we're trying to turn into democracies if I go out of business?"

The county commissioner chews his steak thoughtfully. "You've got a point there."

"Isn't this what our elected officials are for? Isn't that why we vote for people like you, so that our rights will be protected? Isn't that what America is all about?"

The commissioner puts down his fork. "What would you like me to do?"

You try to appear nonchalant. "Oh, nothing much. No big deal. I just thought maybe you could get the county commission to send me along some of those old people in the County Cares Residence, or maybe battered women from that shelter the feminists got you to build, or the homeless people you don't really want on your hands. You know, those folks could be a kind of a business stimulation package for me. Congress does that all the time.

"I wouldn't charge the county much. They don't need the Ritz, those people, now do they? I can get some people who'll be glad of any kind of job at all to come in and baby-sit them. And it would make you look good. Cost less to pay me than to pay those professionals you've got on the public payroll, and for my nice motel to boot."

The commissioner mulls this over. "I *could* do that. But I don't think it would look very good, me and you being friends and all. 'Favoritism' is what they'd call it. It could hurt me in the next election. Then I wouldn't be able to do anything for you at all." He pauses. "Or for myself." He stops, looking troubled. "I really like this T-bone." Then he brightens. "Hey, I know what we can do," he says. "We'll make it apply to all the motels in the county. That way, no one can say I'm favoring you over anyone else. There's only two more of them, anyway. I'd be helping them and I'd be helping you. And it would be sort of like giving people freedom of choice. That's a good American value, there."

For a while, your new contract is your golden goose. The rooms are filled with guests—some of them not very happy, but paid for nonetheless. The freezer locker is stacked with T-bone steaks for your "goodwill" lunches for folks from the county commission.

Then, slowly, business drops off. Three-quarters full, half full, a quarter full. Fifteen cents full. A nickel full.

"I don't understand it," you say to the county commissioner between mouthfuls.

"It's a small county," he says. "We can barely fill up one high school. And now those other two motels have gotten up and running just like you."

"Can't you close the others down? They must be violating something. You know, like the zoning code."

"We don't have one of those," says the commissioner. "Remember? You got it voted down. I believe it was the time you were thinking of putting a toxic waste dump out back of the motel."

"Well, what about the electrical code? Or the plumbing code? That's public safety you're talking about there."

"I'll see what I can do," the commissioner says. "Thanks for the steak."

The moral of the story: If you're in business, you need customers. Lots of them. Even the biggest corporations have this in common with the mom-and-pop grocery stores. No customers = no cash = no corporation.

Because customers are so important, businesses will do just about whatever they can to get them and keep them. Corporations, just like small businesses such as family-run motels, spend energy and cash trying to persuade people not just to become their customers but to be their customers alone.

The second moral: Corporations don't want you out there dating and playing the field. They want you to come home to them, every night.

Motels and hotels know (or at least hope) that, as long as there are a lot of people looking for lodging, they will get a reasonable share of the total business. They don't have to get all the customers, just a portion of them. When the total number of people spending the night in a city goes up, the occupancy rate for all local hotels and motels is likely to go up, too. When people stop coming to the city, occupancy goes down.

It's the same with private prison corporations. The more people there are in prison in the United States, the better their chances of getting some of them into one or another of the prisons any particular private prison corporation owns. So, if you were in the private prison business, wouldn't you work hard to increase the number of people in prisons, jails, and detention centers?

That's exactly what the private prison corporations do. To start with, they make major campaign contributions to candidates running for office. For example, in just one year, the private prison industry gave candidates for state offices in the South over $1 million. The money went to "830 candidates in 14 southern states during the 2000 election cycle, 90 percent of which went to incumbent and winning candidates who would be making policy and budget decisions in their next legislative sessions."[2] That doesn't even count what these corporations gave to candidates for Congress from those same states.

These candidates aren't just expected to advocate and vote for more private prisons. Politicians who support private prisons also tend to be "tough-on-crime" spokespeople who work and vote for harsher laws that both imprison more people *and* do so for longer periods of time. By financially supporting such candidates and elected officials, and through their small army of lobbyists, the private prison industry plays a direct role in increasing the number of people in this country's prisons, jails, and detention centers. It's just common sense. After all, these are their potential customers.

The private prison corporations also work to increase their customer base through the American Legislative Exchange Council (ALEC), which creates model state legislation. Its members, state legislators who generally range from conservative to right-wing, introduce and work to pass this legislation. Not surprisingly, given ALEC's political leanings, its recommended model legislation on prisons and criminal justice tends to support prison expansion, longer sentences, and other harsh tough-on-crime policies.

Guess who chairs and controls the ALEC committee that makes recommendations on criminal justice and prisons? Why, corporate executives from the private prison industry.

Here's the story's third moral. Corporations, and not just prison privatizers, love privatization not only because it gives them a steady flow of customers but because these deals are guaranteed by legally binding contracts and backed by the full faith and credit of city, county, state, and national governments.

It is also just fine with the corporations that these tend to be long-term contracts. In the private prison "industry," ten years is a good average, typically three years initially with the option of seven one-year renewals. That's a lot of guaranteed income. Wouldn't you like to have a written, signed contract stating that you were promised a job and an income for that long? How many businesses owned by individuals and families have a guarantee that their number of customers won't decrease by one person over three, and very likely, ten years?

So with privatization, you don't need a small army of salespeople and an astronomical advertising budget to entice customers. You just need some high-priced lobbyists, some well-placed campaign contributions, and some sympathetic elected and appointed officials. They'll make sure you not only get customers but that you get them for years at a time.

Here is another juicy aspect of these deals. If getting enough customers is one problem for all businesses, getting those customers to pay their bills is another. Most businesses large and small spend a lot of money and time either acting as or hiring a credit agency to collect due debts and back debts. Bad debts, those which are never collected, cost corporations billions of dollars a year.

Not a problem if you're on the privatization gravy train. You don't need to worry about being paid for your services. The various government agencies with which your corporation contracts will make sure you get paid on time. Even if, as happens occasionally, you have to sue them to get paid, they have very deep pockets. If your lawyers charge you more than you'd anticipated, why, just raise your price the next time your contract comes up for renewal and pass those costs on to the people of the United States.

The final moral of the story: We the People are essential to all this deal-making between government and corporations, although we may not even know it is going on. After all, where do governments (federal, state, county, city) get the funds to pay the corporations, so that they can pay their executives, directors, major shareholders, lobbyists, and lawyers? Not to mention, of course, all the rank-and-file employees who do the hard daily work to keep the corporation going.

Why, from us, the people of this country, the everyday workers, the shopkeepers, teachers, nurses, small business owners, armed services personnel, truck drivers, you name it.

The profits of the privatizing corporations come out of our pockets. They don't even need salespeople, cashiers, or credit agencies to collect from us. The government has an agency that will do that for them.

It's called the IRS.

CHAPTER 8

We Love This Problem: Lives for Sale

The classic investment opportunity is where there's a problem. The larger the problem, the larger the opportunity.
—MICHAEL MOE, INVESTMENT BANKER[1]

PRIVATIZERS TYPICALLY CLAIM that they are in the business of solving our problems for us. These days they are also moving into the business of diagnosing problems—defining what they are and what causes them. This allows them to define problems and causes in ways that set them up to offer themselves as the best suited to fix them, as Lockheed Martin has done with welfare services in Texas, Georgia, and other states.[2]

Privatizing Health Care

Health care is another large problem in which corporations are deeply involved. Everyone knows that health care costs keep rising. Annual U.S. health care expenditures now total more than $1 trillion, equivalent to about 14 percent of the gross domestic product: fourteen cents out of every dollar we spend. Why are those costs so high and getting higher? Who benefits, who profits?

Well, corporations do, particularly those that work to privatize public hospitals and health care services, along with those corporations that sell us drugs, medical care, and health insurance. Not surprisingly, they're aggressively opposed to a national health care program to ensure that no one suffers or dies solely for want of money. Were there such a program, health care costs would be lower. If our government played the role of negotiator with suppliers of medicines and services, those prices would also go down. Again, no surprise: proposals for such possibilities provoke massive counterattacks from the corporations that make their profits from our problems.

Corporations that work to privatize health care services often try to redirect the definition of the problem from costs and prices to who pays for these services: Don't blame us, blame the insurance corporations. Of course, more than forty-three million people in the United States do not hold any form of public or private health insurance. But the major fuss that arises when we turn our attention to insurance is that health care coverage costs so much, and keeps getting more expensive.

Lest that suggest we should question the profits being made by insurance corporations, they rush to tell us why they "have to" set their rates so high. In the 2004 presidential campaign, we heard a lot of talk about how "frivolous" malpractice suits brought against doctors by unscrupulous individuals egged on by even worse trial lawyers have cost the doctors' insurance providers so much money that they have been forced to raise the cost of the policies they issue.

The insurance corporations have set physicians' costs for malpractice coverage so high that some doctors are leaving the profession. Blaming what these insurers do on individuals who bring malpractice suits and the trial lawyers who take their cases keeps us from asking more determinedly why, say, having the medical profession police itself and take action against the very small percentage of physicians who are responsible for most malpractice suits wouldn't be a sensible solution. But that might lead to clear evidence that malpractice insurance should cost less, and that might cut insurance corporations' profits.

So the problem continues, with debates that do not get at any heart of the matter. The United States is still the only economically developed country in the world that doesn't have a national health care program that provides access to care for everyone. And as for-profit medical corporations have taken over hospitals and clinics from public and nonprofit providers, the quality of care has not improved, the costs have either not gone down or have risen still further, and growing numbers of people cannot afford the care they desperately need.

A report on health care privatization concludes, "In wealthy communities, we have argued, the various elements of health privatization are riddled with inequities and contradictions. They focus the resources of a highly developed and well-funded medical system on an increasingly narrow segment of the population. For those unable to afford fees and premiums associated with private HMOs, they ensure inferior service at more inconvenience and greater out-of-pocket cost. In many cases they fail to guarantee that all citizens will have access to even the most basic health services."[3]

Behind this not-very-pretty picture is belief in relying on and promoting private insurance plans to cover costs, and instituting or increasing "user fees" for medicines we are advised to take and other things doctors tell us we must do if we are to be cured, such as following diets prescribed by a nutritionist. Neither getting us to buy insurance nor forcing us to pay user fees on top of that insurance moves us toward universal public health care provisions. Doesn't do so in this country, doesn't do so for people in other countries that are being forced to privatize in order to repay their debts to global organizations such as the International Monetary Fund.

The authors of the study on health care privatization observe, "In fact, undermining free health care providers is partly a strategic decision by those who design health care privatization policies." And then they quote an advocate of privatization: "If people can obtain health care for free or at a uniformly low cost, they will not have much incentive to pay insurance premiums to cover unexpected health hazards."[4] Right: So the real problem being solved here is how to make sure people *do* have to pay those insurance premiums, not how to provide decent health care for all who need it.

"Here as elsewhere, the structure and ideology of health care privatization can be lethal to society's most vulnerable members."[5]

And it is hardly promoting good and accessible care for the rest of us, either.

What's going on here? Why is all this not perfectly obvious? Why have people not risen up and rejected such a lethal ideology?

Privatization Ideology at Work

When people hold onto a set of ideas even when the evidence of their own experiences and credible reports warn them that something is very wrong, that set of ideas can be called an ideology. That's what we mean when we call someone an *ideologue*. We're saying that he or she puts some theory, some set of ideas, over open-eyed recognition of reality.

There are ideologues of all stripes, from right to left on the political spectrum, just as there are fanatics and extremists in most if not all religions. They have a right to their views: A healthy democracy depends on all of us hearing the full range of opinions. But it is one thing to stand up and say, "This I believe, and I want to persuade you to agree with me." It is quite another to set out to take over or even destroy the very government that protects your right freely to express your beliefs in order to make it conform to your personal values, your own ideology. In the United States, we elect and then expect our president to listen to all of us, to figure out and do what's best for the country, not to be an ideologue and impose a personal religious belief, a political agenda, and self-interested economic goals on the rest of us.

According to the extreme ideology of privatization, with its roots in the private profit culture and unfettered capitalist fundamentalism, we are not to worry just because the United States has failed to provide for one of the most essential public goods, public health. We are to think ourselves superior to all those other highly developed countries that do have national health care systems, and to believe that imposing our own system on less developed countries will help them.

Why? Not because the United States has the the best health care system in the world. It does not. What's superior is the profitability of our system, not whether we're healthy—which we're not. Key indicators put the United States at the bottom of the list of developed countries, below Canada (that crazy bunch of ice-bound socialists), Japan, and with the exception of Portugal, all of Europe (with its old-fashioned socialist parties and stubborn belief in serving the public good). So, we're superior with regard to health care despite being inferior with regard to health care. If you can wrap your mind around that, please let us know.

A lot of history, a lot of effort, has gone into trying to convince us that private, for-profit corporations are superior to government and the whole public sector *in all regards*. This ideology, of course, serves the privatization agenda and the corporations that both promote and benefit from it. We need to pay attention to some of the ways this ideology has worked in the past, and is working today.

In the throes of today's massive moves by corporations to take over provisions for the public good, we are ideologically primed to cut back still further support for all the good people who today do public health work here and around the globe. The real heroes, we are to believe, are the folks who make big money by leveraging still more capital to privatize more once-public hospitals and clinics and public health providers—or to develop and control the patents for new drugs for which they can charge more than too many of us can pay. And they can and will focus, of course, on the largest markets that will reliably keep paying. Too bad if your child has a rare disease; too bad if people are dying of illnesses that could be avoided if they had clean water, enough food, sanitary toilets, affordable medicines. Those aren't included in diagnoses of the problem by those with profitable solutions to sell.

Why do some of us still trust and make heroes of the corporations and corporate leaders whose primary cause is to make profits? Because by the ideology of privatization, the real and only true heroes are those who produce wealth. Public health, like other aspects of the public good, is then at best to be hoped for as a kind of fortunate by-product.

Set aside for a moment what an insult it is to give the profit motive pride of place over every moral code and religion and ethical philosophy and democratic creed. Even on the level of simple common sense, this is an ideology of which we should be leery. After all, if a corporation takes over a public hospital, its profits depend on there being sick and injured people who can pay or be paid for (by such government programs as Medicare and Medicaid, for example) to occupy its beds, do they not? Do they then have a stake in finding ways to have *fewer* sick and injured people?

Quite the contrary: They need a steady, and ideally, growing supply of paid-for suffering people. Of course, like for-profit private prisons that need to fill their beds, they won't stand up in public and say, "We *love* this problem. Back off from trying to solve it: It sends us our business." No: They solemnly proclaim, "We can solve this problem. We can solve any problem. And we can do it better than Big Government or nonprofit organizations run by bleeding-heart liberals and would-be saints." Never mind that privatization of responsibility for health care shifts the diagnosis of the problem away from failures to keep people alive and well toward enhancing "efficiency" and "choice," which are what advocates of free-market solutions tout.

Choice? Listen to this conversation that took place between a Peruvian patient with multidrug-resistant tuberculosis and her physician in 1997:

"Señora, you have to buy these medicines, or you die—you choose."

"Doctor, I want to live—but I can't afford to buy them."[6]

The privatization ideology doesn't have room for the experiences of such real people. What do you really think of corporations that sell us medicines we need to stay well, even to stay alive, at prices inflated by the desire for high profits? How high, how far beyond what it takes to keep a business running and basically healthy? High enough to pay those monstrous CEO salaries and bonuses, to keep wealthy board members contented and agreeable, to support gleaming corporate headquarters worthy of the old Egyptian pharaohs, to keep the big shareholders and Wall Street happy, to manage public relations, to make people buy what you sell through manipulative advertising, to retain a fleet of lawyers, to support lobbyists in Washington, D.C., to pay for corporate jets, to throw parties to "build relations" with other mega-rich corporate players around the globe—remember all that? That's your money, as surely taken from you as taxes, but in the form of excess profit wrung from controlled markets—and they get some of your taxes, too.

Try this. Look at a government building: city, county, tribal, state, federal. Then look at a corporate headquarters. Which one tells you there is lots of extra money to spend because the cost we pay for the delivery of a service or product has been seriously inflated?

How do you feel when corporations respond to efforts to lower prices for the medicines some of us need—say, by having the government negotiate for them, as it does through the Veterans Administration—by citing the free market as their justification for fighting against any such efforts? Just how much do you value protecting the "right" to price-gouge more than the health of your grandmother, your children, the basic health of the general population?

Remember that the term *general population* refers not just to neighbors and community members but also to all those people living in circumstances in which highly contagious diseases can breed and spread if not stopped where they fester, so often among the poor and overcrowded. The general public also, and these days increasingly, includes the more than 2.1 million people now in this country's prisons, jails, and, as security anxieties are hyped by those who will profit from them, detention centers.

The privatization ideology doesn't even work both ways: It claims its values, but it turns out they hold only for the profit-makers. Let's say we agree that it should be the free market, with no interference from our government (let alone justice movements and unions), that takes care of setting and meeting public priorities for a whole country, or even the world, as the privatizers' ideology holds. We might, after all, believe that prices eventually do find a level at which a profit can still be made where there is great need. Economies of scale might have their promised effects: big corporations, big need, lots of sales, big enough profits so buyer-pleasing lower prices can still rake it in.

Let's say, then, "Okay, let the free market rule. You charge what you think you can get away with, and we, also players in the free market, will comparison-shop. If need be, we'll go to Canada to buy medicine, where there is a national health care plan that provides better and more reliable care than our private and privatized system. You go international, we'll go international, looking for where we can buy what we need more cheaply: multinational corporations, multinational shoppers." That's exactly what some retired Americans, who simply can't afford the medicines they need in this country, are doing: going to Canada to buy them.

What do you think when the corporations, with President George W. Bush lined up on their side, use governmental power, the very power they say they want to shrink, to make that illegal, as they are doing even now?

"Say, Martha. This sure is a surprise. Good to see you."

"You, too, George. You're looking pretty good for an old man."

"I haven't run into you since your eighty-fifth birthday party, and that's got to be at least two years ago. Where've you been?"

"Federal prison, mostly."

"No, Martha, not you. I don't believe it. What were you in for?"

"Arthritis."

"Now, Martha, they don't put you in federal prison for arthritis. The hospital, maybe, if it gets bad enough. But not prison. There must have been something else."

"Well, there was emphysema."

"How'd they catch you?"

"The federal marshals arrested me at the Canadian border."

"What, were you trying to flee the country?"

"Nope, just trying to get back in with my medicines."

What happens to such private profit culture values as *the free market* and *open global markets* when they threaten to work in favor of We the People? The privatization ideologues claim these values and principles, but the last thing they want is for them to apply to everyone. To the privatizers, whatever their rhetoric, the basic market dynamics of supply and demand, of real and equal competition, and of responsiveness to consumers are actually problems. They preach them as solutions for us, but they try to subvert them for themselves. Corporations want captive and therefore reliable buyers who can't take their money elsewhere. They want to control, to dominate their economic arenas in ways no real free market ever could be controlled.

In short, they don't want us wandering around an open, public square comparing prices and the quality of goods. They want to own the square and all its outlets. Why not? That's the way to make *real* profits.

So, no, Martha, you can't go to Canada to buy medicine more cheaply. Instead, why don't you go down to the public library and check out a book by Milton Friedman on the wonders of the free market. That is, of course, if the library hasn't been closed because of budget cuts, or its management contracted out to Halliburton.

The old song comes to mind: *If living were a thing that money could buy, the rich would live and the poor would die.*

No more "if." Living *is* a thing that money can buy, and not just the poor but much of the middle class *are* dying. The corporate privatization of public health has not solved the problem at all. It is making it worse. How, then, can the privatization ideology stand against the evidence of our experience, our own need, the wrench to our hearts and consciences of the need of other people here at home and elsewhere in the world?

Paul Farmer, who has given his life to serving the poorest and sickest people wherever they are, observes that Russia "has recently been demoted to the status of a developing country, and it is embracing, according to many observers, 'Western' (read, American) ways of managing inequality."[7] This is gratifying to people who are triumphant about the collapse of the Soviet Union, who think: See? We were right, they were wrong, and now the Russians will have a chance at our freedom and equality.

Well, once again, not exactly. Privatization ideologues are at work again here. Post-Soviet Russia, is selling off (privatizing) all that was once nationalized (held by the state) to homegrown and international corporations. As a direct result, it is undergoing a massive public health crisis.

"In 1990," Farmer reports, "TB [tuberculosis] incidence in Moscow was 27 percent per 100,000 population; by 1993, it had almost doubled, to 50 per 100,000."[8] Why this disastrous increase in an eminently treatable disease that, untreated, is both highly contagious and deadly? As always, it results from the coming together of many causes. But prime among them, says Farmer, is that "the local TB specialists have had their funding cut, in many instances, by more than 90 percent."[9]

There you see the ideology of privatization at work. Don't support those doctors, those TB specialists, with public funding. Let them get out there and compete for profits, and then, by god, you'll have a fine, all-American system in Russia. We'll show them how it's really done!

Sounds good, perhaps? Farmer, who has in every sense been there, sees it otherwise. "The collapse of the public health system, a part of the broader social disruption, . . . is the heart of the problem."[10] Of course it is. Tear apart a government, open the "market" to the multinational corporations, put everything the government once owned or operated on sale to the most powerful (or best connected, or least scrupulous) bidder, don't ask questions or even think of setting rules and regulations that might make profit-seekers respect the public good just a bit—and heaven help the "little people." They've been liberated. The free-market global, capitalist economy has arrived. What else do they want?

Of course, they now have nowhere to turn when TB comes back with a vengeance, but that's okay. We're bringing them democracy.

But an economic system is not a political system, and multinational corporate capitalism doesn't put out fires or epidemics if there's no big profit to be had (and not always reliably then).

In the ideology of privatization, it is literally not conceivable that privatizing can fail to fix, let alone cause, problems. Inflated by the fearfulness of the cold war era into a theory-on-steroids to make it a match for the globalizing Communist ideology, it is out to win at all cost to fairness and health—just like those steroid-pumped-up athletes we keep being shocked, shocked! to discover in the ranks of the outrageously overpaid, profitable arena of competitive sports. That's another arena where we forget at everyone's peril, including the athletes', that we need democratic rules and referees to keep things safe and fair for all.

Don't Confuse Capitalism with Democracy

We have been encouraged to confuse democracy with capitalism, to confuse a political system with an economic one. How to prove your love of our country? Go out and buy, as President Bush actually urged us to do after the huge shock of 9/11. Why? Surely not because that's what democracy is all about. No: Our shock, horror, and terrible losses had diverted our attention from shopping, and that was bad for business. We needed to be convinced that the killers who had struck us hated freedom and democracy *in the form of shopping*.

The privatization ideologues are also determined to keep us from realizing just how dependent we are on the true heroism of public employees like the New York firefighters, police officers, and EMTs who died doing their job of saving lives.

Firefighters, however, were not always public employees. In the early days of this country, all fires were fought by private companies. You chose the company you wanted to protect your property and paid it a regular fee to do so, kind of like an insurance premium. Of course, this meant that profits were to be made from fires and from peoples' fears of them, not from solving the problems that made fires happen in the first place, like substandard, highly inflammable building materials.

This private system worked fine if, at the particular moment when your home or business caught fire, the firefighting company you'd retained was hanging around in the neighborhood and not off somewhere else fighting another fire.

But, wait! Look! Right across the street from your burning house, there's another firefighting company having lunch, horse-drawn pumper and all. Your home is saved!

Well, not exactly. If you had enough cash to pay them on the spot, they'd fight the fire. But if your cash was still in the burning house, and you hadn't been paying a regular premium to this other company as well as to the first one, they would just stand around and watch the house burn. No contract, no service, no matter what. Nothing personal, it's just that business is business.

Privatizers do not want us to remember what it was really like for the majority of people before we learned the hard way that no person, no household, no neighborhood, no community, no state, no country is an island complete and sufficient unto itself. We all need the food, the water, the air, and the health-and-safety care that sustain us in life, just as we need the arts and philosophies and songs and stories that give meaning to that life. We are all vulnerable to diseases, to injury, to catastrophes from hurricanes and earthquakes to wars and genocidal hatreds, to the power lust and unbridled greed of those who are always among us just as the good, the loving are also always among us.

When we face together the problems we share and draw upon the best in all of us to solve them through social provisions and protections made equally available to all by a good, responsive, democratic public sector and government, we share and thereby grow our power and with it the freedom to make real choices. When we let those problems be defined for us by those who want to sell us their solutions, we hand far too much of our collective power and freedom of choice over to them.

CHAPTER 9

Don't Fence Me In:
Private Walls and Public Rights

It's roof leak door squeak bed soaked window broke
Cat chase a rat chase a mouse
If you ever want to see a man lose his bobbins
Make him live in a company house

It's white beans turnip greens pinto beans streak o' lean
Pay every day you owe more
If you ever want to see a man flip his spindle
Make him buy in a company store

*'Cause it's card room spinning room winding
room weave room
Lint all over my shoes
When I get over to the other shore
Gonna tell 'em 'bout the cotton mill blues*[1]

YOU MIGHT THINK that all cities and towns are public bodies. But this isn't the case, either historically or currently— and the past, as they say, is repeating itself.

Company Towns: Private Worlds of the Past

In the past, particularly in the South and the West, there were what became known as *company towns*.

They were just what the name suggests: towns owned outright by a company. Nothing was public, everything was private. No one could be a resident of the town who didn't work for the company.

Everyone lived in company houses, walked to work on company streets, prayed in a company church. There was often a prescribed and very strict moral code defined and enforced by the owners, and they wanted their workers' religion to reinforce it.

These corporations didn't just build the physical town from scratch—they built the population the same way. In the cotton mill villages, recruiters traveled the back roads of the farm country, looking for workers. In New England in the nineteenth century, the recruiters drove wagons that were known, amazingly enough, as "slavers." They usually recruited young single white women, who left their families to live in company-owned boardinghouses and work in the mills. In the twentieth-century South, they recruited whole families, the larger the better—children as young as eight years were part of the workforce. The recruiters hired mostly white workers, who got the better, safer, and more prestigious jobs. Black workers, if they were hired at all, were recruited only for jobs "on the yard," meaning that they worked outside the physical mill—or in the rarer cases when they were allowed inside the walls, at the lowest-paying and most dangerous work.

The mill owners also made sure that their agents only recruited workers whose beliefs they felt would reinforce the system they were trying to establish. Si used to have a book published by the state of Georgia around 1913, which was circulated to northern textile corporations that were considering moving South. The book boasted that the state's workforce consisted entirely of native-born Anglo-Saxons, rather than foreign-born syndicalist immigrants (*syndicalist* meant union supporters), and that the Georgia legislature had never in its history voted against the interests of business.

> I wish I was in the land of cotton
> Wages there are on the bottom
> Look away, look away, look away, Dixie land
> Down among the alligators
> Where there's friendly legislators
> Look away, look away, look away, Dixie land

I'll move my plant to Dixie
Today, today
I'll lock the gates and close the doors
Goodbye to union wages
Away, away, away we'll go to Dixie
Away, away, away we'll go to Dixie[2]

Those workers played baseball for a company team on a company field. They shopped at a company store, also known as a commissary—the same term used on military bases. If there was a fire department, the equipment belonged to the company. Law enforcement consisted of company security personnel. Workers were paid, not in U.S. money, but in special tokens (sometimes wooden, sometimes metal, sometimes paper) issued by the company, called *scrip*. Scrip was private money, which could only be spent at the company store. Even if people had saved up their scrip, if the company store refused to sell to them—for example, during a strike or lockout—they had no way to buy food and other necessities.

In this closed economic system, where people were trapped and could literally be starved, they were often driven to desperate measures. Here's the legendary midwife and songwriter Aunt Molly Jackson of Bell County, Kentucky, remembering the time she robbed the company store to feed the starving children in her community:

I went into the commissary
and I went in laughing
and I said to the commissary clerk
I said, Well, it don't make any difference
how hard times gets, Mister Martin
I said, I can always have a little money
or a little scrip
or something to get by on
Give me a twenty-four-pound sack of flour

Then I begin to call
for the things that was needed the worst
for them little starving children
And I filled my sugar sack full and I said:
How much is this?

Five dollars and ninety cents

Well, I said, Now, Martin, I'll see you in ninety days
as quick as I can get around
and collect enough money to pay you

He says, Aunt Molly Jackson
don't you offer to walk out
with all them groceries

I reached under my arm
and I pulled my pistol
and I walked out backwards
and I said, Martin,
If you try to take this grub away from me, I said
God knows if they electrocute me for it tomorrow
I says, I'll shoot you six times in a minute[3]

People who didn't work at the company that owned the town were usually banned from entering, a ban enforced with particular enthusiasm by the company's security guards when the visitor was a union organizer or a news reporter. They didn't want any news going out, or outside help or new ideas coming in.

If you drive through the Piedmont and mountain South, through the old coal and cotton country, you will still run across many of the company towns. The companies that owned them have by and large disappeared (usually taken over by other, larger corporations) and the towns themselves are drying up and blowing away. Sometimes you can tell just by the name that a place was a company town: If it ends in "co," as in Vicco (for the Virginia Iron and Coal Company), that's almost certainly what it was.

One of the most famous of the former company towns is Kannapolis, North Carolina, just east of Charlotte. Some twenty-five thousand people worked in its mills. Supposedly, the name means "city of looms" in Greek. "Polis" is, it's true, the Greek word for "city." But "kann" is neither a Greek nor a Latin root, let alone the Greek word for "loom." So most likely someone made this up to make it sound more elegant than your average mill village.

Kannapolis belonged to the Cannon family and was obviously named after them, Greek or not. It was run by the family patriarch, Charles Cannon, known to one and all as Uncle Charlie. There's even a song about Kannapolis, from a film about the town called *Red, White, and Blue for Uncle Charlie*, made in the late 1960s or early 1970s by Public Citizen, the organization founded by Ralph Nader.[4]

Are there any of you people out in TV land
Who haven't ever seen a company town?
There's a few of Nader's raiders down in North Carolina
Gonna take a little look around

The city limit sign says Kannapolis
It's got thirty-thousand people or more
And Uncle Charlie Cannon owns every building
Every house and every street and store

He owns the bank, he owns the jail
He owns the A&P
He'll sell you anything except beer
I wouldn't say nothing to the chief of police
That I didn't want Charlie to hear

And everybody's working down at Cannon Mills
That's owned by you know who
Some folks say that when you get on payroll
Charlie owns a piece of you[5]

According to a common story, sometime back in the 1930s union activists organized a march down the main street of town. They were all arrested for trespassing by the chief of police and ordered to appear in court.

Their lawyer couldn't have been more self-confident. "Your Honor," he said to the judge, "these union members were exercising their constitutional right of free assembly. The first amendment to the United States Constitution, Article I of the Bill of Rights, clearly states, 'Congress shall make no law respecting . . . the right of the people peaceably to assemble, and to petition the Government for a redress of grievances.' That's exactly what they were doing, Judge. They were on public property exercising their constitutional rights as free American citizens."

The lawyer for Cannon Mills stood up. "Your Honor," he said, "we could not agree more with the distinguished attorney. The right of free assembly is sacred. It's sacrosanct. It is enshrined in our Constitution. Far be it for me or for Mr. Cannon to challenge that right. Every American citizen has the absolute right to march down a public street holding a picket sign and shouting as loud as he wants.

"Only problem is, the streets in Kannapolis aren't public property. Mr. Cannon owns the ground under them, he owns the ground next to them. He paid to pave them and he pays to keep them up, out of his own pocket. He has not accepted one red cent of county, state, or federal money to build them or to maintain them. They're Mr. Cannon's personal private property. And if you're walking on one of Mr. Cannon's streets, and he tells you to get off, and you don't, why then, sir, by God, you're trespassing."

Private Communities and Public Rights

Over the years, the Supreme Court of the United States has struggled with the question of what public rights we have in privatized places. The trend since the 1970s has been to limit our freedom to exercise those public rights on corporate-owned properties.

For example, in 1946, in *Marsh v. Alabama*, a Jehovah's witness who was handing out religious tracts in a town owned by a company was arrested. In a ringing assertion of First Amendment rights to freedom of speech, U.S. Supreme Court Justice Hugo Black—remarkably, himself a former Ku Klux Klan member—"emphasized that all citizens must have the same rights, regardless of whether they live in a traditional municipality or a company-owned town." Black noted that "a typical community of privately owned residences would not have had the power to pass a municipal ordinance forbidding the distribution of religious literature on street corners. Why then, should a corporation be allowed to do so?"[6]

But in 1972, in *Lloyd Corp. v. Tanner*, the Supreme Court narrowed its interpretation, and its defense of our rights to free speech, by finding against activists who were distributing leaflets in a shopping mall. Justice Lewis Powell, who in 1971 wrote an extremely influential memorandum to the U.S. Chamber of Commerce issuing a call for businesses of all sorts to go on the attack against activists,[7] argued that the public was only "invited" to a mall "to shop." "According to Powell, political activists misunderstood the invitation if they turned the mall into a public forum." Furthermore, he said, "because the First Amendment only limited 'state action' there was no constitutional basis to apply it to private entities."[8] What that interpretation means is that the Constitution limits *governmental* power to deny your freedom of speech, but it does not limit *private entities*—read, corporations—from doing so.

Back to the Future: Gated Communities

Gated communities provide an interesting modern parallel to the old company towns.[9] Here's how they work. A developer buys up a major tract of land and constructs what is in effect a self-contained city. The developer not only puts up the houses but builds and pays for everything else: roads, sidewalks, water lines, sewer lines, electric cables, emergency generating facilities, community buildings, sports fields, swimming pools, lakes, ponds, walking trails, fire station. And more: the gate that keeps people from coming in without permission; the guardhouse next to the gate; the stone and brick walls that surround the community; the high-intensity floodlights that illuminate those walls, the guardhouse, the gate; the alarm system that lets the security guards know if anyone is attempting to sneak through the gates or climb over the walls.

It's ironic that in the United States today there are two groups living behind locked gates: those who can afford them, including growing numbers of the wealthy and famous, and the poorest in prisons (whose numbers are also growing).[10] But of course that's not really anything new: Once upon a time, the wealthiest had castles with moats and drawbridges, palaces with guards, ancestral mansions with gates. And once upon a time, the poorest had debtors' prisons.

Gated communities are kind of like Kannapolis with a wall around it and a locked gate to control who goes in and out, or those old moated castles that were small towns inside. If you're not a resident of a gated community, someone who works for one of the residents or for the corporation that maintains it, or someone approved by one of the residents or by the corporation, you can't get in.

Think of it. No unapproved strangers on your streets. No people you don't know wanting to mow your lawn or rake your leaves. No door-to-door canvassers raising money to help protect the environment. No college students selling magazines to pay their way through school. No homeless people to make you feel guilty.

All clean and neat and controlled. All private.

And again: As in Kannapolis, roads, sidewalks, water and sewer lines, electric cables, emergency generating facilities, community buildings, sports fields, swimming pools, lakes, ponds, walking trails, fire station, security systems are all privately financed—and private property. If public funds were used to construct, say, the playing fields and walking trails, they would be public. Anybody would have the right to come through the gate and use them. Your kids might even play with them.

But someone has to pay for all this, since these services are not coming out of tax dollars. Those "someones" are the people who live in the gated community. In addition to buying or renting their home, they pay large fees to cover these costs.

But the people living inside that community are still taxpayers. (See how irritating government is? You just can't shut it out, even if you have the money to build gates and lock them.) They pay taxes to the city and county in which their gated community is located. They pay city, county, and state sales tax. If the state they live in has an income tax, they pay that. They pay federal income taxes.

Now, no one likes to pay taxes. We forget to pay attention to what they pay for. When the bill comes due in April, we just feel the bite. But people in gated communities have special reasons to resent the taxes they pay. Talk with one of them about city taxes and they're likely to say, "I'm already paying for the things the city would do for me if I lived there" (actually, of course, they do live there—it's just that, when they're inside their gated community, they don't feel like they do). "If I have to pay high property taxes to the city on top of everything I'm already paying to my community and to my kids' private schools, that's just not right. I believe in being a good citizen and in helping those less fortunate than I am. But we need to lower city and county taxes so that people like me aren't paying more than their fair share."

So people in gated communities often become tax conservatives, advocates for the lowest taxes possible. Because they are wealthy and connected, what they have to say often gets listened to.

But despite the story they tell themselves, people living in gated communities do rely heavily on public services. They don't spend their entire lives inside those gates. They drive on public roads when they go out to shop, to go to the publicly supported airport, to attend an open-air public park concert along the river in the summer. They use public libraries. They vote. They surely do want police protecting them outside the gates patrolled inside by their own guards, and they surely do want there to be public laws to be used by those police.

Suppose the people living in gated communities are successful in getting city and county taxes lowered. Who suffers? Well, everyone who depends on the public goods and services that the city provides. This includes them, of course. But the heaviest burden falls on the low-, moderate-, and middle-income people who can't afford to live in a gated community, who depend on public services to survive.

Public education, for example, is expensive. It costs a lot to have good public elementary and secondary schools, community colleges, vocational schools, colleges and universities. But public education doesn't just help those who go to public schools, whether those are elementary and secondary schools or colleges and universities. Everybody benefits, even those who go to private schools.

Don't believe it? Compare communities in states that have some excellent public education programs with those that don't. The states with the best public education programs do better economically. Because they have an educated workforce, they're able to attract better-paying jobs. People make higher wages and salaries. They have greater job security.

In those states with the best public education systems, people not only make more, they get better benefits. Again, these are benefits not just to them but to the community as a whole. If someone has a pension plan in addition to her Social Security, when she retires, she'll be better off financially. She'll continue to spend more money locally.

Such people are likely to remain healthier, and to volunteer for community projects and services: helping out in nursing homes and hospitals (both public and private), coaching community soccer teams, delivering meals to homebound seniors. And more: volunteering for political campaigns and voter registration drives, acting as poll watchers on election day, being members and leaders of community organizations—all those things that give a democracy strength and vibrancy.

Like public education, public health benefits all of us. But good public health is also expensive. You need a lot of money to have excellent public hospitals, health clinics, and educational programs about HIV/AIDS, teen pregnancy, domestic abuse. Plus a strong public health system is the best way to insure against epidemics. One of the major threats to everyone's health today is communicable diseases like HIV/AIDS, hepatitis C, and tuberculosis (believe it or not, TB is back—at least in part because, with over two million people in prison, we've re-created the concentrated populations and crowded living conditions of the nineteenth-century tenements and slums that originally made this disease into an epidemic).

HIV/AIDS, hepatitis C, and TB are called communicable diseases because you get them from another person. It's not like heart disease, which you're not going to catch from someone else. Someone may persuade you to spend an afternoon watching football on TV instead of playing it outdoors, which isn't exactly helpful to your heart, but that's not the same as catching the disease from him.

If these diseases are out there in the community, your chances of getting them are just plain higher, no matter how careful you are. And don't even think about what your children can get into, and come home with.

No private health care system, whether it's an HMO or a for-profit hospital, has as its overall responsibility making sure that these communicable diseases are under control to the extent possible. That's not their job. It is the job of our country's various public health care systems. That's another reason not to privatize. In some cases, it literally is "your money or your life."

Think positively, too. A community, a city, a state without much public money can't become, or stay, a good place for even a gated community to locate in. No public concerts, no good universities, no strong arts community, no beautifully planted boulevards for your guests to drive on from the airport to your house, no great parks to picnic in, no local school football, basketball, soccer teams worth cheering for.

Gated communities are private from the start. If they were originally built by the city, and then sold or leased to a private developer, that would obviously be privatization. Or if the city built the gated community, and then gave a private company a contract to manage it, that would also be a classic case of privatization.

Still, it's not always easy to figure out what's private and what's public. Even private property (like the house you own, if you're fortunate) makes use of all sorts of public provisions, such as roads and schools and police. And if you build your house, there are all kinds of public inspections required as part of the process—electrical, plumbing, fire—that protect not just you but your neighbors. If you build a firetrap, you threaten not just your own but also your neighbors' safety.

But there's a tipping point in this mixed and meant-to-be balanced and reasonably cooperative situation. We have reached it when, as today, the public sector is being used for the benefit of the private to such an extent that private interests and profit-seekers can call the tune, and citizens are reduced to dancing to it. We have reached it when the owners of a private place, like a mall or a gated community that must have public people—their customers—coming and going, can control the information available to those people.

Here's what private space means to free speech. In 1994, the New Jersey Appellate Court found that the owners of the Galaxy Towers, a large apartment building, could ban signs and leaflets—not all signs and leaflets, but certain ones. The case came about because the Guttenberg Taxpayers Association had been banned from distributing information about candidates it supported for the school board and the town council, but another political organization, one that was in favor with the owners, was not banned.

So what happened? The condominium residents, most of whom had only seen the literature from one side, voted close to unanimously for the candidates that the owners wanted to win. All the other residents of the town, who had access to information distributed door to door from both sides, voted two-to-one for the candidates supported by the organization locked out of the Galaxy Towers. The corporation that owned Galaxy Towers had taken a political position, restricted the freedom of speech of its opposition, and won. It worked, and the New Jersey Appellate Court said that was just fine.[11]

There are evident conflicts between the public good and private interests. Picture a gated community with its more or less expensive houses and all its amenities—but with restricted access to the residents' fellow citizens who want to give them information about pressing public issues to which they might not otherwise be exposed. Picture the middle-class communities in the same area outside those gates starved ever further of tax money and the public commitment to keep up public streets, public schools, local libraries, community centers. And think of the poorest areas of town, often the hardest hit by cuts in taxes—their deteriorating streets, their run-down school buildings, their weed- and broken bottle–littered bits of "playground" surrounded by metal fences. This is not a healthy picture for anyone. Diseases, drugs, ignorance, and selfishness, once set loose, spread. You really can't fence them in, or out.

CHAPTER 10

Privatizing Against Equality

My hands are as cracked as an August field
That's burned in the sun for a hundred years
With furrows so deep you could hide yourself
But I ain't chopping cotton no more this year
I'll just sit on the porch with my eagle eye
And watch for a change of wind
The rows are as straight as a shotgun barrel
And long as a bullet can spin

Black clouds gathering on the edge of town
But no rain's gonna fall on us
Hoes rise and fall in a distant field
Earth takes a beating for all of us
I thought I heard the angel of death overhead
But it's only the crop duster's plane
Hoes rise and fall like the beating of wings
Lord, send us freedom and rain

> *You know how hot it gets*
> *In Mississippi*
> *You know how dry it gets*
> *In the summer sun*
> *The dust clouds swirl*
> *All down the Delta*
> *I just hope that I don't die*
> *'Fore the harvest comes*[1]

I N THE DAYS OF legal segregation, southern counties and cities had two school systems: one for whites, one for "Negroes." Robeson County, North Carolina, even had three systems: one for blacks, one for whites, and one for Native Americans. This, too, is a history that is repeating itself as we lose control of a democratic government that must be responsive to all of us.[2]

Privatizing Our Public Schools

While there were always some private schools in the South, mostly for the white upper class, during the segregation era the majority of white parents sent their children to the public schools. So those white parents had what they firmly believed to be a self-interest in making sure that the white public schools were as good as possible. That included paying reasonable property taxes to support the public school system.

African-American parents were in a different position. They also paid taxes, of course. But they were—often violently, always relentlessly—kept from having any political say in how those taxes were spent. The schools their children went to didn't get nearly the public resources that the white schools did. The buildings weren't built as well to begin with, and with little publicly funded upkeep provided, quickly became run-down. Black schools often lacked gyms and auditoriums. Classroom equipment and supplies were inadequate at best. Textbooks were often worn-out, outdated hand-me-downs from the white schools.

In this situation, African-American parents and students usually tried to make up the difference themselves. This meant that parents who had already paid taxes to support the public schools their children went to had to raise money on their own to bring these schools up to a minimum standard. They used this additional money to buy things that the school board, using public tax dollars, provided to the white schools but not to the black—everything from chemistry equipment and new textbooks to chalk and football helmets. African-American plumbers, electricians, roofers, carpenters, concrete finishers, bricklayers, and glaziers donated time and materials to repair broken-down equipment and build new classrooms, cafeterias, and gyms for the children of their community.

African-American parents knew that education was crucial for their children; they loved and valued and respected learning. They also believed in freedom and worked for equality.

The Levine Museum of the New South in Charlotte recently put together an exhibit called *Courage*. It remembers and celebrates the people of Clarendon County, South Carolina, who filed the first of the five cases that were eventually consolidated into *Brown v. Board of Education*, which undid legal segregation in the United States. Looking at the photographs and montages, we remembered the South as it was when we first arrived forty years ago: Si to work with the Student Nonviolent Coordinating Committee (SNCC) during the southern civil rights movement, Elizabeth to help found a neighborhood center to bring together and serve black, migrant, and poor white communities in rural Florida. We recalled the barefoot children picking cotton and oranges; the mules and plows; the overcrowded, broken-down cars in which migrant workers arrived at the camps run by the grove owners; the shotguns over the doors of the homes of local civil rights leaders whose lives were at risk just for speaking up for their most basic rights; the small-town Florida sheriff—known for shooting people of color—who rode his prancing horse at the head of the annual Fourth of July parade; the constant threat of the Ku Klux Klan; the black churches destroyed by white arsonists who called themselves Christians and patriots; the trailers, hot under the southern sun, set up for the few children of migrants who made it out of the grove owners' camps and fields to go to school at all.

In the margins of his program book for the museum's exhibit, Si wrote down the simple statement that greeted people as they walked in:

Try to imagine people who could
change American history.

You probably wouldn't think of
farmers in Clarendon County, S.C.—
African American, country folk, poor,
laboring by hand and mule, barred
from any role in government,
often unable to read or write.

But they knew that schooling offered
a better life. And they decided,
no matter what, to open the door
of education for their children.

Public, governmental action undertaken to undo the deep wrong of segregation was supposed to open the door to good education, to create for African-American children the same educational opportunities that white children enjoyed. It didn't entirely work out that way.

Faced with the prospect of having their children sit next to African-American children in the classroom, eat with them in the lunchroom, dress and undress with them in the locker room, play with them at recess, compete with them at sporting events, and (God forbid) dance with them at the prom, many white parents developed a creative response.

They abandoned and then sabotaged the public school system.

White parents in droves pulled their children out of the newly desegregated public schools. To provide for their children's education, white parents and grandparents set up private schools, popularly known as "segregation academies," "seg academies," or "Christian schools"—as if the great majority of African-American students weren't also Christians, and as if fleeing people to whom you believe yourself superior is being a good Christian. Being private, the segregation academies didn't have to abide by what was now, as the result of a people's movement to which government finally did have to respond, the law of the land.

It is never irrelevant to privatizers that many of our public rights don't apply on private property.

But then white parents whose children were attending a local segregation academy faced a financial problem. They were paying a lot of money to send their children to private schools. They resented having to pay taxes to support a public school system their children and grandchildren weren't even attending—and on top of that, a school system that was now almost entirely black, except for the few poor white children whose parents couldn't afford the segregation academies and the children of principled white parents brave enough not to participate in this refusal to bring equality into the public schools.

Remember, this was often taking place in rural communities in the late 1950s and early 1960s, before the Voting Rights Act of 1965 reaffirmed that African Americans have and must not be denied the right to vote. Some of the leading white families in these counties called the shots on the (all-white) county commission, the (all-white) city council, the (all-white) school board.

So what did these leading white citizens, these pillars of society in these cities and counties, do? They used their political power to force a disinvestment in public schools. They lowered property assessments and property tax rates, often substantially. For the white community, or at least the 95 percent or more of the white community who now had their children enrolled in the segregation academies, this meant they often saved almost enough in taxes to cover the cost of private tuition. Money from the public purse went into the private sphere. This wasn't called privatization then, anymore than the convict lease system was, but that's what it was: Public assets were transferred to private pockets.

If poor people or people of color benefited from such a transfer, it would be called *redistribution of wealth* and roundly denounced by many, from politicians to preachers. But when wealth is transferred from poor and working people to those who are already wealthy, it's called *fighting for our freedom*, *standing up for our way of life*, and *protecting the American Way* by those who confuse preserving their inequitable privilege with the promise of democracy.

For the black community, for the poor whites, and for those white people acting on their principles whose children were still in the public schools, the result of the cut in property taxes was a disaster. Funding for public schools plunged. Schools that before desegregation were "high-achievement white schools" became "low-performing black schools." "See?" said the white parents who had caused this to happen. "These schools are no good. We *had* to pull our children out."

Privatizers then and now do this: They claim a public system is failing, disinvest and otherwise make sure it *does* fail, create or support private alternatives, and justify the shift from public to private by saying, "We had to do it because the public system was so terrible." And if subtler methods such as disinvestment seem too slow, and they can get away with more, sometimes what was public is outright sold to private buyers. In the South, (white) school boards sometimes closed a school and then sold it for next to nothing to a segregation academy.

So, in South Carolina and all over the South, the people in power in effect re-created the segregated school system that existed prior to *Brown v. Board of Education*, with two critical differences. First, instead of all students attending racially segregated public schools, African-American students now went to technically desegregated but practically speaking all-black public schools, while most white students went to private all-white segregation academies.

Second, whereas in the old black public schools all of the personnel were African American, from principals and teachers to cooks and custodians, in the new (black) public schools most of the good-paying jobs, all paid for with public funds, were held by whites. African Americans who had been principals became assistant principals. African-American teachers became assistant teachers. African-American coaches became assistant coaches— all with less responsibility, less authority, less pay, less respect. Decent public jobs were downgraded. Black students lost the

African-American role models and the support of a stubbornly proud and responsible community that had inspired them in their poor but valued segregated schools.

Whether or not it is directly intended or openly admitted during specific instances of privatization, loss of status, power, and pay by historically underserved people may be one of its goals and is often one of its effects.

From our "what goes around comes around" department: Governor Mark Sanford of South Carolina (unsuccessfully) proposed to make payments out of public funds to parents who want to send their children to private schools, another move in his overt privatization agenda—and a clear link to the ugly past of the segregationists. More than a few of the private schools that would have been eligible to participate in this program started out as segregation academies.

But remember that, even if belatedly and only as a result of courageous grassroots activism, our government did try to right a great wrong, to do its proper work of protecting and providing for the public good and civil rights of all people. We ignore at our peril what happens when any public good, including the schools on which any democracy depends, is deliberately undercut and then privatized. And we ignore at our peril what will happen again if we allow ourselves to be turned against movements and organizations that have held our government accountable to the democratic principles of equality and justice, rather than to the privatizers' "ownership" society.

Evidence of the effects of today's privatizers' agenda and tactics is increasingly available. In some poor urban areas, privatization via charter schools is once again drawing money away from already underfunded public schools, putting it into private pockets, and failing to strengthen publicly run education so it can be equally good for all students.

A Case Study: Dayton, Ohio

We know the agenda and the usual tactics. Here's a case study of their effects in midstream.

Locate a problem. There was an evident problem in the public schools in Dayton, Ohio, which were reportedly among the worst in the state.

Apply your usual diagnosis. A Washington D.C.–based education advocacy group named for a wealthy businessman from Dayton, the Thomas B. Fordham Foundation, has worked nationwide to increase the number of charter schools. Its president, Chester E. Finn, Jr., is a longtime critic of and consultant on both public and higher education. The foundation and Finn were eager to apply their national agenda to the foundation's hometown schools.

Offer the usual solution for the usual diagnosis. Privatization in the form of charter schools was offered as the solution to Dayton's problems.

Emphasize that "the market" offers people more choice and healthy competition. The charter school movement in Dayton started with schools founded by people who cared about making things better. Then, for-profit competitors moved in. "'We're the No. 1 charter school mecca in Ohio, if not the country,' said William Peterson," who had "founded three charter schools in Dayton and one in Cleveland." He reportedly hoped "to open two more here in the fall. But the only one of Mr. Peterson's schools that has been rated so far under Ohio's school report system was classified in an 'academic emergency' because of low test scores."[3]

National Heritage Academies, another for-profit school corporation, also moved into Dayton's new market. NHA has its base in Michigan, and has fifty-one schools in five states. Edison Schools, a for-profit corporation based in New York, moved in. So did Electronic Classrooms of Tomorrow, based in Columbus, Ohio.

By spring 2005, 26 percent of Dayton's public school students were in charter schools. With 166,000 residents, Dayton had "about as many charters as are in New Jersey, which has a population 50 times larger. . . . Gail Littlejohn, a former corporate lawyer who supported charter schools as part of a menu of changes when she was elected president of Dayton's Board of Education in 2001," said, "'Never in a million years did I think we'd end up with 50 charters in a community of this size.'"

Prove the correctness of your diagnosis by making the problem worse for the public sector. The pool of experienced educators was not adequate for all the new charter schools. The privatizers recruited the people who were trained and experienced from the publicly run schools. Things got worse in the publicly run schools. A slate of school reformers was elected to the Board of Education in Dayton. Instead of being able to improve the schools, the leader of the reform slate said she found herself only "redoing budgets and figuring out how to downsize schools." The publicly run schools got worse as they got less state money because they had fewer students.

"Supporters of charter schools, while acknowledging that quality"—the original problem—"has been a disappointment so far, say the schools have given parents new educational choices. Critics of the movement say Dayton has become a playground for entrepreneurs who are proficient at . . . marketing their schools through television campaigns but who are mediocre educators."

Say privatization saves taxpayers money. But in Dayton, $41 million in taxpayers' money went from the state to the charter schools. Taxpayers also continued paying for the still–publicly run schools. Dayton is now paying for two school systems, neither of which has improved public education. Taxpayers are paying $108 million more than they were.

Say you can do a better job than the public sector. But most of the charter schools are no better than the publicly run schools. As already noted, some have been classified as in academic emergency (others have not even been rated). That classification has not stopped their founders from opening still more charter schools, getting more public dollars, taking more public dollars away from the remaining public schools.

Say privatizers are "more accountable" than publicly run services. But public laws and regulations are not available to control the quality of the charter schools, or to shut down those that are failing in Dayton. A Republican, the speaker of the Ohio statehouse who helped with legislation to get privatization via charter schools going, now expresses "frustration over [their] financial and academic mismanagement." He asks, "How do you write a law to shut down the ones that aren't any good and let the others flourish?" He also says that the publicly run schools shouldn't blame their new competitors for their own failures.

Take over the "market" so that the public sector becomes dependent on the privatizers, whether they work out well or not. In California, in the fall of 2004, some charter schools folded. In Dayton, there is already concern that public schools can no longer step in should that happen in Ohio. The dean of the education school at the University of Dayton "worries about whether the public schools could respond if several charters collapsed simultaneously." Handing public education over to the "market," he now says, is "experimenting with young peoples' lives."

A reporter writes of public education in Dayton, "For decades, conservatives have dreamed of an America in which public schools would lose their monopoly on government education financing and face the harsh reality of market competition. Here in Dayton, their dream has come true with a vengeance."

> Did you go to school this morning
> Did you sit there in the classroom
> Were you sure to pay attention
> Were your ears both open wide
> Did you listen to your teachers
> Did they make some good suggestions
> Did you think about their questions
> Could you see the other side
> > *What did you learn, what did you learn*
>
> Did you learn about your neighbors
> Could you understand them better
> When you heard their different stories
> The histories in their names

How the things that make us different
Across lines of race and color
Give us strength to know each other
Could you see how we're the same
> *What did you learn, what did you learn*

Did you learn about the history
Of the working men and women
In the office and the factory
The classroom and the field
Did you learn how hard we've fought
To get the dignity that's owed us
Do you understand our dreams
Will you help to make them real
> *What did you learn, what did you learn*

I dreamed about a country
That I heard of in my childhood
The streets are paved with justice
The schools are built with care
The leaders of the nation
Are the teachers and the learners
The questions and the answers
Are the road that takes you there
> *What did you learn, what did you learn*[4]

CHAPTER 11

Minds for Sale

We want our poets back. What can you do without poets? How do you find your moral compass as a nation?
    —PARTICIPANT AT THE ARTES LIBERALES CONFERENCE, WARSAW, POLAND

I N 2000, THERE WAS a big conference in Warsaw called Artes Liberales, at which Elizabeth was invited to speak. Provosts, chancellors, and intellectual leaders from all over Eastern Europe and the former Soviet Union came. They had experienced what it means to live under a government controlled by people with one ideology. For too long, their schools had been turned only to the purpose of training productive workers and docile citizens.

Liberal Arts Education

We know that education is essential to honesty in conserving and facing up to the past, preparing us to engage thoughtfully with the present, and choosing our future wisely. It is essential to learning to love what the human spirit reaches for in all times, in all cultures, on the horizon, and just as mysteriously, close at hand. Do we want to hand control over so much that matters to profit-making corporations?

Professor of public policy David L. Kirp thinks not:

> Embedded in the very idea of the university . . . are values that the market does not honor: the belief in a community of scholars and not a confederacy of self-seekers; in the idea

of openness and not ownership; in the professor as a pur-
suer of truth and not an entrepreneur; in the student as an
acolyte whose preferences are to be formed, not a consumer
whose preferences are to be satisfied.[1]

But universities, colleges, and schools are today under great
pressure to attract and to "service" their "consumers" and "stake-
holders" by offering more courses to satisfy job-scared students'
more or less well-informed preferences. "No one," David Kirp also
observes, "is warring over prospective philosophy majors," but
many are competing for those who are seeking no more than
degrees and the training to start, change, or advance careers. This
includes ever more for-profit corporate-owned schools, such as the
huge University of Phoenix with 150,000 paying customers, which
trades on Wall Street as the Apollo Group. Between 2000 and
2003, its stock value rose 368 percent.[2]

Customers of such providers (terrible terms for students and
educators, but that's the language in use as corporations take over)
may emerge with the training they spent their money for. They
may get the jobs they want. But there are no guarantees that they
will do so. Furthermore, training for one job at one point in time
may not prepare you to change, to relearn as work requirements
change—which, in today's world, they do rapidly.

And what about life beyond the job? What about the personal
relationships that are so central to the lasting experiences of
schooling? What about the experiences with people you would
otherwise never have come to know, the courses that turned out to
be life-changing even though you signed up for them only because
they were required? What happens to *education* (from the Latin
educare, to lead out), that turning around of the whole soul, as
Plato long ago described it?

Is the public good served when more and more citizens are
trained in corporate for-profit schools rather than educated in public and private institutions of higher learning? Even as schools in
the formerly Communist countries are hungrily turning back
toward the liberal arts (the *artes liberales*), education in the United

States, under pressure from market competition and legislators forced to cut budgets because of tax cuts, is moving away from them.

In March 2005, a watchdog official at the U.S. Education Department had to warn legislators to "go slowly" in relaxing rules that for-profit colleges have been required to follow to get federal student-aid funds.[3] Let's see: We tighten restrictions on public and nonprofit educational institutions—as President Bush's underfunded and more work-demanding No Child Left Behind initiative does—but we loosen them for the private profit-making ones? Stacking the deck, wouldn't you say?

Actually, the libertarian Cato Institute is pressing Congress to go ahead and get rid of federal student aid altogether. They say it "drives up the cost of tuition." It might, if all our schools were out to make a profit. But as long as truly public institutions of learning remain in existence, financial aid is just one of the ways in which they are enabled to serve all of us equally.[4] What bothers those who want everything privatized is that publicly supported schools are, as they like to put it, "unfair competition in the marketplace." They want us to have no alternatives to having to buy what they sell. Set all of education up that way, and what you have is a quick route back to a locked-in economic and social class system.

Imagine what is no longer far-fetched but is actually happening: corporate logos on textbooks, corporate boards setting course requirements and checking the contents of those courses, corporations deciding what original research will be supported and what will not. Is this the kind of education we want for ourselves and our children? In letting corporate-dominated markets define education and knowledge, are we not at risk of selling out our connections to the rich complexities of the past and the openness of a future of which few have yet dreamed?

Let's not forget why we have public higher education in the first place. Just like public schools, public universities were set up to enable as many people as possible to have a real chance at getting a good education. To differing degrees, they were—but were not only—training schools for productive workers. They have always also nurtured the poets to whose words we turn when we seek sustenance of a different sort than working and shopping provide. They have educated theologians and sculptors and anthropologists and historians and philosophers and physicists who think in their different ways about things for which no one has yet found, and maybe no one ever will find, an immediate, concrete, or financial use. But many of these "useless" thinkers and dreamers have nevertheless changed our lives, and helped us find meaning in them. Past, present, and future, thinkers free of the immediate competitive pressures of the economic sphere are the heart and soul of cultures worth preserving.

Public schools, colleges, and universities have kept much that makes our cultures meaningful, beautiful, and interesting alive, growing, and accessible to many more people. In doing so, they have taught courses in the very subjects that dictators fear and hate, the ones that invite people to think for themselves, to create, to dream. The struggle for an education that is free in all senses is as old and as ongoing as the struggle for democracy. Privatizing literally means selling out these twin dreams.[5]

Privatizing Knowledge

In 1998 one of the premier research universities in the United States, the University of California, Berkeley, formalized an agreement with Novartis, a Swiss company that produces pharmaceuticals and genetically engineered crops. Berkeley got $25 million. Novartis got the right to license about one-third of the research done by the university scientists—including research funded by you and me, through state and federal monies. There we are, subsidizing profits of global corporations again. Novartis also got two of the five slots on the university committee that decides how research money will be spent—what will be studied, and what will not.[6]

Even knowledge, even truth, is being privatized. We support public universities because knowledge is a public good, a commons of the mind in which all who desire to know should share. The purpose of research, like that of teaching, is to share, to spread what is known as widely as possible.

This is why, until 1980, public higher education institutions were not allowed to apply for patents on findings of research paid for by government tax dollars. The Bayh-Dole Act, passed in 1980, changed that. Now universities can seek patent protection. People who supported the Bayh-Dole Act argued that it was good for universities. With the right to own patents, they could enter the marketplace and seek to profit from inventions. It seemed a win-win situation: The public would still support research universities, but successful universities would eventually need less tax money. The market would provide—which is the dream that privatizers keep trying to tempt us into believing.

But the market is never neutral. For example, research in the area of biotechnology began to swamp other areas, because that's where the money was to be made. A kind of gambling fever set in. Deals were made. "As Denis O. Gray, an expert on university-industry relations, has pointed out, because so much federal research support is now tied to corporate matching grants, cost sharing, and other cooperative research arrangements, industry now directly influences an estimated 20 to 25 percent of university funding overall."[7] Collectively, in 2003 165 higher education institutions made more than $968 million from licensing fees.

Because in-house corporate research in the biotech area was also going on, and corporate employees' findings, data banks, and other resources are privately controlled, some public university scientists agreed to such deals because they had no other way to access the privately held knowledge.

But the price of publicly employed researchers' access to knowledge monopolized by corporations is that the monopoly is made stronger, not broken up. When corporations "partner" with universities, what they are after is not openness or public sharing, but ownership—theirs. The idea of a community of scholars who openly share their ideas, correct, refine, and extend them, is anathema to those who want to profit from what can be made and sold based on those ideas.

So much for the metaphorical free marketplace of ideas that our support as taxpayers, tuition payers, and donors to educational institutions used to serve. When the real marketplace moves in, ideas too become commodities to be "branded" and controlled so they will be, not free, but profitable. And their producers—that is, professors, teachers, researchers—must then be reined in lest they give away the goods or sell them independently. Quality suffers: Intellectual evaluation by academically recognized journals and presses that use expert readers to screen submissions yields to protective secrecy.

The rationale for all this privatizing of knowledge is that new, marketable products enhance economic growth, provide job opportunities, and enrich the research institutions. Well and good—indeed they can and have done so in a few instances. Some very useful and exciting research breakthroughs have resulted. But of course we'll never know about all of the research that was not undertaken in profitable fields like biotechnology, let alone the other fields that have been starved of support because they are not considered hot in the marketplace, will we?

Every once in a while, we do get glimpses of what is not done when the marketplace rules, though.

Listen to this story:

> A three-month-old baby named Miles "needed a heart transplant. Though he was born healthy to Ms. Bills and her husband, [Mr.] Coulson, his heart began to fail when he was only a few weeks old, possibly because of a viral illness. By late June he was on the transplant list.
>
> But donor hearts from infants are so scarce that doctors feared Miles would not live long enough to receive one. Older children and adults waiting for transplants can be kept alive by mechanical pumps implanted in the chest, but none of the pumps approved in the United States is small enough for an infant. *There has been little incentive for companies to develop pumps for babies, experts say, because the market is not large enough.*" [italics added][8]

Well, that sort of makes sense, when you think about it. Do you really believe it's the corporation's responsibility to save every little kid who gets sick? That could cost them millions. Of course, they wish they could help, and they would if they could. But they do have a legal and fiduciary responsibility to their shareholders, right?

The imperatives of the market are simply not the same as the imperatives of our hearts, of living and dying, of a decent life for us all. They *can* serve those imperatives, but there is nothing in them to ensure that they do—and there is something in them that often ensures that they do not.

Five days after Christmas 2004, Peter Rost, vice president of marketing for Pfizer, one of the world's largest pharmaceutical corporations, wrote a special piece for the *Los Angeles Times*:

> The U.S. health-care system is the best in the world. Or so we are often told. But is it really the best?
>
> It is certainly the best system for drug companies, which can charge the highest prices in the world to some U.S. consumers. The Congressional Budget Office has estimated that average prices for patented drugs in 25 other top industrialized nations are 35 percent to 55 percent lower than in the United States.
>
> And it is a pretty good system for hospitals and insurance companies. Americans spend about twice as much per person for health care as do Canadians, Japanese, or Europeans, according to the World Health Organization.
>
> But it's not a good system for American citizens. The United States has shorter life expectancies and higher infant and child mortality rates than Canada, Japan, and all of Western Europe except Portugal, according to the WHO.[9]

Mr. Rost finds this wrong, and outrageous. "I'm a drug company executive," he writes, "who has spent twenty years marketing pharmaceuticals. And I'm troubled. I'm most troubled by the fact that we stick it to the people who can afford it the least"—the "67 million Americans who lack insurance, having to pay cash, with no rebates, at double the prices that most-favored customers pay." Most-favored customers include federal agencies like the Veterans Administration, which is allowed to negotiate with the pharmaceutical corporations for the drugs it uses. It's good that the government agency entrusted with the care of our wounded, disabled, and aging veterans can get drugs at a less inflated price. Shouldn't we all?

Peter Rost also confronts the issue of patents, the very things the Bayh-Dole Act allowed public universities to seek so they could get in on the profits of privatized knowledge. Patents, which are granted by a government agency, were designed to do two things. First, they encourage researchers and inventors by giving them control in the form of ownership of their discoveries and works. That means they can sell them, and make money. But because patents expire, they also allow the commons of knowledge to continue to grow. What was owned reverts to the public domain.

Having patents expire is good for the public, for you and me and future generations. But it is not good for profit-dependent corporations that precisely do not want what they sell to be out there for free. These days, it is also not good for public universities that were forced by cuts in funding and rising costs to set about owning and marketing ideas.

Today, a number of brand name drugs "with annual sales of $72.9 billion" are about to emerge from patent protection. This will seriously hurt the bottom line of pharmaceutical corporations. And it is one of the big reasons, says Peter Rost, that "we in the drug industry are fighting reimportation"—like buying drugs from Canada.

"But when we have to choose between that and the lives of those who can't afford drugs, we have to choose life. I joined this industry," Peter Rost says, "to save lives, not to take them. And that's the reason I've chosen to speak out."[10]

Too bad public research universities are not adequately supported to develop and supply the public with some of the medicines we need most. That, surely, is a public good for which we could share the cost. Brazil's government, faced with the HIV/AIDS epidemic and unwilling to let people die because medicines made by private corporations cost too much, set up its own labs and is supplying its own people with the medicines they need.

Too bad the pharmaceutical corporation that decided not to develop a mechanical heart for infants because there wasn't enough money in it was not balanced by a publicly supported laboratory that would have. Too bad if soon we will no longer have independent public research universities at all. Remember Governor Sanford of South Carolina? He still wants to privatize the whole education system there, and he's not alone among governors. Jeb Bush, George W. Bush's brother and governor of Florida, wants to do exactly the same thing.

But some researchers are coming together to stand firm even where their universities will not. For example, the Committee on Scientific Freedom and Responsibility of the American Association for the Advancement of Science drafted a pledge. Scientists can sign it, just as physicians sign the Hippocratic oath.

> Aware that, in the absence of ethical control, science and its products can damage society and its future, I pledge that my own scientific capabilities will never be employed merely for remuneration or prestige or on instruction of employers or political leaders.[11]

CHAPTER 12

Privatizing Social Security: A Case Study of Ideology, Strategy, Tactics

We live in a world in which none of us knows who will lose a job or become ill and need a helping hand. Real reforms in Social Security should express our core conviction that we're not isolated, self-made men and women, but a society of individuals who should care for the most vulnerable.

—RUTH ROSEN, "OLD WOMAN OUT IN THE COLD," *The Nation*[1]

I T WOULD BE HARD not to know that in 2005 the Bush administration's full court press to privatize Social Security turned into a major struggle. Privatization finally became of public concern, if not in its full sweep and agenda. Not a surprise: Social Security is the safety-net provision on which the greatest number of Americans count, 48 million of us—30 million retirees, 6.7 million survivors of deceased workers, 6.2 million disabled workers, 4.8 million children of retired and disabled workers.

More of a surprise: The Bush administration privatizers chose to use retirement benefits as their opening wedge to undoing all of Social Security. Why would they do that, when those thirty million retirees make up the largest group involved? Perhaps it's not quite so easy to argue that children and people who are disabled should be forced to take their chances in the risky, competitive ownership society promoted by Bush's privatizers. So much for respect and care for our elders in this youth-worshiping country.

Trying to Win Over the Public

The Bush administration has already made it evident that the reasons they give for what they are doing are designed to play on our fears first and then on highly charged ideals. They have made it equally evident that they will change what they say without changing what they have already decided to do. In Iraq, they spoke to our fears by saying Saddam Hussein had weapons of mass destruction. Not true. About Social Security, they spoke to our fears by saying it was in crisis, about to go bankrupt. Not true. In Iraq, they spoke to our ideals by invoking democracy and freedom. About Social Security, they spoke to our ideals by invoking independence, freedom of choice, and providing for our children by creating an inheritance. The question, of course, is not what they say but what they actually intend, and actually do.

For example, although they continue to talk about "liberating citizens" from too much government, and about giving back to us what "Big Government" takes, the move to privatize Social Security makes it evident that they plan *both* to inflate centralized government power where it serves private profit and corporate interests *and* to radically weaken government power where it serves the long-term public good—yours and mine, and for generations to come.

The corporate privatizers have had our most widespread safety net—and most trusted government program—in their sights for a long time. Like affirmative action, which kept the commitments of the great civil rights movement going, Social Security has kept alive the great achievements of President Franklin Delano Roosevelt's New Deal. Both affirmative action and Social Security are symbols as well as programs—symbols of governmental commitment to making equality real, and to the public good. They are levers the long privatized—the disenfranchised, the poor, disabled people, the old and the young, women, the unemployed—have used to move from being dependent on the dicey protection of the economy and of charity, to being independent holders of equal rights. The privatizers want those real and powerfully symbolic levers gone.

As Grover Norquist, Republican strategist and founder of Americans for Tax Reform—who, not being elected, need not pretend to "compassion"—said, "The problem is that the federal government hands out billions of dollars, and people will lie, cheat, steal, or bribe to get it. If you have a big cake, and you put it under the sink, and then you wonder why the cockroaches are in your kitchen, I don't think any sprays or blocking the holes in the walls are going to get rid of the cockroaches. You've got to throw the cake in the trash so the cockroaches don't have something to come for."[2]

Norquist doesn't mean we should throw out the cake of corporate subsidies and tax breaks and bailouts to get rid of those supersized cockroaches. He means the cake we baked for ourselves and our neighbors and children by pooling our tax money to be sure no one starves.

It's the familiar story. The privatizers couldn't move on Social Security until we had been painstakingly prepared to believe that it is unjust, that people who benefit from this kind of community insurance are no better than cockroaches, that the system is "in crisis," and that, for all these reasons, it "needs fixing." This took time, and had to wait until the privatizers had a true friend in the White House. They do now: Years of work have paid off.

So, now they are using the same old foxy ploy to get us not only to fail to resist but positively to welcome them into the henhouse. "What are you doing all cooped up like that?" asks the fox with his slyest grin. "Locked behind all this so-called chicken wire. What an insult to poultry pride! Dependent on the farmer's handouts, forced to peck the ground for dry corn kernels—what kind of life is that? Be like me, free to roam, free to eat whomever—I mean, whatever I choose. Feather or fur, are we not all animals under the skin? Come, let me in, and I will show you the way to freedom and true security."

That's how you get into the henhouse. Here's how you get people to fail to defend the public good, to hand their assets over to you. First, you make them anxious about their safety. You keep saying (repetition does wonders, whether it's of a truth or not) that their "chickens," their assets, really aren't safe, that they are escaping, shrinking, being eaten up (but not, of course, by foxes). You get them used to the idea that they just can't count on Social Security being there when they need it in the future.

Some years ago, we said something about our Social Security to a young friend. He just smiled skeptically at our naïveté. "My generation," he said, "doesn't count on Social Security at all. We already know it won't be there for us." He's not likely to be outraged enough to join others in protesting its destruction; never believed in it anyway.

Having undercut opposition to your plans, you then say what you have yourselves presented as obvious, despite the fact that it is not true. You say that Social Security is bankrupt, that there is an immediate crisis. And then you present yourself and your plan as its only saviors. How? By handing it over to the foxes, of course— to the profit-seekers, who, need we repeat, do *not* have the public good, or your retirement, health, and safety held nearest and dearest to their hearts. Those who are seeking profits may not mind if you benefit from what they do; they may even convince themselves that benefiting you is a fine secondary effect that they also have in mind. But that is not their primary goal.

What the Social Security privatizers want is for your money to be at risk in their marketplace, the one they always call the "free" market. We should recognize this line by now and realize that it is their freedom to profit they are serving, not ours, not individual or political freedom. It is a marketplace, do not forget, in which they, not you, have all sorts of power—power that will be enhanced significantly if they can get control of all our Social Security money. They are doing just what an unscrupulous con man would: trying to convince you to turn your paid-up insurance plan into cash so he can invest it for you. This is, as anyone knows, not the way to become more secure than you were. Nor is handing the money you and your family need to live on over to the market, where investors, investment banks, and private investment managers make their fees whether you win or lose. You are free to get fleeced; they are free to fleece you.

As always, the details of this particular scam are complicated enough to get your eyes to glaze over, but here are some of the key points and some ways to understand them.

You have been encouraged to be anxious about Social Security. You are told that the shortfall is estimated at $3.7 trillion over the next seventy-five years. You are set up to be open to something radical to save it for the future—but you are also protective of the provision of Social Security for yourself and for everyone else. Even if you aren't the sort who is inclined to contribute to projects that other people also benefit from, you understand that we pool our money through Social Security so the risks we all face are evened out, just as they are with insurance. Some will get a lot from the common pool; some won't. But when we share the risk, we all sleep a whole lot better. Who knows, after all, which group he or she will turn out to be in? If we pool our money, no one person will necessarily win big, but no one will lose everything either. So, not knowing which will turn out to be our lot, we choose to even the odds for all.

This is like pooling our money through taxes to provide good and safe roads. If the government budget showed a coming shortfall for adequate maintenance of our roads, would that suggest we should just decide to let them go to potholes? That we should abandon the whole idea of pooling our money for something we all need but can't afford to do individually? That we should throw out a system that's worked for years, even if not always perfectly, and come up with some new, dicey plan? Not even George W. Bush has (yet, anyway) suggested that states invest their highway trust funds in the stock market.

If responsible public officials expect that a critical highway is going to need major repair ten years from now, they plan in advance to fix it, including budgeting for the money to do so. So why can't a Social Security shortfall that is projected for the future be made good long before it's expected to hit? Surely there are creative ways to do that. The government finds ways to pay for wars that aren't adequately budgeted for ahead of time. It finds ways to pay for essential public work when natural disasters hit, like the four hurricanes in a row that decimated a great deal of Florida in 2004. It contributed to the international effort to help when the tsunami devastated countries around the Indian Ocean. It finds ways to put more police on the streets if the public demands them, even if that expense was not planned for in advance. And it finds ways to subsidize as well as to bail out corporations when they are tottering, too.

Why can't Social Security retirement benefits be preserved, when thirty million of us depend on them, when so many have contributed to them throughout their working lives, and when we already know that the bill will come due in about forty years—not today, not right away?

What we face is a choice about what, and whom, to care for. In fact, well before this privatizing administration arrived in Washington, D.C., a trust fund *was* set up to cover the retirement bulge of baby boomers. It's set up to last until about 2042—and even in 2042, tax income will still cover about 70 percent of benefits due.

The people who want you to believe that there is a crisis and that it is financial, rather than political—that it has to do only with dollars and cents, and not with a government's obligations, commitments, and priorities—did not factor in that trust fund when they started their campaign to privatize Social Security. They "overlooked" it, so they could make the shortfall sound as if it would hit in fourteen years, in 2018 rather than in 2042.

Having frightened us about the general situation, the privatizers tried to silence those of us who were most personally vulnerable and so most likely to be galvanized into action. The new plan they were working on, they told us, would not change anything for people fifty-five years and older.

Even if you were reassured by that, though, honoring the commitment to people age fifty-five and older doesn't do anything except make things worse. Why? Because the proposal allows younger people to shift money from the payroll taxes that have contributed to Social Security into private retirement accounts. Sound good? More control, perhaps more money if those private accounts are well invested?

But if chunks of money are taken out of the Social Security fund to be invested, there is less money left to honor the commitment to those who are fifty-five and older. There is less money to cover the remaining benefits to everyone else. We've gone from a projected shortfall that had already been deferred by responsible planning (the trust fund), so that we had forty years to do something, to an immediate budget crisis *and* an even larger projected shortfall. And of course it also has to be said that if some people were to invest their money, the ups and downs of the stock market would mean that some would lose it.

There's the familiar tactic again: Privatizers create the crises they then propose to fix. But privatization is not about fixing real problems, other than the problem the privatizing corporations have in trying to push their profits higher and higher. No, privatization is an agenda to serve an antidemocratic ideology in service of corporate rule. Creating problems to "fix" is the way they get us to welcome them into the henhouse.

But why should we trust privatizers to fix Social Security? Their track record is hardly a good recommendation. The corporations are themselves $450 billion in the hole for their own pension plans—and as usual, they are asking our government to bail them out. The Pension Benefit Guarantee Corporation was driven into a $23 billion deficit by the corporations' demands in 2004 alone. The corporations milk the government for all it's worth to cover their failures—and then want us to trust their marketplace rather than that same government to make sure we have security in our old age.

If they win this both real and intensely symbolic struggle, government will be still further weakened. The shrunken government will be kept in the nasty role of collector of the Social Security taxes that remain.[3] The corporations will look more and more like the good guys—if you trust Las Vegas dealers. Risk your money with us, they will keep saying. Dream that you'll beat the odds. Those odds are always in our favor, never in yours, or we wouldn't stay in business, but never mind: Follow your dream. It'll be exciting, we promise.

And Then Get Us Deeper in Debt

In the first decades of their plan, if we agree to it, Social Security will see the loss of trillions of dollars—the money people are supposed to take out of Social Security and hand over to be gambled in the private sector. Government would then have to borrow, it is estimated, up to $2 trillion to cover those of us who were promised we *would* get our paid-for benefits. That, of course, would balloon the national debt still further.

Debt requires payment of interest, which makes the whole deal even worse. How to solve this created problem, the monstrously growing indebtedness of government? Bush's budget plan, submitted to Congress in 2005, guts both mandatory and discretionary government spending—*discretionary funds* for public provisions such as housing assistance and public transportation, *mandatory funds* for—you guessed it, Social Security and other programs on which many of us count. They want to cut financial aid and grants that help people go to college. They want to cut supports for public transportation that might get us out of our cars, thereby cutting consumption of oil—not exactly a plus for the Bush family.

The monster deficit this administration created after having inherited a huge *surplus* is being used as a reason either to eliminate or to privatize our government's provisions and protections for the public good. Once again: First they create the problem (in this instance, the deficit), and then they propose to solve it by privatizing—a radical change that was on their agenda all along—not by simple, sensible adjustments.

President Bush, while saying the deficit forces us to accept cuts to environmental protections, to health and safety oversight, to the veterans administration, wants to *increase* spending our money on national security, and on the military. Again, no surprise: These are areas in which privatization has proceeded rapidly since he took office. Just listen to the news from Iraq—mercenaries and contractors are all over the place. Halliburton is getting fatter and fatter.[4] The huge new Department of Homeland Security started out as a bonanza for corporations that feed off of public-sector contracts.

But the struggle over Social Security has awakened many more of us to what is really going on. The press, as corporate-dominated as it is, has been covering this issue thoroughly. The Internet has been teeming with facts, analyses, discussions. There is growing discussion and debate about it in Congress. Senators and representatives who fanned out across the country to make their case for or against Bush's plan found themselves having to listen even more than they talked. More and more organizations are joining in active opposition to Bush's plan.

We know all that is having some effect: The privatization speechwriters changed their language again. Those private investment accounts they started out with? No, no—they're not "private." They're "personal." Not a sign that the privatizers are backing down, as we know, but it does cheer us up to know that the word *private*, when used for a public good, was turning people off. Can *privatization* be far behind? Too bad the only change will be verbal. (What do you suppose it will be, though? *Personalizing* won't fly for selling off, say, national parks to logging companies; well, we'll see.)

George W. Bush and the privatizers, who knew they were taking on one of the most potent symbolic as well as real bulwarks of the public good, are going all out to win in the face of all this good democratic response. Their methods are being more openly observed, and commented on. When President Bush holds what he calls town meetings with "real citizens" to "discuss" his plan, some commentators have finally said the obvious: These aren't town meetings. No one gets in who hasn't pledged support for the president's plan. These are sham democracy, public relations productions.

The privatizers have staked an enormous amount on this takeover effort. If they win, if they are actually able to privatize some and cut the rest of the largest, most successful public program in this country, they will have won big. Our independence will have suffered a very large blow. Not only the millions of people on Social Security but our government itself will have become more dependent on corporations. Why is that? Because once you've privatized something large and complex, you can't just start it up again overnight when you realize your mistake—whether it's our current Social Security program, or a real citizen-based military, or national parks, public schools, or public transportation. Once these public goods are in profit-making hands, those hands hold the reins.

But if they do not win this one, we will have preserved some of the heritage of democratic movements of the past. We will have strengthened the kind of open, active democracy that has been under attack for so long. We will have reanimated organizations that work effectively for the public interest. We will have reminded our elected representatives that we voted them in, and we can vote them out. And we will have rediscovered some of our real power even in the middle of a very scary, hard time.

> It's hard to watch it all go down
> Drowning like the setting sun
> Hard to watch our freedoms taken
> Hard to lose what we had won
> It's hard to watch the towers tumble
> Hard to watch the struggling town
> Hard to watch the bastards smile
> While they tear the Constitution down
> > *Hard times*
> > *It's hard times*

> But it's hardly time to take a seat
> Hardly time to lose your voice
> Hardly fair to just complain
> As if we never had a choice
> For we are born to work and choose
> We are born to rip and mend
> We are born to win and lose
> We are born to rise again
> > *Hard times*
> > *It's hard times*
> > *Hard times*
> > *It's our time*[5]

PART III

THE GREAT DIVIDE

FLORIDA'S FIRST two-term Republican governor . . . spoke wistfully of a day in the future when state employees won't even be needed. "There would be no greater tribute to our maturity as a society than if we can make these buildings around us empty of workers," said [Jeb] Bush, standing on the steps of the Old Capitol, which is surrounded on all sides by state buildings containing thousands of offices for employees from dozens of agencies, from auditors who examine state contracts to lawyers who advocate for consumers, to the officials who run state elections. These empty buildings, Bush said, would be "silent monuments to the time when government played a larger role than it deserved or could adequately fill."[1]

Bush . . . has exposed his devious libertarian thinking for all of Florida to see. . . . Will privatization leave Florida a pawn to corporate interests? Who will fill the void of compassion and thwart the greed of industry? When tumbleweeds gently blow through the empty halls of Tallahassee's state office buildings, who will find Florida's lost children? Certainly, our governor will not.[2]

CHAPTER 13

The Two Cultures of the Twenty-First Century

Recently, when I was traveling to Rajasthan's capital, Jaipur, in Western India, for a public hearing on drought and famine . . . we were served bottled water, where Pepsi's water line Aquafina was the brand of choice. On the streets of Jaipur . . . at the peak of drought, small thatched huts called *Jal Mandirs* (water temples) were put up to give water from earthen water pots as a free gift to the thirsty. *Jal Mandirs* are a part of an ancient tradition of setting up *Piyaos*, free water stands in public areas. This was a clash between two cultures: a culture that sees water as sacred and treats its provision as a duty for the preservation of life and another that sees water as a commodity, and its ownership and trade as fundamental corporate rights.

—VANDANA SHIVA, *Water Wars*[1]

THE GREAT DIVIDE and the looming struggle of the twenty-first century is between two cultures, which, with Vandana Shiva in mind, we call the *private profit culture* and the *public good culture*. What does it mean for our lives when these two cultures have become so unbalanced that one of them, the private profit culture, is increasingly encroaching on the other?

There are basic things all people must have to sustain life before talk of liberty and the pursuit of happiness can have any real meaning. When these basics are taken over by corporations driven by the need to make private profits, the public good itself becomes just something else to put up for sale. And when the public good is for sale, freedom is on the auction block with it. As the international economist Amartya Sen says, "Sometimes the lack of substantive freedom relates directly to economic poverty. . . . In other cases, the *unfreedom links closely to the lack of public facilities and social care*, such as the absence of epidemiological programs, or of organized arrangements for health care or educational facilities, or of effective institutions for the maintenance of local peace and order." [italics added][2]

More vividly, the writer Wendell Barry says, "Rats and roaches live by competition under the law of supply and demand; it is the privilege of human beings to live under the laws of justice and mercy."[3]

Just so does the imperative to compete for ever larger profits lead to domination by a few huge economic players. Just so does the political choice made by free people to provide and protect the public goods of equality, justice, mercy, and freedom for all people fall prey to all-out economic competition. Little is then protected as essential, of worth beyond price, sacred—from water and other gifts of nature, to help when we need it most, to art and poetry, to the teachings of most if not all of the world's religions.

But the profit-making culture tells us that a competitive economic system driven by an unending, ever-escalating quest for wealth is good for us—for all of us—because profit-making "grows the economy," and a growing economy means more jobs and so more money in more pockets. A public good culture, by contrast, remembers that *even if* this economic agenda worked as promised, more jobs for more people with more money avails us naught when crops shrivel for lack of water, when we cannot drink the water we have, when drought and floods and famine are created and do their deadly work.

Because of the dominance of the private profit culture, such disasters are no longer to be blamed on Mother Nature alone. She still provides for us when we cooperate with her, but she also takes vengeance when we mess with her too much—a vengeance that falls first on the poorest and most vulnerable but eventually hits us all.

As Vandana Shiva writes:

> The impact of climate on all forms of life is mediated through water in the form of floods, cyclones, heat waves, and droughts. Water fury can be tamed only if the atmospheric saturation by carbon dioxide is contained. While subverting international struggle to avert climate disaster makes economic sense for oil companies, it spells political and ecological disaster for much of the earth's community.[4]

The public good culture, which respects the earth and knows that its most essential gifts must be honored and shared for the survival of all, is not some leftover hippie, ecological fad indulged in by privileged people. It is based on scientific assessment of present pressing realities, and requires an open-eyed realism. The culture of the public good is also rooted in many traditions. It can be found among Hindus and Jews and Jainas and Muslims and pantheists and animists and Christians, among scientists and poets and farmers and small business owners and corporate officers and workers and rich and poor. But around the globe, the public good culture is pitted now against the private profit culture.

The private profit culture too contains a diverse array of people. They believe that they are the realists, and that realism requires us to admit that only the market matters, that all things and all people have their price, that competition for profit and wealth and the power they confer is what makes the world turn and life worth the living of it. The profit-making culture holds that it is, and should be, the "free market" alone that can and will protect us from problems, and even disasters, caused by an unfettered economic system. But the free market has not stopped corporations, which in reality do not operate by the historic laws of the marketplace, from creating social and environmental problems. The free market, unchecked and unregulated, has time and again led to monopolies that choke off the competition that sometimes kept businesses subject to, and limited by, the law of supply and demand. That law turned out not to be reliable: The growth of corporations has been neither limited nor balanced.

Small businesses, smaller corporations that limit themselves to what they were created to do, and that will not do *anything* to keep growing, are driven out of business. The divide between rich and poor widens still further, and with it the divide between the powerful and the powerless within and among nations. Essential resources become depleted, polluted, and, unleashed from the balances of a healthy environment, themselves wreak havoc.

Birds may not foul their own nest, but humans can, and do. Check the air pollution index in your area, and if you have a faucet, think about why it is that you are considering buying a water filter, or why you now feel the need to spend money to buy bottled water. And remember the people around the world who do not have faucets, cannot afford bottled water, and have nothing but polluted water where once it ran free, and clear.

The Private Profit Culture Versus the Public Good Culture

The public good culture in the West as in the rest of the world has many roots. Among these are philosophical as well as religious traditions that distinguish between quite different kinds of value, of worth.

In one of the ancient Greek philosopher Plato's dialogues, the main character, Socrates, is trying to help a young man sort out what makes something *good*. "Tell me," he asks, "this physician of whom you were just speaking, is he a moneymaker, an earner of fees, or a healer of the sick?"

Socrates, it's probably worth noting, was eventually put to death by the democratic rulers of Athens, allegedly for corrupting the city's youth, but more probably, as Elie Weisel says, for "speaking truth to power."[5] This was thousands of years before the rise of "Big Pharma" and the American Medical Association, neither of which has exactly a sterling reputation for wanting to hear the truth about itself. Socrates' example still helps us reflect on public good values.

As public health care has been increasingly privatized so that all of us, health care providers as well as patients, are forced to submit to the rules of corporations, we too are asking that question: Are health care providers healers, or are they "earners of fees"? It isn't, of course, that we begrudge a doctor her or his reasonable fees. We don't live, and don't want to live, in a society in which, as in the past, some professions can only be practiced by those who have no need to earn money. We believe in equal opportunity as a public good. It is not approved, in most U.S. cultures, to hang onto the old aristocratic male scorn for people who have to work to support themselves and their families. In fact, sometimes we go so far in the other direction that the word *amateur*—the root of which means love; an amateur is someone who does something for love, not money—is said with some scorn: "Well, what did you expect? He's just an amateur." And there is a certain lack of respect even for very rich folks who do not work, who do not at least tend and "grow" their money.

The need for people, including physicians, to make a decent living does not work against the public good. After all, an economic system in which work is respected and people are decently paid is something for which we have struggled. What has come to be called a living wage was an early union rallying cry that still resonates today in cities where community organizers and unions are working together on living wage campaigns. It is unjust for workers to be forced to accept wages that cannot cover their most basic needs, and the needs of those who depend on them. It does not serve the public good to trap people in poverty.

So of course we do not scorn the physician or anyone else who takes money for what she does. "The laborer is worthy of his hire," as the Bible says, whether a heart surgeon or a hotel clerk—and the pay should be worthy of the worker. And we do not mind if the fee is reasonably high where better pay might attract people to do dangerous or especially demanding jobs, or jobs for which education and training far beyond the usual are required. This is one of the ways the system works to draw people into doing the things society needs and wants. Within reason, it seems to most of us to be fair to individuals as well as a way of realizing the broader public good.

But that's hardly the end of the story. Even in a genuine market economy—one not taken over by corporations that skew the rules beyond recognition—it is a terrible thing to reduce everything and everyone to no more than a monetary value. Some things have a worth entirely other than their price. Remember the story of King Midas, who, in his lust for wealth, for ever more gold, asked for and got the privatizers' dream—the ability to turn everything he touched into gold? He touched his beloved daughter, and she turned into dead gold. He touched the food he needed to eat, and it too turned into gold that even the oh-so-powerful King Midas could not eat.

We do not want our doctors, our teachers, the builders of our bridges and buildings, our public servants to be motivated solely, or too much, by money lust. We want them to see us—each of us in our precious uniqueness, and all of us, their clients and neighbors and fellow citizens—as worthy of respect and care regardless of our wealth or poverty. Just as we need the water on which all life depends, we need the basic respect without which spirits too can shrivel and die.

When people do their work only for the money—whether a bare subsistence level or a vast pileup of wealth—the quality of commitment, care, and responsibility that we all need from each other is eroded and sometimes erased outright. That is always a possibility, but it is made less likely when pay scales are not tremendously discrepant, when most jobs and professions pay decent wages. It is mitigated when individuals and groups long subject to prejudice can count on public goods like quality education that make equal opportunity a real possibility. Then the economy is what it should be: a means, no more, to many differing kinds of decent and good lives, to the public and private freedom a good government protects.

But when pay and profit scales break through the top or the bottom of fair limits set to protect these public goods—limits such as a livable minimum wage, a progressive tax system by which those who make more money, including corporations, contribute more—a healthy balance is lost. When some jobs pay so little that only the threat of no job at all, which today can mean deprivation unto death, can force desperate people to take them, no profits in other hands can outweigh the loss of human dignity and worth. Nor should people be reduced by unfettered, cutthroat competition to running their business or their farm on the backs of such labor. Exploitation warps the heart, divides us from other people, and breaks the spirit even when it does not also starve the body.

When some corporate jobs pay far, far beyond what anyone can sanely be said to have earned, their attraction is just as likely to be purely monetary and the jobs held onto almost as desperately as when want and fear are the spur. Just take a look at the young people in jobs that pay more from the beginning than what the very few people who worked their way to the "top" used to make. If they do not rise before dawn and work until after dark, they risk losing their jobs to someone who will. Their young adulthood, the time in which we become most fully who we are, find and establish the love and family and community relationships, the real work and values that sustain us, is swamped by the frenzy of competition.

According to a recent article about young professionals in New York City, it seems that a single person earning $100,000 a year can no longer feel as if he or she has made it. The new golden plateau has become $200,000.

People in the United States often believe that "we have it good" and that other countries are envious of our "lifestyle." But there are people in Europe as elsewhere who alternately pity and scorn us for being so driven, and there are people in some countries we think of as nothing but miserably poor who are horrified by what they see of us on TV, in the movies, on the news. The private profit culture, the passion for profit-making, seem to them nothing but ugly, even when they are indeed forced by today's poverty, too often made worse in a globalizing economy, to leave all they find of worth at home to come here.

But those who are caught up in the private profit culture readily see all those who immigrate, willingly or unwillingly, as testimony to the rightness of their own lives. They have no truck with efforts to include these newcomers in even the most meager of our provisions for the public good. Insecure themselves, and girding themselves for flat-out competition, hard-driven Americans can become defensively scornful of any talk of the public good. They can scorn, too, the far lower salaries made by those who work for that good, even the teachers to whom they entrust their children and our collective future—or the salaries of those paid by regular old businesses that make no more than reasonable profits.

All this makes it easier to convert people to the private profit culture, including the escalating drive of its real players today, the corporations, to privatize the public good functions and services that are barely still standing against it. Convince enough people that wealth is *the* reward worth seeking, and they'll start to believe that anyone who lives by other values is a loser, or a fool, or some kind of bleeding heart to ridicule and avoid. This is happening today—but it has also happened before.

A Little History, with Present-Day Analogies

This is hardly the first time the profit motive has threatened to swamp the public good. Read this true story carefully. What the privatizers are seeking once existed, and the lesson it taught to those who suffered through it is that the private sector cannot be trusted to serve the public good—or even, ultimately, its own good.

In the eighteenth century, when England faced serious problems from the rise of an unfettered capitalist market economy, "the government promulgated . . . a considerable body of regulatory legislation. But this did not initially entail a corresponding growth in government. What we would now regard as governmental functions were 'farmed,' that is, contracted to private enterprise."[6]

And how did it work out when there was what we today call contracting out and outsourcing by a weak government such as the privatizers keep telling us we should have? Some examples from this history:

Naval officers and crews were paid in part or whole from prize money from captured ships.

Prisons were run by businessmen getting their profits from sale of food and privileges to the prisoners.

Queen Elizabeth's ambassador to the Ottoman Empire was appointed, paid, and his embassy maintained by the joint-stock Levant Company.

Volunteer informers were rewarded for denouncing criminals.[7]

We can't resist adding the story of one Mr. Jonathan Wild. In those days in England, this Mr. Wild ran a "profitable conglomerate" through which he "recruited and trained thieves, and set up a rental service in burglar's tools," while also negotiating with "the original owner for the return of stolen goods for a price." Mr. Wild, conglomerate owner, also diversified his operations: He was "a thief-taker" who delivered "uncooperative thieves to the courts" and turned in any thief with a large price on his head. Seventy of them were hanged.[8]

Now, there's a man who knew how to sell his services to the government and do better than the usual contractor. He figured out how to make his services needed by making sure there were well-equipped burglars plying their trade, and then went out and caught the ones who would bring a good price because they were so successful. Got rid of potential competition that way, too. Sort of like today's manufacturers and sellers of armaments: Arm to the teeth any nation that has the money to buy from you, then arm the countries they threaten, and then serve your government by giving it advice on how to deal with those well-armed "rogue" nations—by buying still more arms from you, of course. Very profitable, and very little room left for your competitors.

Today, in the corporations that are trying to take us back to the days when government depended on such imaginative profit-seekers to do its work, there are also a few people who are making out like bandits. Some corporate executives make five hundred times more than the workers who actually produce the company's products or deliver its services; not so long ago, the top executives' salary premium over workers was around forty times as much. CEOs also make significantly more than the middle managers who, day by day, help keep the corporation running. And increasingly, those CEOs are accountable to almost no one—quite unlike the workers and managers who are readily fired if "the bottom line" suggests cuts.

It's not surprising that such CEOs find it more than mildly irritating when government sets limits on what they can do. Corporate bosses are used to having everyone snap to and do just what they say; obligations to the public good just get in their way. Although they may pride themselves on listening to "the little people," they surely do retain the right to make the final decision with the bottom line most firmly in mind. And they will tell you that this is how they do, not just well, but good: They're powering the economy and creating jobs (forget those "lean and mean" cuts, and relocations that lost many jobs, and replacement of decently paid public employees with nonunion, cheaper labor through privatization).

Although the U.S. government today seems often to look the other way while these executives run roughshod over their employees and the rest of us, the English government finally decided almost three centuries ago that it had had enough of Mr. Wild. Parliament passed a law against returning stolen goods without prosecuting the burglar, and in 1725 used it to arrest and hang him.

Corporate boards, which hire and could fire (if not hang) their CEOs, are made up largely of other people with huge salaries. They have a stake in keeping top corporate jobs secure and the largesse flowing. They as well as the CEOs they supposedly oversee are well-served by the myth that monstrous pay is the only way to get "quality" executives. If CEO pay were kept reasonable by boards of directors who were really responsible to the bottom line, to the profit margin, to shareholders, rather than artificially inflated by the very people who stand to make out like Mr. Wild (at least in the early phase of his career), good people would work for good pay, pure and simple. But when corporate board members are given their famously super-generous perks, they want to please the CEO and their fellow board members who set those perks. This cozy situation creates a closed circle of people who line each other's pockets. It does not establish a system of accountability, even to the bottom line—let alone to the public good.

Where the only value to which people are loyal is profit, even honor among thieves fails. Here's a contemporary story that, like Mr. Wild's, is ludicrous, ugly, and terrifying, because now global in scope.

> The current global market for PMFs (private military firms) is essentially unregulated, lacking both formal controls and limits. So, the firms make the choice of whom to work for. . . . Rebel groups in Angola, Sierra Leone, and DRC [Democratic Republic of Congo] are all reputed to have received military help from private companies. . . . Likewise, less transparent firms such as Stabilico, Niemoller-Group, and GMR have been accused of engaging in illicit arms and diamond dealings, sometimes on multiple sides of conflicts.
>
> Indeed, there has also been a link with terrorist networks. In the late 1990s a number of firms targeted the lucrative market of training young Muslims who were being recruited globally to join radical groups engaged in jihads, or "holy wars" in places such as Chechnya and Afghanistan. For example, Sakina Security Ltd. was a British firm that offered military training and weapons instruction to these recruits, as part of its "Jihad Challenge" package.[9]

America has its own Jonathan Wild, a Mr. Kelvin Smith, who, while a government employee, started his own business in western Pennsylvania. He "provided military training to groups purporting to be headed to the fighting in Bosnia and Chechnya," where there were many mercenaries on all sides already. Not wanting to leave his clients unsupplied, Smith also bought assault rifles and ammunition on their behalf. Six members of Smith's classes, in which they were also trained in "mock terrorist-type attacks on utilities plants, later turned out to be members of al Qaeda who were convicted in 1993 of planning a series of attacks around New York City."[10]

Was Mr. Smith hanged? No. Because he broke gun laws, Mr. Smith was arrested and given two years in prison.

A bad apple, one slipup of justice? Well, between 1994 and 2002 U.S.-based private military firms signed over three thousand contracts with the U.S. Defense Department that are estimated to be worth over $300 billion. P. W. Singer, author of the book that gives these examples, writes, "Ironically enough, despite being the dominant power on the international scene today, the United States may make the most extensive use of the privatized military industry."[11]

Wouldn't want to do anything *too* bad to Mr. Smith. Might irritate the PMFs on which the U.S. military is now virtually dependent—and making a big deal out of one entrepreneurial adventurer in the business might lead to highly unwelcome publicity all around, mightn't it?

Yes, there are far less terrifying corporations than the private military firms. Yes, there are corporations that try to play by what rules there are—and even call for more so that they have a chance to compete with those that skirt, flee, violate, and work against those rules. And yes, there are those corporations that we mentioned back in the preface that are committed and trying hard to live up to the values of the public good culture that are among the reasons their customers buy their products.

But do we want a system that not only allows but richly rewards loyalty to nothing but profit-making to own and operate provisions and protections for the public good?

Siamese Twins

There is a great divide between the private profit culture and the public good culture, but the struggle between them is not between opposites that have no relationship. They are historically and politically connected, joined at the hip.

We know that it is a startling thought that privatizing corporations, which justify themselves by invoking the freedom of the market and attacking what they see as both the threat and the ineptitude of "Big Government," actually need governments committed to the public good. But they do. The international economist Andrew Kamarck, reflecting on history, makes the thought-provoking claim, "The welfare state and modern capitalism are Siamese twins." Think about that: Siamese twins are two people who differ from each other, who think for themselves, who can and do disagree—but their bodies are organically joined. Like it or not, they need each other to stay healthy, to stay alive.

Kamarck explains:

> In feudal times, people knew where they belonged, their position in society might be lowly but it was as secure as it had been for their parents and grandparents before them. Capitalism brought in constant change and insecurity. The capitalistic market economy allows enterprises to fire workers, to restructure, downsize, or reengineer firms, to abandon towns, regions, or even countries that depend on them. To make the resulting insecurities socially and politically tolerable, there has to be some provision to blunt the sharp edges. A *major contribution of the welfare state is that unfettered capitalism could never survive politically or socially without it.* [italics in original][12]

The clash between the public good culture supported by democratic governments and the private profit culture that has spawned privatizing corporations is a serious moral, religious, practical, political, and economic one precisely because the two sectors are both different and related. If the corporations, through privatization, succeed in their efforts to tear ever more chunks out of their Siamese twin to make themselves bigger, it will leave not only all of us but those very corporations in big trouble.

Without the welfare state (a term they have worked hard to turn into an insult), who will provide the schools that educate their workers, the public health care that protects us all against the kind of epidemics that kill hundreds of thousands of people? Who will provide the police and firefighters who keep all our homes and neighborhoods safe? Who will protect the water, the air, the soil on which all life depends? Corporations depend on all these, just as we do. But corporations do not want to spend money on them. It hurts their bottom lines, cuts their profit margins, makes them less competitive on Wall Street, less attractive to investment bankers and stockholders who only care about their profitability.

Do we want to go back to the old company towns from which it was very hard to leave, into which few outsiders were allowed? Do we want feudalism back, now with corporate heads free to act like monarchs, and managers who serve as the lords and ladies who led the good life as long as they could keep the people on their lands producing wealth for them?

The public good culture, including its welfare state, remains essential to us, and precisely because it is so different from it, to a healthy profit-making culture as well.

CHAPTER 14

Appreciating the Public Sector

I T IS IMPORTANT to remember that the public sector has an
enviable track record stretching back over many years. How
many of us were born safely in public hospitals? How many of
us were educated in public elementary and secondary schools?
How many of us went to public community colleges, four-year colleges, and universities, both because they offered good education
and because we couldn't afford the tuition at private schools, colleges, and universities? How many of us received public financial
aid that got us through school?

We drive across the country on high-speed interstate highways,
a public project conceived and initiated during the administration
of President Dwight D. Eisenhower in the 1950s. We pitch our
tents in national parks and wilderness areas that were preserved for
future generations by government in response to public campaigns.
We canoe down rivers that were cleaned up by government action.

We work at jobs for which some of us would never have been
hired if it weren't for public laws prohibiting discrimination in hiring. Our safety on the job is protected by government regulation
and inspectors. The safety of our food, medicines, water is overseen
by public agencies. We can report consumer fraud to the government. We can get on the "do not call" lists of our state and federal
governments to stop telemarketers from intruding into our lives
whenever they want to.

If we become disabled, our income is maintained by the public
Social Security disability program. If we die while working, our
children under eighteen are provided with income through gov-

ernment Social Security survivor benefits. When we retire, we are guaranteed a certain level of income by the public Social Security insurance system.

Our community health is protected by public sewer systems, public systems of disease control, public health clinics and hospitals. Our community safety and security, that of our families and neighbors, is protected by public firefighters and police. Our national security is guarded by a public military system. (If you're feeling insecure anyway these days, would it help to know that Si learned speed-typing while in training at Fort Jackson, South Carolina, in 1967? Kept his skill honed and ready through the years, too.) Without this country's public military, who knows what would have happened in World War I and World War II?

Lord knows, none of these public services is perfect. But they were all begun to respond to real need and the collective realization that if we did not provide for them as goods for all of us, everyone would be the poorer for their lack. They were not set up for, and are not held accountable to, the making of profits. We can call them and the elected officials and public agencies responsible for them to account—while they remain in the public domain. We saw what they could do in the tragic moments of 9/11. Since then, private security firms at airports, for example, have been replaced with a federal system.

When the chips are down, we remember what we forget when times are good. We remember basic beliefs that both experience and conscience have taught and held us to.

One is a belief that when we act together, we can make all of our lives better, safer, healthier, and fuller. It is a belief in the moral, political good and power of cooperation. Together, we can refuse the injustice of discrimination. Together, we can preserve national parks so that all can share in them. Together, we can provide schooling for the generations that will inherit what we cherish of our cultures, and renew them. Together, we can ensure that the young, the dependent, the ill, the old, the disabled—among whom all of us either are now, could be at any moment, or will be at some future time in our lives—can live with safety, freedom, dignity.

Related to the belief that we can make things better when we cooperate is the belief that we are all at risk when any of us is. It is a belief in the *necessity* of cooperation. Pollution does not stay where it is caused; it spreads, it sickens and kills without regard for who caused it, who profited from it, on whom it was imposed without choice or chance. Poverty can breed sickness and crime that spreads far beyond the ghettoes into which too many are crowded, and no walls, no police, can stop that spread. Individuals and corporations that are not controlled by the rule of law turn the law-abiding into victims with no recourse. Without cooperation, the most unscrupulous win, and not only individuals but whole societies and cultures lose, and are lost.

Even the shrink-government advocates' favorite economist, Milton Friedman, reluctantly concedes that government is needed to do what "the market cannot do for itself, namely, to determine, arbitrate, and enforce the rules of the game" and to "do through government some things that might conceivably be done through the market but that technical or similar conditions render it difficult to do in that way."[1] We agree, as today's privatizers do not, that government is essential as the rule-maker and umpire to restrain economic powers from destroying, through increasingly worldwide monopolistic control, the very competition of free markets they claim to be defending against government. And we are glad that Friedman and his followers recognize—albeit exceedingly grudgingly—that there are also "some things" that are "difficult" for economic, profit-seeking players to do. Friedman says there are two kinds of such things: those that have *neighborhood effects*—the kinds of effects we mentioned to show the necessity of cooperation—and those that are *paternalistic*, a label that shows how much he hates to put anything at all on this list, which we call the moral and political good of cooperation.

Neighborhood effects need public action because they "arise" when "actions of individuals have effects on other individuals for which it is not feasible to charge or recompense them"—curious language for pollution, the example he gives. Friedman says, "The man who pollutes a stream is in effect forcing others to exchange good water for bad."[2] Well, it's not so often a man (or a woman) who does that; more often it's a corporation. And the corporation isn't really *exchanging* good water for bad. It is turning water, a necessity of life, into a threat to life. If we must use market language for what shouldn't be a market matter at all, it's rather more like theft—the corporation has taken away from us what nature provided.

Sometimes you've got to take a lot
Sometimes you've got a lot to give
You can talk all you want about a life of crime
It's a crime the way some people live
'Cause if a rich man steals a dollar
And a poor man steals a dime
One ends up as the president
The other ends up doing time

But you know I've had a lot of time to think
I think I've got it figured out
It don't really matter what you do
It's who you are they care about
So when I get back to my hometown
You're gonna see a change in me
I'm gonna put on a suit and be a businessman
I'm gonna take your money legally

You know, freedom
Freedom is a funny thing[3]

Friedman then actually says, "These others"—the ones whose water has been poisoned—"might be willing to make the exchange at a price." How's that for a thought? Wonder how many people it would take to be party to that exchange, and for how many years, to make it even a fair *economic* deal? Say the Joneses downstream from the chemical plant accepted $100 for the polluted stream on their property (you know they wouldn't get much). What about the people downstream from them? And those further downstream? How far would this go? And what about their children, and their children's children? And what about the people who used to swim or fish in the river? And the people whose lands are affected by the change in the environment that was once thriving all around the stream?

Friedman doesn't go there. What makes him give up and admit this is a public matter is that "it is not feasible for them [the people with poisoned water], acting individually, to avoid the exchange or to enforce appropriate compensation."[4] Which is to say, what he sees as being violated is not the environment, or the life it sustained, or social or moral responsibility of the public good sort. No, it's the market principle of a free and equal exchange between individuals that he does not want violated. Still, here he recognizes that public action may indeed be needed.

He also has to recognize that something may need to be done by public providers for "madmen and children." Why for madmen? Because "we are willing neither to permit them freedom nor to shoot them." Okay. Grudging, as we said. Economic reasoning doesn't do well with moral claims on care and compassion, which go in Friedman's paternalistic category.

And children? Well, if absolutely necessary, we can provide care for them through public support systems because "children are at one and the same time consumer goods and potentially responsible members of society." That children are "consumer goods" is why we're stuck with dealing with them, Friedman explains. Since we "use [our] individual resources . . . to have children—to buy, as it were, the services of children as a particular source of consumption," having children is just one of many free market choices.[5] He wants us above all to protect the right to make those choices, so he accepts that we're stuck with the children who result. That children are also "potentially responsible members of society" means that they don't go in the category of people we can shoot, either. Add children to madmen, then, as unavoidably public responsibilities.

Not morally inspiring, this line of reasoning. But, however grudgingly, even Friedman thus recognized a role for public action to set rules for economic powers, to protect the environment, children, the mentally ill and incapacitated. In 2002, when he reissued his 1962 book, he left those passages in. Today, even the public provisions he accepted are likely to have been sold to privatizers.

Child support programs, for example, are very strong revenue producers for Affiliated Computer Services, an outsourcing company based in Dallas. Lockheed Martin IMS, itself set up as a subsidiary, is now a division of ACS. Lockheed Martin IMS grew 32 percent a year, contributing rather significantly to "the $25 billion Lockheed Martin IMS empire" before it was sold to ACS in 2002.[6] Little children can be part of making mighty big bucks.

Meanwhile, *privatization* is heralded around the world as *the* political solution for public problems, and *the* way to strengthen both democracy and free markets around the globe. A global agenda that radically changes the lives of billions of people who have no say is *private?*

In the public sector, we are citizens and political actors. We make decisions together about issues of general significance. We vote for our representatives, and they are accountable to us. We have basic rights enshrined in the Constitution. Among our other rights are those to certain services that support the common good. We pay taxes to share the costs of those services and the ongoing functions of our government. We call the people who provide those services and fulfill those functions public employees, because we collectively pay them to do our shared work. We also have other public obligations and duties, such as serving on juries, and of course, obeying the laws passed by our elected representatives.

In the private sector—which does not mean the same thing as in our private lives—we are not citizens, or political actors but, rather, economic actors. We do not pool our resources for the common good but, rather, buy and sell. We are able to do so according to our income level: The rich can obviously buy things the poor cannot. The providers of what is bought are motivated by profit. That means that they charge more than it costs them to make a product, or deliver or perform a service. Exchanges between buyers and sellers that yield profits to the sellers take place in what is called the market (so the market is not a place, but rather a kind of relationship—an economic exchange).

Despite all the rhetoric, image advertising, movies, and TV shows that glorify private corporations, there is no evidence that the private sector is superior to the public. The private sector is not the source of our freedom, of all that is good about and for life. We are not most who we are as consumers. Our most important relations are not marketplace, buy-and-sell, profit-driven.

It is in the tradition of this land, of different peoples in different times and places, to refuse to be subjected to economic domination and exploitation and to value the public good. The poor in America have resisted exploitation by the more privileged. Enslaved people have resisted. Women have resisted. The Native Americans resisted the colonists before the colonists resisted the Crown. The founders of our country learned from the Constitution of the Iroquois Confederacy[7] as well as the English Magna Carta and the ancient Greeks how to think about democratic governance for the public good.

We need to continue resisting the takeover of our government and the public sector. When the promise of democracy is twisted to justify domination, as George Orwell so famously wrote in *Animal Farm*, "all animals are equal, but some animals are more equal than others."[8] In Orwell's fable, it was the pigs who had made themselves more equal than others.

CHAPTER 15

A Fable, and a Fabulous True Story

The scene was so familiar
With farmers all around
The auctioneer was standing there
He brought his hammer down
He started off the bidding
The crowd let out a roar
'Cause we heard something on that day
We'd never heard before

> *What am I bid for the White House*
> *Come on now don't be slow*
> *They've overspent their credit*
> *So they'll just have to go*
> *If they can't learn to manage*
> *It's time they're moving on*
> *The leaders of this country*
> *Are going going gone*

He said, Let's start the bidding
With that Congress on the hill
They're awful fond of spending
They just don't pay their bills
But with a little honest work
They'll be as good as new
I hear they're handy on the farm
Once they learn what to do

Then the crowd grew silent
You could hear a needle drop
He motioned up the White House
And he put it on the block
But no one bid a nickel
They just stared so hard and cold
'Cause you can't bid on something
That's already bought and sold

When the sale was over
I sure did thank my luck
I paid for both my Senators
And put 'em in the truck
Now one has gone to milking
And one has gone to seed
By wintertime they'll understand
Just what the farmers need[1]

The Fable

AROUND THE WORLD, every year, there are semisecret private retreats for the top corporate movers and shakers. Secluded in some elegant rural resort, the leaders of industries, armies, and nations gather, greet, congratulate, honor, and plan for the future.

There is always a theme around which the retreat is organized. In the year of which we are speaking, the retreat theme is *We Did It—80 Percent!* Slogans on bright banners hang everywhere in the massive banquet hall, variations of this main theme. One reads, "80 Percent Pays the Rent!" Shouts another, "80 Is Great!" Proclaims a third, "8! 0! Watch Us Grow!"

A hush falls over the hall as the evening's speaker approaches the podium. Tall, graying, handsome, his cultivated white-man's tan proclaiming his health and vigor, impeccably dressed in a

British tailor's bespoke suit, he moves with the self-assurance of a corporate leader whose name is whispered with reverence in boardrooms and backrooms around the world.

"My friends," he begins, "we come here tonight to celebrate a stunning achievement. Thirty years ago, this seemed an impossible dream, a vision shared only by the most courageous and far-sighted among us.

"The timid, the unsure, the unconfident laughed at us. Nervous laughter, to be sure, because of who we were even then, but laughter nonetheless. Impossible, they carped. The vision is flawed, they complained. The strategy is defective, they whined. It will never happen. It can't be done. It *won't* be done.

"Too many of these naysayers were hunkered down in defensive positions. They were worn out, worn down by too many losing battles, trying to fend off the intrusive attacks of Big Government, those bureaucracies that owned and ran great hunks of our countries.

"Big Government laughed at us, thinking us puny. They used their legions of public employees, those gray, faceless, worthless bureaucrats, to limit us, to regulate us, to hold us back from our proper place in the world. To add insult to injury, they used our own money against us—*our* money, stolen from our hard-earned profits, taken from us by confiscatory taxes. We, who did the back-breaking work that created this wealth, saw all the bounty we had made ripped from us and used against us.

"In those days, my friends, Big Government told us what to do and what not to do. They closed off markets we could have profited from. They passed laws against cheap labor we could have used. They forced us to deal with power-hungry unions, as if our employees—*our* employees, people we paid *our* money to—had a right to tell us, the captains of industry, how to run our businesses.

"Oh, we had our spheres of influence, and we did as well as we could, considering the adverse circumstances under which we labored. It's hard to stop the great-hearted, the truly competitive, creative, hard-driving warhorses that we are, every one of us in this room. But we could only go so far before we hit their fences and their walls, before we had to account for ourselves to them. I repeat: *We* had to account for ourselves to *them*, those 'public servants,' those pigs slopping at the public trough.

"But did we let hard times grind us down? No! We broke through those fences when we could. We smashed through those walls. We found ways around them. We undermined them. We're hard to stop. We won't be stopped. We *can't* stop.

"And we held on to our dream, our dream of freedom, our dream of conquest, our dream of opening the whole glorious globe to be a free and open market, where no one and nothing can stop us from making profits by any means necessary.

"We set our goal: 80 percent of everything. Impossible, they said.

"But tonight even those who scoffed must recognize that the dream was real. The vision was true. The strategy was brilliant.

"My friends, we have accomplished what we set out to do. The multinational corporations represented here, and the family dynasties who are our closest partners and allies, have achieved our proudest goal.

"We now own 80 percent of everything worth owning in the entire world!"

The crowd goes wild, springs to its feet as one, shouting, screaming, applauding. Champagne corks go off rat-a-tat-tat like machine-gun fire, champagne sprays from a thousand bottles and sloshes over the rims of a thousand glasses. Confetti and music fill the air.

Slowly the crowd settles back into its chairs. But in the farthest corner of the room, one young man stays visibly if somewhat unsteadily on his feet. This is Eddie, a rising star in the world's largest petrochemical corporation. This is his first time at a meeting like this. He's here as the guest of the corporation's president, who is sitting just to his left.

"Sir!" he shouts. "Sir! I have a question."

"Yes?" the presiding officer asks.

"What about the other 20 percent?"

The room is so still you can hear a pin drop. Eddie's president kicks him hard in the leg and hisses at him, "Not now, you idiot! Sit down!"

But the speaker is in a generous mood. "Let me explain," he says. "We didn't just pick the number 80 percent out of a hat. We arrived at that goal through a long process of strategic analysis. Obviously we didn't want to go so far as to provoke a counterreaction, which could have upset not just this plan but many others. We set a realistic goal, which, through careful, coordinated work, could be achieved in a reasonable period of time.

"We know how to do strategic planning. Economic planning is our rock, our base. To that, we added local, national, and global political planning: an unbeatable combination. We did it, we did it together, we did it well, and I am very proud to say, we achieved our goal."

Eddie replies, "Thank you. I understand what you're staying, and I appreciate it. But I still want to know: What about the other 20 percent?"

Eddie's boss kicks him again. But the presiding officer is still in a generous, expansive mood, riding the crest of victory and fame. "You have to understand what that other 20 percent is. It's people's personal property, the things they've worked all their lives to achieve: their homes, their small businesses, their yards, their gardens, their cars and boats.

"But it's not just the things they own individually. It's also other, bigger things these people actually believe they have a right to share in, just because they've decided they're part of that so-called public sector, just because they bought that old textbook stuff about 'government of the people, by the people, for the people.'

"And what is this government of, by, and for the people, this great public sector? It's the public schools and day care centers their children go to. It's the city, county, state, and national parks they play in. It's the public hospitals that heal them when they're sick even if they can't pay the cost—appalling as this is to those of us who always pay our way and our fair share. It's the institutions that protect them and keep them feeling secure: the police forces, the fire departments, the courts, the prisons, the military forces of our great nation. It's the affordable public housing, the neighborhood libraries, the local health clinics, the community centers, and the roads they drive on to get to all of these places. It's the Social Security they've paid into all their working life.

"They've paid for these with their tax dollars. They've contributed millions of dollars of their own money to make them better. They've spent thousands of hours volunteering to keep them going. They honor the people who led the movements that won these things for them. They won't let those things go without a fight—and that's a fight we don't want to have."

But Eddie, high with excitement and champagne, doesn't know when to quit. "I still say," he says, "what about the other 20 percent? *Why can't we own it all?*"

Finally, a scowl crosses the presiding officer's face. But in that same instant, the man seated next to him rises slowly, painfully to his feet. He is the dean of all multinational corporate leaders, a man whose name inspires respect and fear in the seats of power around the world. Gently moving the presiding officer aside, he grabs the sides of the podium to steady himself and leans into the microphone.

"I think this young man has a very interesting point," he says. "*What about the other 20 percent? Why should those damn governments own and control anything at all?*

"Big Government is vulnerable, I tell you. This young man is right. We know how to get people to change their loyalties, to need—not just to want, to *need*—what we offer. We've already got the best minds money can buy. Let's turn them loose on the public sector. Let's tell the people of the world that the system is broken, that it's not working. Tell them the schools aren't working. Tell them public transportation isn't working. The welfare system isn't working, Social Security isn't working. And if we have to do some work to make sure the public sector really is broken, we know how to do that. We just keep saying it, and we get our"—a knowing wink—"friends in government to starve the public sector by cutting their funds to the bone. Voilà! Broken, just like we said.

"The need to fix what's broken—how can they argue with that? Then we offer ourselves as the fixers. Why should they turn to us to fix public services? Because we're the Free Market. We stand for Freedom to Choose. They understand that, because they love to shop. They *have* to shop to feel alive.

"Let's affirm that! Let's tell them, Yes, that's who you are, and what you do, and it is good. Go to it, but remember that you have your freedom to shop because we, and we alone, protect the Free Market for you!

"How can we fail?

"So, by God, it's time we really got together and went for it all. What's this measly 80 percent? We've got nothing to lose but our chains, and a world to win for our"—again the pause, the low voice to announce the sacred phrase—"bottom lines.

"I say to you: This young man is right. We *can* own it all.

"We *will* own it all."

The Fabulous True Story

Although there really are meetings of global economic and political powers (such as of the World Trade Organization and the Organization for Economic Cooperation and Development), we made up our fable to bring together some key threads that run throughout this book. Here, though, is a story we didn't make up. Honest: We found it in the *New York Times*.[2]

In May 2004, invitations were issued to a corporate governance retreat scheduled for March 2005, in Pebble Beach, California. The retreat was planned and the invitations were sent by the former chair of the U.S. Securities and Exchange Commission, Harvey Pitt. Mr. Pitt left that position under a cloud during the corporate and investment fraud scandals that erupted in 2004. Now back in the private sector, he is one of the founders of the Stillwater Directors Summit, the name he has been pleased to give the retreat that caught the *New York Times*'s attention.

Joining Mr. Pitt as hosts were Joel Kurtzman who is—hold on— "global lead partner for thought leadership and innovation" at

PricewaterhouseCoopers. You may remember Pricewaterhouse-Coopers: It's the accounting firm that was as blind to improper financial shenanigans perpetrated by privatizing corporations in Russia as the accounting firm Arthur Anderson was to Enron's. Peter Ueberroth, formerly the commissioner for baseball, was the third host.

And what was slated to be discussed at this retreat? The letter from Mr. Pitt says, "Government has overlegislated, overregulated, and overprosecuted. As a result, a new type of [corporate] director has emerged—some through appointment, some through 'conversion' with a new sense of mission. In many cases, collegiality has been replaced by skepticism and boards have become more risk-averse."[3]

Very interesting. To just what risks have corporate directors become averse? Are Mr. Pitt and his cohosts worried that corporate directors might stop and think twice before cooking the books, or polluting a river, destroying a wilderness area, poisoning a community's water supply, depleting the ozone layer, tearing off the top of a mountain to get to the coal underneath? Are they worried that these new risk-averse managers might just go limp and comply with laws and regulations prohibiting discrimination, dangerous working conditions, sexual harassment? *Exactly what risks do they want corporate leaders to be free to take?*

Corporate directors, you recall, have limited liability. The corporations they are supposed to oversee can go down without taking the whole personal fortunes of the so-called risk-takers with them. Employees will lose jobs and pensions and benefits, whole communities will suffer, small stockholders will lose their investments. But the risk-takers eventually bounce back, if not to where they were, to something not, on the scale of things, to be pitied.

Still, in the shadow of the fallen Enron, some corporate directors have apparently grown a mite more cautious. So Mr. Pitt says in his letter, "People have to seize control of the situation and make necessary changes." Right, "people" do, but it's doubtful if he means you and me, or the corporations' rank-and-file employees—let alone government regulators and prosecutors, none of whom were invited to this summit.[4]

What's the likely solution to the problem Mr. Pitt and his cohosts invited the summiters to consider? Well, the problem is governmental intrusion on their independence. Quite likely, don't you think, that they would reflect on how to fend off our government's efforts to keep the Enrons of the world from engaging in risky (read, unethical, illegal) practices that led to those irritating regulations? Which suggests weakening the government that is exercising oversight on behalf of the public good—or, still better, gaining control over it, no? Another step toward Bush's ownership society in which they own, and the public good is on its own.

Speaking of Enron: The whole story of how Enron made so very much money for its major players is now emerging. The same government that Mr. Pitt fusses about for "overregulating" corporations has, in fact, also been subsidizing their profit-making. So have some international financial organizations.

In 2001, Enron had foreign revenues of $23 billion. It got them through deals with countries including India, Panama, Columbia, the Dominican Republic, and Guatemala. Enron had help from the World Bank, and the U.S. government generously kicked in over $3 billion. Mr. Pitt doesn't seem to have put that interference with the free market on his agenda.

Privatization plays a significant role in such cozy, lucrative international deals. The International Monetary Fund, which was created along with the World Bank as the result of a perceived need for international economic planning after World War II, makes short-term loans to national governments. In return for those loans, the IMF has required recipient nations to cut back social services established for the public good of their people. The IMF has also demanded that these nations privatize big chunks of their governmental functions, such as providing and maintaining public roads and utilities, as well as national resources, such as oil and natural gas. Privatizing corporations gain; the people lose.

This is all supposed to strengthen the economies of the nations that get loans. Unfortunately, these nations are not consulted about whether they think cutting social services and selling off their national assets really will do that. They are told what to do by international financial organizations that force privatization on them. The people in those countries simultaneously lose crucial social services and find themselves with increasingly indebted governments that, as "debtor nations," fall further under the control of supranational corporations and international finance organizations. Whether or not the people had genuinely responsive leaders in power before these transactions, afterward they surely do not.[5]

That's the free market as privatizers have long planned for it. Even nations are subjected to their dictates, forced into their plan to own it all. And this is called spreading the free market, the free enterprise system, which, we are to believe, means exactly the same thing as spreading democracy.

CHAPTER 16

An Offer No Corporation
Could Refuse

Democracy and capitalism have very different beliefs about the proper distribution of power. One believes in a completely equal distribution of political power, "one man [person], one vote," while the other believes that it is the duty of the economically fit to drive the unfit out of business and into economic extinction. "Survival of the fittest" and inequalities in purchasing power are what capitalistic efficiency is all about. Individuals and firms become efficient to become rich. To put it in its starkest form, capitalism is perfectly compatible with slavery. The American South had such a system for more than two centuries. Democracy is not compatible with slavery.

—LESTER C. THUROW, FORMER DEAN OF MIT'S SLOAN SCHOOL OF MANAGEMENT[1]

W E NEED TO EVALUATE what is being planned by any group, to ask, "Whom does it benefit? Who will suffer? Whose power will be enhanced, and whose weakened? What values does it claim to serve, and which do we actually see in action?"

Changing Corporate Relationships to Government Since the 1970s

Before today's hyped-up globalizing economy, corporations got together mostly to press for their interests in specific industry situations. Coalitions across industry lines were not unknown, however, and those could be formed to take on issues that were more broadly social and political. People's movements for equality and social justice have more than once occasioned such corporate coalitions. For example, "prior to World War I a number of corporations, led by liquor and including textiles, mining, and railroads, had joined forces to block women's suffrage." Now, why would they want to do that? To protect the all-male club of big owners and bosses? Sure, but also because they thought voting women were a threat to their baseline cause, their profits: "The liquor industry feared women's support for Prohibition; other industries worried that giving women the vote would add momentum to such 'home-and-hearth' issues as higher wages and stronger social benefits."[2]

In the 1970s, corporations again began seriously to rethink the nature of their relationship to governments and public sectors throughout the world. There were two other dynamics that helped drive their thinking then as now. American-based corporations were rushing to beat all others by sending their manufacturing work to other countries, while also buying up those countries' assets—privatizing them. But although they were already expanding their operations transnationally, they needed to be sure they could keep doing so.[3]

At the same time, they realized that the public sector at home represented a set of very large economic units that were not yet under corporate management, ownership, or control. Think public education: thousands upon thousands of public day care centers, kindergartens, elementary schools, middle schools, high schools, community colleges, colleges and universities, in every town, city, and county in the country. Think Social Security: billions of dollars in management fees there for the taking, the dream of every stockbroker and investment banker. Think public prisons: over two million regular, paid-for "customers" who can't take their business somewhere else even if they want to. Looked at strictly from a financial point of view, the public sector consisted of a series of already developed economic sectors just hanging there, ripe for the picking.

It was a corporate CEO's dream—not, in fact, a public market where individuals and small traders meet to make fair and equal exchanges (your goods or services traded for mine, my money for your goods and services). No, it was a dream of turning the whole country into the biggest private mall of all—a privately owned and controlled stage set, a not-at-all free market entirely dominated by corporate stores where the sellers are not managers, the managers are not owners, and the owners are far away and rich beyond the wildest dreams of any small, independent vendors.

Furthermore, owning once-public goods, including the spaces around shops, the sidewalks and streets and squares that connect them, also means that you can control—you can even eliminate—people's public lives. In privately owned, for-profit malls, there is no right to public political activity. There are no striking workers, advocates for reproductive choice, environmental activists handing out leaflets, talking to people. There are no political candidates seeking votes, no people gathering signatures on petitions. You may not even be allowed to wear the wrong T-shirt. Stephen Downs, a lawyer, bought a T-shirt at the Crossgate Mall near Albany, New York. He paid for it. He put it on. His new T-shirt read, "Give Peace a Chance." Mr. Downs was arrested by the security guards.[4]

A privatized world, as we can already see it in malls, in corporate headquarters, on corporate "campuses," no longer has the public spaces that "are the last domains where the opportunity to communicate is not something bought and sold."[5] Take over what was public, including the airwaves, and even communication is yours to sell.

So there were powerful economic reasons for the corporations to develop and move a strategy to increase their control of the public sector. But there were also compelling political reasons. By the competitive dynamics of the economy, the political realm is turned into both a barrier to doing whatever it takes to win, and a prime plum to harvest.

Barriers to Corporate Control: Government, Labor, and Activist Movements

In the approximately four hundred years since the invention of the corporation, corporate power has been growing more or less steadily. In all those years, there have only been three forces that succeeded in challenging not only that growth but the sometimes harmful ways in which corporations did business and made money: government, organized labor, and activist movements for justice and equality such as the feminist movement that so worried corporations before World War I. All three had, in different ways and with varying but some consistent successes, opposed critical elements of the corporate agenda.

Now, it's not necessarily true in human affairs that, as Sir Isaac Newton decided when that apple fell on his head (as the story goes), what goes up will fall down. But history suggests that at crucial moments of change in any one system, and particularly when that system is either static or shrinking, when someone's power and money go up, someone else's fall down. This tends to please the ones who got more, and they rarely take lightly organized efforts to share in the new division of spoils or to rebalance the system.

People in business understand this right away. Many years ago, a spokesperson for the U.S. Chamber of Commerce, who suspected that Newton's law applied to economics as well as physics, said, "It will be a hard pill for many Americans to swallow—the idea of doing less so that big business can have more. . . . Nothing that this nation, or any other nation, has done in modern economic history compares in difficulty with the selling job that must be done to make people accept the new reality."[6]

The corporate power players who were rethinking their relationship to government understood this all too well. They, like the retreaters in our fable in the previous chapter who were dreaming of anything but retreat, knew that any growth in the corporations' share of the public sector would come at the expense of government. If the public sector had less, who but they would have more? And if the corporations could find ways to radically reduce the interdependent powers of government, organized labor, and activist movements, what would be left to stand in their way when they redistributed the wealth and power of the public sector in their favor? It would be like a football player who catches a pass, looks downfield—and doesn't see a single opposing player between him and the goal line.

And, ah! the sweetness of it all! To take down to size the very government that in U.S. history has more than once horrified the corporate economic players by trying to find ways to keep them from consolidating their winnings, from stacking the deck against any real competition with their monopolies. By taking over as much as they could of the public sector, they could cut down government's power and size. Then, when labor and other organized movements made demands on the corporations, there would no longer be even a governmental hand brake available to slow the corporations' triumphant progress toward owning and controlling it all.

Furthermore, weakened state and national governments could not bother the globalizing corporations by imposing their different laws, rules, and regulations. People who could organize and make their state governments set limits on corporate polluting, for example, had "forced" those corporations to move to states where there were no such people's movements—just as nations that set federal minimum wage laws "forced" them to move to other countries.

So here was an irresistible combination, a genuine three-for: government, unions, social justice movements. If corporations could gain control of that part of the national economy that was currently in the public sector—including the millions of jobs at all levels of government—they would simultaneously destroy much of the power of government and of those unions that represented public employees. Without the reinforcement of government and the labor movement, activist movements for justice and equality would be increasingly isolated and less effective. The three main barriers to corporate expansion and power would have been cut down to irritant size.

These goals could be furthered by transnational organizations, economic agreements and compacts, such as the World Trade Organization (WTO), the North American Free Trade Agreement (NAFTA), and the General Agreement on Tariffs and Trade (GATT). The corporations would be able to achieve the increase in market share they needed to continue expanding and to push profits higher without any organized or governmental barriers worth a moment's thought. And transnational economic, corporation-driven financial organizations could even "shrink" the power of international organizations of governments and international law. NAFTA, for example, goes WTO one (or more) better: It makes it possible for a corporation to sue another country's government all on its own. There is no need even to go through its home base government to do so. And such suits are decided by arbitration boards that meet in secret—no public present, no publicity, no representatives of the public good.[7]

As these plans and organizations were made, and made real, the corporations could look down the field and see only daylight between them and the goal. The corporations *could* own it all. In a privatized country in a privatized world, they *could* have their cake and eat it too.

Public Employee Unions

But there was not only this delicious, gigantic economic cake just waiting to be sliced, divided, and eaten. There was rich frosting on the cake. Even though the U.S. labor movement had fallen on relatively hard times compared to its most powerful years, had been declining in numbers and strength, it was still a troubling, troublesome, and often surprisingly effective opponent. From the proverbial shop floor to the halls of Congress, unions were, from the point of view of the corporations, a serious impediment to their plans for expansion and domination of both the economy and politics. And some of those damn unions had even taken in recent years to joining forces with the movements of feminists and disabled people and racial and ethnic minorities, and those oh, so cheap to hire "illegal aliens" who brazenly dreamed of decent pay, and tree-hugging environmentalists, and queers, for heaven's sake, and all those other radical kooks that, whatever they said, were really out to destroy corporate profits and privileges.[8]

Among the many unions in the U.S. labor movement, some of the most irksome to the corporations were those that represented public employees (although 13 percent of U.S. workers overall are covered by union contracts—down from 35 percent in the 1950s

—over 30 percent of public employees are). These, by and large, tend to be the more progressive unions, more open to taking on social as well as economic issues and even to seeing these as the same fight. These unions would be even more inclined to figure out how to make common cause with, say, environmentalists, rather than lobby for a new nuclear plant because it would create temporary construction jobs. Even worse, the public employee unions were growing, putting major resources into organizing and winning over new constituencies.

What if their strategy worked? What if the unions that already represented several million public employees were twice or three times as large, and therefore that many times as powerful? What if public sector unions were large enough, as they are in some other countries, to call a national strike to protest corporate or governmental policies?

How could the corporations deal with a possible reawakening of the labor movement, led in part by the unions that represented public employees, which were themselves far too prone to work in coalition with other movements for justice? It was a well-known fact in corporate as well as in labor circles that newly organized union members tend to be the most militant. And these weren't just new union members, they were new constituencies: women, people of color, immigrants, low-wage workers. What if this turned out to be the 1930s all over again, the time in U.S. history when organized labor came closest to threatening corporate control of the economy and the country? *What could be done to head them off at the pass?*

As they say, you didn't have to be a rocket scientist working at Lockheed Martin to figure this one out: *No public employees, no public employee unions.*

Even though they made it to themselves, it was an offer the corporations could not refuse. And to refuse was the last thing on their minds. They had watched *The Godfather.* They knew what was expected of powerful leaders. They had seen *Patton* and *Julius Caesar.* They knew how the captains of any industry, the true commanders-in-chief of warriors on a crusade, were supposed to behave.

We're not making this up. Among other observers of this scene, the neoconservative Carnes Lord, author of *The Modern Prince: What Leaders Need to Know*, urges Americans to fight against "the progressive 'feminization' of politics," and a reviewer of Lord's book comments on a neoconservative obsession with overcoming "the decline of 'manliness.'"[9] Surely not all corporate leaders and privatizers subscribe to this macho scenario, but it's hard to ignore it as an, um, potent script in the age of "lean-and-mean" corporations, and "tough, straight-talking," gun-toting presidential candidates like George W. Bush and John Kerry.

So for the privatizers of today, their successes in turning us against our own government, in convincing us that their license is our individual freedom, are not enough. They want government, unions, and grassroots organizations to be as weak as possible. They want the provisions and protections for the public good that so many struggled so hard to win to be handed over to them to run for profit. That's why they started planning, strategizing, devising tactics. In doing so, they both drew on and re-created a contemporary version of an ideology that has roots in the founding of this country.

The corporations and their political allies can wave flags, and wear flags, and speak eloquently about freedom and democracy in front of huge flags. But try to remember that other spirit of '76— the one that refused to be exploited and dominated by government corporations, some of which had visions, as the Massachusetts Bay Company Puritans did, of founding a theocracy, in which a required religion made not just religious but political dissent into heresy. What *are* we doing being taken in by an ideology that is so obviously threatening democracy?

FREEDOM, REVOLUTION, PROGRESS

A long time ago, but not too long ago, a man said:

> ALL MEN ARE CREATED EQUAL . . .
> ENDOWED BY THEIR CREATOR
> WITH CERTAIN INALIENABLE RIGHTS . . .
> AMONG THESE LIFE, LIBERTY
> AND THE PURSUIT OF HAPPINESS.

His name was Jefferson. There were slaves then,
But in their hearts the slaves believed him, too,
And silently took for granted
That what he said was also meant for them.
It was a long time ago,
But not so long ago at that, Lincoln said:

> NO MAN IS GOOD ENOUGH
> TO GOVERN ANOTHER MAN
> WITHOUT THAT MAN'S CONSENT.

There were slaves then, too,
But in their hearts the slaves knew
What he said must be meant for every human being—
Else it had no meaning for anyone.[1]

CHAPTER 17

The American Dream—Always at Risk

President Bush will talk about two concepts of freedom in a Thursday inaugural speech. On the international front, aides say, he will discuss the importance and world-changing impact of giving people the freedom to form a government. Domestically, Bush will talk about freedom from government.[1]

From the Beginning: Balanced Government Versus Privatization Ideology

THOMAS JEFFERSON SAID long ago that preserving liberty is always likely to require ongoing revolution.[2] The revolutionaries who created our government therefore set up a balanced form of governance that had to be responsive to the people so that future revolutions could be orderly and peaceful rather than violent.

But the seeds of the ideology of privatization were also planted in the seventeenth and eighteenth centuries. When capitalism overtook feudal aristocracies and monarchies, the change seemed to some people nothing but good, a win for freedom and equality, a loss for the rotten old orders in which wealth stayed in the hands of a very few for generation upon generation. But like most that is human, that win was also a mixed blessing, even though Western stories of our progress tend to skim over its downsides.

Economic historian Esther Kingston-Mann starts the story of privatization with the enclosure movement in seventeenth-century England. That was when common lands, long used by open-field farmers, began to be enclosed—fenced in by new own-ers. This takeover of what had been public, common land was romanticized just as corporate takeover of the modern economy has been. The hero of that early story and of theories made to explain it, Kingston-Mann tells us, were "courageous architects of private property rights."[3] The "man of property" was—and still is, in many histories—characterized as the progressive, hardworking man (not woman) whose stake in making his owned land more productive led him to modernize farming, to increase productivity. The villains, in this story's terms, were the "backward country bumpkins" who could not and would not change and so had to be—deserved to be—shoved aside.

The problem with this romanticized tale of progress driven by privatization of public lands is not only that it casts the victims, the dispossessed, as villains, but that, by telling a partial story, it falsi-fies history and keeps us from learning about other ways of doing things. For example, Kingston-Mann's research reveals that, "Despite their lack of schooling and the meagerness of their resources to bear the costs and risks of change, open-field farmers in seventeenth-century Oxfordshire appear to have secured the consent of their neighbors to the village-wide introduction of many-field systems of crop rotation. As a consequence, the use of fodder crops spread more rapidly on the open fields than on the large-scale private estates of the Thames district."[4]

Why does that matter? Because the ideology of privatization is built on the notion that only private ownership gives people the motivation to work hard, to take creative risks, to improve their land and their products. That private ownership sometimes does so can indeed be demonstrated historically and cross-culturally—but that is not the only or the whole story. When it is assumed to be the whole story, serious mistakes can be and have been made.

For example, "in the 1980s, the World Bank's structural adjust-ment program in sub-Saharan Africa required the wholesale pri-vatization of common, public, and socially controlled resources." This was supposed to jump-start a new, far more productive economy that would benefit everyone and so be worth the social and cultural destruction of the traditional way of life. But "economic output in sub-Saharan Africa fell by 30 percent in the 1980s; by the mid-1990s, per capita income in sub-Saharan Africa stood at 80 percent of the 1980s level": It fell, and kept falling. Women were particularly affected, because their traditional right to shares of land was also judged to be "backward."[5] Individual land claims were given to men. The privatizers scorn paternalism, but they actively promote patriarchy.

The same ideological blindness led to similar disasters in the former Soviet Union, where privatization led to a fall of 50 percent in economic output by the year 2000. There, too, women suffered the most: They became 80 percent of those without jobs. That was not because they were unqualified for the new economic order; 75 percent of the unemployed women were well educated and highly trained.

Back in England, where the tale of the heroic individual male property owner carrying the torch of progress took root and then took over so much of future economic theory and planning, vast divisions between the rich and the poor developed right along with the capitalist industrial order. The poor, including children, were forced to work twelve-hour days with no weekends off in miserable, life-threatening conditions for just as miserable pay.

No school this morning
The whistle's blowing
Children by twos and threes
Tumble down the hill
Out of their childhood
Into the world for good
Out of the schoolyard
Into the mill

Dressed in her mother's shirt
Too small to reach her work
Worn as the wooden box
On which she stands
Torn from her books and games
She stares at her spinning frame
The threads of childish laughter
Break in her hands

Seasons don't shift in here
Smog doesn't lift in here
Snow doesn't drift in here
When the nights turn cold
Wind doesn't blow in here
Rivers don't flow in here
Children don't grow in here
They just get old

> *Silk and satin*
> *No time for dreaming*
> *The dawn is breaking*
> *The twelve-hour shift starts soon*
> *Ribbon and lace*
> *Go take your place*
> *Within the shadows of this spinning room*[6]

Outside the factories and workhouses, air and water became poisonously polluted. Remember those famous fogs of London, so dramatically reproduced in movies and novels about those times—pea soup fogs, into which villains could disappear? That was what we now call smog: It was industrial pollution. It took organized governmental action even to begin to fix all that this new liberator, industrial capitalism, had brought.

But the seeds of belief that freedom and equality were best and even only served by a free-market capitalism had been planted, and the real successes of this new economic system kept the new growth watered and healthy. Then as now, pointing out capitalism's obvious failures to protect the public good was taken to be dangerously radical—especially, of course, by those it was enriching and all the wannabes before whom it dangled the promise that you, too, can grow up to be a rich owner, a corporate officer, director, shareholder.

Some of those seeds have grown into today's rigid ideology of privatization, even though a theory from the early days of capitalism that it often invokes—Adam Smith's famous free market that was supposed to be kept in balance by its own dynamics as if by an invisible hand—is radically insufficient for today's global corporate capitalism.

Those seeds of belief in the righteousness of unregulated capitalism were kept from taking over the whole field of political economics by vivid experiences. People *were* impoverished as well as enriched. Economic insecurity *was* a constant and increasing problem. The economy swung back and forth between growing, productive periods and horrific depressions and failures. All this made it evident that the invisible hand was by no means reliable all by itself.

But when you listen to some of the staunchest advocates of the privatization ideology that says government should get out of the way of corporate pursuit of profits, it becomes apparent that the lesson they learned was *not* that capitalism needs to be kept from the harms it can do for our sake, and also for its own sake. The privatization ideologues don't readily admit that economic systems *need* governments to make and enforce the laws and regulations that keep competition fair and safe for all concerned, that we *need* a welfare state—a state committed to the welfare of its people—to provide for the public good, backed up by the rule of law on which a healthy economy also depends. Those who are blinded by the ideology of privatization persist in seeing the state as a problem, not a necessity.

Of course, it's also true that, while a strong state is necessary to balance competing economic, political, and social forces, a state that becomes too strong can create problems of its own. It is hardly new in the United States to be suspicious of "the state." The colonists, the revolutionaries, the founders of the U.S. government knew from their own experiences that too much concentrated power means tyranny.

But there's another aspect to the still-resonant story of the early days, one that is familiar but that, somehow, just hasn't been emphasized in the U.S. mainstream. Here's a simple version of that story as we don't usually hear it:

> America was actually settled by early corporations. In 17th-century England, companies were chartered by the Crown to help colonize the New World. Investors pooled capital and launched massive trading ventures. These joint-stock companies created colonies in America that served as sources of raw material and as markets for exports from England. The Massachusetts Bay Company and the East India Company were two examples of these trade monopolies.[7]

And how did the colonists feel about the corporate monopoly that was enriching both the wealthy investors and the British Crown?

> Early citizens of the colonies, burdened by increasingly onerous taxes and import duties imposed by the Crown, had no say in how they were governed and taxed. The Boston Tea Party in 1774 epitomized the growing wrath of the citizenry and presaged the American Revolution. The War of Independence, which began the following year, was not merely a revolt against the Crown; it was a fight for independence from royal-chartered corporations.[8]

Having learned the lesson that the Crown could and did exploit them, "America's founding fathers purposefully created a new nation in which government could not interfere in the individual wealth-creating activities of its citizens. The result, according to Professor Paul Tiffany of the Wharton School, one of the country's leading graduate schools for business, is 'a long history of abuses.'"[9]

They were remarkable men, the founding fathers, but their identification was not firmly with the exploited of the world. The American revolutionaries—although they were by no means all wealthy—were outraged to find themselves among the exploited. This was treating them, they felt, as if they were slaves, like those being bought and sold in the then-flourishing slave trade. It was treating them as if they were Indians whose lands could just be taken, as if they were women who did not have, as they did, rights as Englishmen. What a bunch of insults! So they set up a government in which they would have the rights to which they felt entitled. What they did *not* do is set up adequate protections for the exploited they themselves never intended to be among again.

Within those limits, they did a magnificent job. They knew that a government aspiring to democratic ideals must be strong, and they took a huge step when they chose to base its strength in the authority of "We the People."

The final paragraph of the Declaration of Independence invokes the authority not of a Crown, not of a church, not of a corporation. Its authors acted, they wrote, on the "Authority of the good People of these colonies."

You might want to bear this in mind when corporations and churches are handed our government goods and functions and services by elected officials wearing flags on their lapels and talking about democracy, liberty, and the independent Spirit of 1776. That spirit was outraged by the rule of the corporations and churches of the time (which had actually united in the infamous Massachusetts Bay Company). Unfortunately, the men moved by that spirit did not hold on to what they had learned about the tyranny of the not-so-holy trinity of state, church, and corporation.

Consider John Winthrop (1588–1649), scion of an aristocratic, wealthy British family that had seen its fortunes reversed, which was not a happy situation for young John. He succeeded, though, in being made governor of Massachusetts by the Massachusetts Bay

Company. And in chartering that company, the Crown slipped up. The king failed to make the usual specification that the company's directors, or governors, were required to live in England. So the Puritan directors of this company took advantage of a charter that, under the laws of England, gave almost absolute power, and took off for the new land. Their real goal? To set up a religious state—a theocracy. Profits for the corporation, political and religious power for them. Who could resist?[10]

Winthrop delivered a sermon on the good ship *Arabella,* en route to the New World. It begins with this: "God Almighty in His most holy and wise providence hath so disposed of the condition of mankind as in all times some must be rich, some poor; some high and eminent in power and dignity, others mean and in subjection."[11] Government, therefore, said Winthrop, is to "manifest" God's spirit, "first, upon the wicked in moderating and restraining them, so that the rich and mighty should not eat up the poor, nor the poor and despised rise up against their superiors and shake off their yoke." You might describe this as *compassionate economic puritanism,* an early version of today's so-called compassionate conservatism.

Winthrop also preached that government is to "manifest" upon "the regenerate"—which is to say, the good and godly folk at all levels of society—so that "sensibility and sympathy of each other's conditions will necessarily infuse into each part a native desire and endeavor, to strengthen, defend, preserve, and comfort the other."[12]

There is in that brew a seed of a notion of the public good, but it rested on *religious* principles that were used to justify an *economic* hierarchy. A spiritual but neither a political nor an economic democracy.

Nevertheless, in Massachusetts as in other colonies, the experiences in self-governance of the colonists, far away from England, made the notion of the public good more political. The colonial men got used to independence. They became practiced in self-governance. They began to want more.

In 1791, Thomas Paine gave voice to a distinctly political vision of liberty and justice that the revolution for democracy had birthed. Its principles were these:

> I. Men are born, and always continue, free and equal in respect of their rights. Civil distinctions, therefore, can be founded only on public utility.

Public standing in the new republic thus was to come only to those who served the public, and did so well. Here is a breach in the old order, a notion of a genuinely political *public* good not subservient to economic power, aristocratic blood claims, or religious authority.

> II. The end of all political associations is the preservation of the natural and imprescribable rights of man; and these rights are liberty, property, security, and resistance of oppression.

The old fear that democracy would provide license for the poor to try to overthrow what had been preached as God's ordained social order had been dramatically weakened. There was a *right* to resist oppression, and a vision of a political order in which government is to protect human rights.

> III. The nation is essentially the source of all sovereignty; nor can any INDIVIDUAL, or ANY BODY OF MEN, be entitled to any authority which is not expressly derived from it. [caps in original][13]

The concern had become how to keep *any* "individual, or any body of men," from claiming authority over a government that derived and exercised its sovereignty from and on behalf of the nation's people.

Sharing Power by Dividing It Up

One of the extraordinary insights of some of the revolutionaries and founders was that power can be used to check power if you spread it around effectively. You want to be sure that any one powerful group, or any one kind of power, does not get altogether too big. When that is taken care of, groups are more likely to try to find their common interests than to try to dominate unilaterally.

As James Madison wrote:

> In a society under the forms of which the stronger faction can readily unite and oppress the weaker, anarchy may as truly be said to reign as in a state of nature, where the weaker individual is not secured against the violence of the stronger; and as, in the latter state, even the stronger individuals are prompted, by the uncertainty of their condition, to submit to a government which may protect the weak as well as themselves.[14]

Unlike the corporation-appointed John Winthrop, Madison was no longer preaching at people of different economic and social classes to be kindly to one another in the hope that their religious obedience would fend off rebellions of the poor. The whole point of the U.S. government system is that *no* power and *no* faction should be allowed to get so big that it can take over the others.

Great idea, brilliant political insight. Unfortunately, the founders checked and balanced pursuit of too much power by state and church, giving each its separate sphere, but they did not adequately contain in its sphere the very corporate domination of government against which they had waged a revolution. The seeds of confusion between a form of government (democracy) and an economic system (unfettered capitalism) were planted. The door was held open for wealth and power to try to take over government.

This is not to say that the founders and their early successors did nothing at all to control corporations. What they did just wasn't thorough, determined, or deeply enough entrenched in governance and legal systems. It therefore failed. Furthermore, because few of us were taught the history of corporations as the essential thread in the story of our ongoing struggles for democracy, few of us have learned from the lessons of the founders' real opposition to corporations or their failure to contain them. Here are just a few of those crucial lessons:

+ We should know that, in 1816, Thomas Jefferson wrote, "I hope we shall crush in its birth the aristocracy of our monied corporations which dare already to challenge our government to a trial of strength and bid defiance to the laws of our country."

+ We should know that the effort that was made to do that was undercut by too few protections against the rich and powerful getting charters for their corporations.

+ Nevertheless, the new government did set limits on early corporations through the charters that corporations must have to become legal. Back then, there were fixed time limits on how long a corporation could exist, what today we'd call a *sunset clause*. There were also strict specifications about what they could do. Clearly, the founders knew better than to allow corporations to go on indefinitely, do whatever they decide to do (from establishing militaries for sale to the highest bidder, to running child care offices, to providing janitorial services—or all of the above), or to grow without limit. Today's charters do not impose these limitations.

+ Perhaps most importantly, in the early days our government retained the ability to revoke a corporation's charter if, for example, that corporation caused public harm. The founders were committed to serving the people and the public good, not "the aristocracy of our monied corporations."

But, despite all this, because individual states insisted on and won the right to set their own rules for the charters they issued, pretty soon corporations were doing what they do today—picking up and moving from more to less restrictive states. And when states, such as New Jersey in 1896 and Delaware in 1899, enticed corporations to relocate there by gutting the controls of charters, all the other states pretty soon found themselves having to do the same or lose employers that had made themselves central to their economies. Delaware still has 59.2 percent of the Fortune 500 corporations incorporated there.[15]

This not only reminds us that corporations always have gone wherever they can go to get the best deal but also explains something about conservatives who support corporate power and, today, argue for privatization. Conservatives have long stood for stronger state than federal government. This made sense for them when corporations benefited from the lack of uniform federal controls on their charters. But today, with privatization on the top of the corporatist agenda, some conservatives find it desirable to (a) strengthen the federal government they now at least partly control, and (b) use that centralized strength to sell off the federal government to the corporations. The differing states are not to be allowed to block this takeover, which will end by providing the very uniform federal posture toward corporations that the founders failed to provide, but now for the opposite purpose—to unleash, not to restrain the corporations.

CHAPTER 18

Differing Visions, Conflicting Values

The long night falls on cannonballs
That stack upon the White House lawn
Like sentries posted just before the battle
The air is filled with sounds of guns
The country torn, the death of sons
The cannon's roar, the saber's angry rattle

Affairs of state, the wheel of fate
The devil's dance of luck and chance
Have picked you out to lead where men will follow
And while you deal with complex things
Alliances and deals with kings
The bodies mount at Gettysburg and Shiloh

You struggle with the faith begun
By Jefferson and Washington
The eyes of all the nation now are on you
You hold the key to Tom Paine's dreams
Ben Franklin's hopes, Sam Adams' schemes
One hundred years of history lie upon you

But if you could come back again
And see the mean and selfish men
Who deal in lies and compromise the nation
Would you consider all the pain
The battles fought the loss and gain
Still worth it for the Union's preservation
A tired man, a lonesome man
Abe Lincoln walks tonight[1]

"GOVERNMENT OF THE PEOPLE, by the people, and for the people shall not perish from the earth."[2]

That's Abraham Lincoln speaking, calling people in a new nation torn by civil war to remember what the gaunt, weary, but determined president held to be the heart and soul of the Union purpose.

The leaders of the Confederacy differed. They fought for their way of life, for the preservation of their property—including enslaved people who made that way of life possible but were owned as if they were things rather than people. The owners of the South understood that what they saw as their liberty, their life, their pursuit of happiness required an economic system that protected their rights to have and to deal with their human property at home and in a marketplace free of intrusion from government—that is, the federal government, which was finally trying to undo slavery.

So like today's corporate privatizers, when Confederate leaders said they wanted to "get the government off our backs," they didn't mean all government, only that part of the government that got in their way. They were happy to have the Confederate government, which they virtually owned and operated, and which helped them maintain economic power, including the power to continue to be slaveholders. So they fought for what they called southern independence—as if anyone is free and independent when ownership takes precedence over the respect and love and care between people that have no price.

But then as now, the independence and desire to be free of intrusion of the privileged actually did not mean hands-off. The plantation owners certainly did not want government to keep hands-off the laws that made slavery possible, protected, lucrative—and importable to any new states trying to join the Union. If capitalism, as Lester C. Thurow, former dean at MIT, observed, is compatible with slavery, the not yet thoroughly industrialized economy of the Confederate states downright required it. That made it seem necessary to spread slavery, rather than to limit it. Free states were far too attractive to the enslaved people who always knew that human beings are not property, and who loved freedom as few who have not lived without it can.

The cause of the North was not without its own economic self-interest, of course. Whatever the publicly affirmed purposes of the Civil War, there were money-driven property and profit interests involved on both sides. And again on both sides, as always, the poor bore more of the brunt of the war than the rich who declared it.

It is not news that monied interests drive a great deal of human conflict, and can profit from it as well. But the American Civil War was also fought against slavery, and to preserve a new and still fragile form of government. Lincoln, with the Declaration of Independence and the Constitution in mind, could speak of that government as "of, by, and for the people."

These ideals were hardly realities. But like all ideals, they called people to consider their self-interest from a deeper and more far-reaching perspective—and even to transcend that self-interest. We human beings are not just creatures of self-interest; we are not just buyers and sellers. We are, heaven knows, much more than owners and owned.

The American Revolution as well as the abolition movement that worked for the end of slavery, early and continuing feminism, the labor movement, the civil rights, disability rights, and Native American struggles—as well as many more—have all held before us the ideal of a democratic government that is of, by, and for *all* the people. Of course these movements also had and have their specific grievances and demands and purposes, and none is without various, even clashing, self-interests.

But they are movements of people who have experienced exploitation and been targets of violence. They are movements of people who have been silenced, insulted, ignored, rendered marginal, and denied economic and political power. They are movements of people who know that "silence = death."

CHAPTER 19

"Trickling Down" into the 1980s and 1990s

The President stepped off the silver screen
He said, People, put your lives here in my hand
We can turn our country's honor white again
Let the sulphur smoke of progress fill our land

> 'Cause we've got government on horseback again
> Back to the days when congressmen were men
> We can make it on our own
> Running on testosterone
> It's government on horseback again

Help me give our land a golden goose
Turn our native corporations loose
High voltage lines will go the extra mile
Now it's power to the people, nuclear style

Blow out the lamp beside the golden door
We don't need cheap foreign labor anymore
Without our unions and the ERA
We will all have twice the jobs at half the pay

> Back again, back again
> We've got government on horseback again
> It's back to home for mommies
> Bomb the hell out of the commies
> It's government on horseback again[1]

IN 1981, George Gilder published a widely influential bestseller, *Wealth and Poverty*, that became a virtual bible for conservative policymakers. David Stockman, then director of the U.S. Office of Management and Budget, said it was "the best thing written on economic growth in 15 years." William F. Buckley, one of the conservatives' most important theorists and publicists, wrote that Gilder's book "points us in the right direction." The financial publication *Barron's* called Gilder's book "at once a defense and celebration of capitalism and capitalists," and exulted, "Its call for liberty and free men smacks of the spirit of '76."[2]

Yet again: freedom and liberty identified with capitalism, capitalism identified with democracy, and this brew equated with the spirit of '76. Flags begin to appear on *very* expensive suits.

The popular magazine *Newsweek* is quoted on the back cover of Gilder's book: "Anyone who wants additional insight into the thinking of Ronald Reagan's economic planners doesn't have to look far. . . . *Wealth and Poverty* has all the right elements."

Favoring Business Over Government: Reaganomics

So what did George Gilder have to say about the relation between the free enterprise system and government? This:

> Our central problem arises from a deep conflict between the processes of material progress and the ideals of "progressive" government and culture. . . . The result is that all modern governments pretend to promote economic growth but in practice doggedly obstruct it.[3]

How does progressive government obstruct economic growth? Progressive government, it appears to Gilder, cares about the public good and is—gasp—democratically inclined.

What's wrong with that? It's wrong, he says, because "material progress is ineluctably elitist," which, for Gilder, is to be understood as a good thing. Why? Because "it makes the rich richer and increases their numbers, exalting the few extraordinary men." *All* the rich are extraordinary? Well, Gilder thinks so. Rich men are extraordinary because they are so rich; they are rich because they are extraordinary. Shades of preacher/Governor Winthrop again? Not quite. Gilder doesn't invoke God to anoint the rich as superior. It's money he's interested in, and unfettered capitalism does the anointing.

Thus, rich men (he does say *men*) are extraordinary because they "can produce wealth," which is what differentiates them from "the democratic masses who consume it."[4] So We the People are the masses, just as we were to the European and British aristocrats who feared our uprising.

But what does Gilder mean by saying that we—us masses— "consume" wealth? Who does the actual work that produces products, delivers services, keeps the offices and homes of the supermen running? Whose wages are held down to increase profits? Whose dollars are enticed out of pockets by massive advertising and marketing so the supermen can get rich?

But let's not get resentful of the very few supermen to whom Gilder gives all the credit, the forerunners of today's downright idolized corporate bosses, some of whom even have their own TV shows. "Material progress is difficult," Gilder tells us sternly. "It requires from its protagonists long years of diligence and sacrifice, devotion and risk that can be elicited only with high rewards, not the 'average return on capital.'"[5] Ah, I see. *These* are the real hard workers, the ones who risk everything—for what? To make an extreme return on capital.

And there's nothing merely selfish, let alone greedy, in this. In Gilder's view, the whole world depends on the supermen making that massive return on capital because "a world without innovation succumbs to the sure laws of deterioration and decay."[6]

Rich men are the only innovators who save the world from decaying? The supermen who will do anything for more than the average return on capital are the geniuses, the inventors, the creators? Gilder even gives astronomer Galileo as an example of such creativity. Got that? Here we thought Galileo was studying the stars, but what he really wanted was a greater than average return on capital.

Gilder has obviously lost his balance here. An overeager bunch, these PR men for the super rich.

Nevertheless, Gilder had a huge impact, and we have been subjected to a great deal more of this stuff since the 1980s. Did you notice when first class was joined by corporate or business class in airplanes? That tells us *not* that we no longer have a class system but that now we have a class system with corporate executive types moving on up (so much for outdated scorn for "crass commercialism"). Have you noticed the spate of best-selling books with titles like *Excellence* that are about business success? What a painful shrinkage of the meaning of excellence. Hard not to say "Jesus weeps," but of course now there are also super-wealthy televangelists who tell their flocks that faith is rewarded by—you guessed it—wealth. One of them is actually named "Dollar." Really: the Reverend Creflo Dollar. Proves to him, he told a reporter, that God called him to his mission. The Reverend Dollar has a $5 million private jet, a Rolls-Royce, and a home behind the heavy gates of an elite community in Atlanta.[7]

Rich men, in all these views, not only can pass through the eye of a needle but are the only ones who can. Us and the camels: We're all just the wrong sort of beasts. Even if we're poets, and inventors, and astronomers, and songwriters, and teachers, and firefighters, and organizers, and artists, and nurses, and medical researchers, and scientists—productive workers, and volunteers for all sorts of causes just because we care about them, we're not innovators. If our goal isn't seeking extreme return on capital, we're just consumers of wealth.

The rationale—or rationalization—for the non-"progressive" political economy offered by Gilder and espoused by the Reaganomics folks came to be known as *trickle-down economics*. That's the theory by which those super-rich people were told to get richer still without qualms about the rest of us, because their wealth would sort of somehow run over the edge of their golden bathtubs and drip into the basements the rest of us could afford, and all would therefore be well. We could take showers on their overflow. And if our ceiling got soggy and collapsed, why, that's a job created right there and then. We'd have to hire someone to fix it, thereby spreading the money around. Meanwhile, the penthouse folks, not having to contribute much to the rest of the building underneath them, would love to hire people to do lots of work for them to help the economy, if there weren't those damn unions to make it so expensive.

President Reagan, you may recall, started off his term in office by breaking the air controllers' union. Don't know about you, but we prefer having the people who get airplanes off and back on the ground safely well paid, well rested, and well respected. We tend to believe that they should have significant say in judging whether their working conditions help them do their life-saving jobs. Does your boss know what it takes to do your work well, or do you and your co-workers? Does your boss have more respect for the work you do than you and your co-workers? We're glad to know that the people operating and maintaining the planes on which we fly still have unions protecting them—and us.

The 1990s: The Era of Big Government Is Over

Bill Clinton was supposedly elected in 1992 because his centrist Democratic campaign managers kept him on message: "It's the economy, stupid." This is hardly a slogan that implies that the government does not and should not have an important economic role. In fact, it exaggerates what any president is able to do. The curious thing is that today we in the United States seem to believe simultaneously that the freedom of capitalism must be protected from the state *and* that the government is responsible for the health of the capitalist economy.

Curious, yes. But this apparent contradiction is not untrue to the mixed, messy model of our government of separated, mutually checked and balanced powers. We do want it both—and all—ways. We want the government to stay out of our way. We blame the government when things go wrong, but still we turn to it for help when needed. After 9/11, when we had to face how badly private security at airports had failed us, we demanded that the federal government take it over—even though the head of the federal government, George W. Bush, allied as always with private profit-making corporate interests, opposed having our airport security protected by public employees. Wrong direction, from private to public.

We want the protection that government provides, and we want freedom. Put those together, and what we really want is for our government, and the whole public sector, from firefighters to voluntary organizations, to be both responsible and responsive. We do want public services to be better run. We do recognize problems, and dislike governmental bureaucracies that are too large to be adequately responsive to us. But we don't want weak, removed, almost absent government and far fewer public services, any more than we want huge, intrusive, omnipresent government. It's quite simple, actually. We want problems fixed, but we don't want to throw the baby out with the bathwater (as Grover Norquist does, once he's drowned it).

Bill Clinton's other message—"The era of Big Government is over"—need not have meant, "So, welcome to the era of Big Corporations." But the arguments for shrinking government, the attacks on Big Government, have in fact grown stronger and more influential, and are now being used to drive the ideological and very real economic, political agenda that supports the corporate privatizers who gained control of the White House.

The everything-for-profit ideologues also gained more power in Congress, and set about renewing the administration's efforts to do just what the anti–New Deal people swore at FDR for doing—trying to control the Supreme Court and every judicial body to which they can nominate and appoint judges. In March 2005, President Bush renominated all twenty of the judges Congress did not confirm during his first term. One of them, William Meyers III, has never even served as a judge. He was a lobbyist for the cattle and mining industries. It is in the public written record that he thinks interfering with potential profit is unconstitutional—even when profiteers are destroying natural habitats. No environmental protection laws for him.

Another, Terence Boyle, formerly a legal aide to Senator Jesse Helms, was a judge. His major cause has been trying *not* to enforce laws pertaining to employment discrimination. Allowing discrimination on the basis of disability, race, and gender seems to be so important to him that basically sound legal judgment doesn't matter. The Fourth District Court of Appeals, itself known to be conservative, has had to overturn Judge Boyle's decisions 120 times, apparently because they were found to be so significantly erroneous.[8]

The presidency, or executive branch; the Congress, or legislative branch; and the courts, or judicial branch: that's all three of the founders' carefully separated branches of government being turned to the service of weakening and selling off government. Add the Bush administration's claims to speak for "all-American" moral values and his carefully tended base in fundamentalist Christianity, and the effort to centralize—not genuinely shrink— power and authority is frighteningly evident. But that power and authority is also being privatized, so the centralized power is in corporate, not governmental hands.

To keep us from defending the values of the public good culture, the privatizers go all out to discredit government and the public sector. They do not want us to defend the values of the public good culture, to stand up for them so that we can hold onto an equitable system in which a strong economy is balanced by a strong, independent government. They express nothing but scorn for those who, they like to say, "feed from the public trough" (or when they are really wound up, "suck at the public teat"), by which they mean those who work for the public sector. Such people, we hear, can't be trusted to be practical, efficient, or even just plain capable, because they have "never been responsible to the bottom line." Which is to say that *they* don't take the risks the profit-makers do, because the government is there to pay and to bail them out if they mess up. This, from businesses that incorporated precisely in order to limit the liability of the individuals involved so they could protect their personal assets from losses and lawsuits the corporation might incur if those individuals mess up.

In fact, many corporations do quite a lot of public feeding and sucking, and their bottom lines are often well-padded with public money. Conservative journalist David Frum writes:

> On principle, of course, the Republicans champion free enterprise and smaller government. But all too many of their friends—agriculture and ranching interests, logging and mining companies, export-oriented manufacturers— have come to expect a helping hand from Uncle Sam.[9]

Frum then quotes Stephen Moore from the Cato Institute, a libertarian think tank, who "counts 125 federal programs that subsidize business at an annual cost of $85 billion." He also says that "the liberal Progressive Policy Institute identified $131 billion . . . along with $101 billion in highly targeted tax exemptions." When a conservative writer quotes a liberal think tank and agrees with its point, it's worth paying attention. The privatizers' argument that corporations are superior to the nonprofit and public sectors because, being run for profit, they don't depend on government money simply ignores, and hopes we will not know, just how much corporations feed at the public trough.

The corporations rail at government when they're doing well, often enough with that same government's help, but when they get into trouble (corporate executives really aren't superior to everyone else), what happens?

The public bails them out. Think Chrysler. Think Lockheed. Think airlines. But we don't see corporations standing in line to bail out, say, public transportation, or Social Security, now do we? When public services fall on hard times, financial or political, it just proves, would-be corporate privatizers are sure to say, how inept the public sector is. You wouldn't want to reward bunglers by bailing them out. Why don't you let us just take them over and do it right (padded and protected by the usual government subsidies, of course)?

If that reasoning went both ways, the federal government would have taken over and operated Chrysler when it went broke. It would have taken over the airlines that have failed to compete successfully since President Jimmy Carter deregulated them in 1978 so they could do what they say they do best: compete in a free market. Need a national carrier, like many other countries have? A little paint, two periods, an extra space and USAirways—which was in bankruptcy in 2005—could really be U.S. Airways.

When the government takes over corporations, that's called *nationalization*. And nationalization, you should know if you've managed to miss it, is what privatization around the globe is presented as *the* solution for. Don't even try to go there these days if you're sensitive. Defending the idea that some things should remain, or become, the property of nations rather than corporations will get you called a supporter of the *failed Communist system*.

But the next time you hear about how we need to tighten up standards for schools, make them specify the outcomes of their work, impose standardized tests on them that a set proportion of students must pass for the school to go on receiving public funding, think of Wal-Mart with its government subsidies. Think of the corporations bailed out by our government. Imagine their outrage if the government were to move in to standardize and regulate and test them with anything like that same determination. Both public and private sectors do need to be accountable, but the freedom to pursue maximum private profit that is so fiercely defended by corporations is surely no more important than the freedom of teachers to teach the best way they possibly can.

We repeat: There is precious little democracy in the corporations to which privatization hands over public goods, resources, and functions. They are not set up to serve the public good, nor are they impressively accountable to it out of the goodness of their hearts—or even under pressure from laws and regulations. For example, Boeing was subject to federal ethics probes throughout 2004 and 2005. It fought them, but in February 2005 it changed its legal strategy to try to negotiate a comprehensive settlement. Meanwhile, Boeing, along with Northrup, hauled in significant Pentagon spending even though Boeing's net fell 84 percent, certainly in large part because of the ethics charges.[10]

So a corporation can be subject to ethics charges, negotiate a settlement to avoid full public exposure and possible punishment, see its net fall drastically—and still go on getting fat Pentagon contracts. Where that is already the case, full privatization is hardly even necessary: The for-profit culture has already subverted the care for the public good that government is supposed to provide. And yet the privatizers continue to put themselves forward as the proper and best folks to take over our government, and as much of the public sector as they can get. If they succeed, they won't even have the temporary bother of fending off such things as ethics probes, ineffective as they may be most of the time.

CHAPTER 20

Methods That Affect Our Lives

Patents had expired or were not in effect on the first drugs Brazil produced, so there were no legal constraints against making generic versions. But then other new costly AIDS drugs came on the market, many of them on patent. Quietly, scientists at Fiocruz figured out how to make those drugs, too. Then the Brazilian government issued global pharmaceutical companies an ultimatum: They could continue to sell the patented drugs to Brazil, but only at deeply discounted prices. If not, Brazil would invoke provisions of global trade law that permitted the country to respond to a public health emergency by making the drugs itself. The companies opted to slash prices.

—SUSAN DENTZER[1]

I do think they were surprised when they saw a developing country, like Brazil, that could develop the technology to produce these drugs, and that it was being used in a socially responsible way. It wasn't for profit. It was to meet the needs of the Brazilian people and the people sick with AIDS.

—JORGE LIMA DE MAGALHAES

PRIVATIZATION IS presented to us as a practical, realistic way to solve problems. But the way problems are solved is never neutral. It shapes the world and our relationship to it by its own logic. For example, if we have a "problem child," we can try to "fix" her by hitting her whenever she does something we believe to be wrong. We have then taught her that violence is the way to deal with behavior of which we don't approve. We have taught her not to be good for its own sake but to be obedient out of fear of physical pain and emotional humiliation.

When we choose a method, we are also revealing who we are, what we value, the kind of power we understand. We are reflecting the kind of world that shaped us, and we are modeling that world for others.

Because a method and the solution it may achieve has effects, we need to assess those effects. It is not enough just to say, "Well, it worked this time," particularly if one apparent success leads us to use the method more and more often, to advise others to use it, to persuade many people to see it as the solution. When a method becomes a movement and the movement develops its own ideology, we really must stand back and take stock of what it is actually doing to our worlds.

So, what is the method of privatization doing on a large scale?

+ Privatization has escalated the dominance of corporations here and around the world. The privatizing corporations are increasingly telling nations what to do, using governments to do what serves their driving purposes.

+ Privatization is dismembering our democratic republic, handing it over in small and huge chunks to be used for purposes other than the public good.

+ Privatization makes corporations increasingly immune to regulation, to being held accountable to those who are affected by what they do in their quest for profits and growth.

+ Privatization undercuts and disempowers the democratic sovereignty of We the People.

+ Privatization turns our government into a provider of money and of legal, police, and military force to be used to protect and enforce the primacy of corporate interests.

+ Privatization destroys the balance of powers among nations, as well as the careful separation and balance of powers that the founders designed to protect our own governmental system from the potential tyranny of too much wealth and power in too few hands.

+ Privatization sucks monies out of the public sector, reducing what we can choose to do for our public schools, our parks, our social safety net, our roads, our libraries, our firefighters, our public health services—our provisions for the equality and public good for all.

+ Privatization stacks the deck against people of conscience working at all levels of corporations, because weakening government means hamstringing the referee who keeps the dirty players from winning.

+ Privatization increases governance without representation: We don't vote for the corporate bosses or the policies they make and follow.

+ Privatization leaves us with unreliable service providers, because a corporation will move elsewhere, or cut corners, or change its employees' job descriptions whenever its bottom line so dictates.

+ Privatization reduces the public good to no more than a by-product of a search for higher and higher profits rather than a purpose that is to be achieved for its own sake.

+ Privatization spreads the values of profit-seeking beyond their proper sphere. The ethic of public employment, of being truly a *public servant*, becomes something to scorn.

+ Privatization leaves the responsibility to care for others to individual consciences, so those whom no one chooses to help are left to suffer alone.

+ Privatization turns hard-won rights back into favors.

Privatization thus refuses the moral and political premises of democracy—that we are all created equal; that we all have rights to life, liberty, and the pursuit of happiness; and that to protect and provide for such rights, governments were established among us.

Today, powerful words like *freedom* and *justice* and *equality* are used by just about every group that wants us to support it. We therefore need to judge what any group, organization, or political party really stands for, with and for whom it works, what the effects of its values and methods are. Strong corporate ties, heavy dependence on corporate money, are obvious markers that an organization may not be a reliable defender of the public good. But because it is difficult today to do without such money—particularly as the public sector and independent funding sources continue to be shrunk precisely in order to increase our dependence on the private sector—we recognize that many groups of all kinds do depend on corporate money. This doesn't necessarily mean that all those groups are unreliable or have sold out. Some are bought, paid for, and subservient to the sources of that money, some maintain a fierce independence, and some, perhaps most, are a mixed bag.

For an example of the latter, consider the Democratic Leadership Council. The DLC is partly funded by corporations that include Philip Morris, Texaco, and Merck. It was set up as the 1992 election approached to help Democrats take back "the center," which some Democratic analysts thought was necessary in order to compete with Republicans. The DLC partisans saw themselves as saving their party from election-losing identification with what they saw as old-fashioned, rust-belt-industry-supporting, union-loving diehards. It maneuvered Bill Clinton into becoming the party's presidential candidate, and instructed Democrats not to shoot themselves in the foot by objecting too strongly to corporate dominance, the privatization agenda of Republicans such as Ronald Reagan and George Bush, Sr., and the privatizers' drive to shrink government.

Once elected, Clinton dutifully carried out the Republican goals of joining so-called free trade agreements like NAFTA, giving out still more corporate welfare to the tune of $300 billion a year, working for "smaller government," putting an end to "welfare as we know it," and either privatizing or abolishing 130 government agencies.[2] He also remained true to some recently important Democratic values and causes, notably civil rights, women's equality, gun control, and reproductive rights.

The Democratic Leadership Council is not the same as the George W. Bush administration's rabid privatizers. But it has bought into the conservative analysis of what constitutes the center and how to appeal to it—and in its effort to shift the Democratic party in a more centrist direction, has adapted much of the right's uncritical relationship to privatization and privatizing corporations, along with significant elements of its agenda and methodology.

As the DLC should have learned the hard way by now, in one losing campaign after another, most Americans today don't buy the line that what's good for corporations is good for the rest of us—whether that line comes from Republicans or Democrats. A *Washington Post* poll taken in 2002 found that "88 percent of Americans distrust corporate executives, 90 percent want new corporate regulations/tougher enforcement of existing laws, and more than half think the Bush administration is 'not tough enough' in fighting corporate crime."[3]

Many other major polls show similar findings. The Service Employees International Union (SEIU) did a large-scale poll and found that most of us think there are better ways to solve the real problems of the public sector than selling it all off to corporate privatizers. Ninety percent of respondents favored giving public employees the tools they need. Ninety-one percent favored better training for public employees. Ninety percent favored more community input into service delivery. Eighty-five percent favored rewarding employees for doing the best job of serving the public. Sixty-two percent did not want child support enforcement privatized because they trust the public sector more to preserve fairness and reliability. Only 39 percent believed corporations are more honest than public officials.

These polls were taken before the flat-out effort to privatize in Bush's second, go-for-broke (actually, go-for-wealth) last term in the White House. So centrist Democrats are *not* responding to the views most of us hold. They too are hearing the siren call of the privatizing corporations, and it has thrown them—and the country—badly off course.

So with the privatization ideology of the profit-making culture moving across established party lines, and with all that corporate money going into pockets of all sorts, we find ourselves in the middle of a confusing squabble among various groups that don't differ as much as they should in a healthy democracy.

Instead of responding to evidence of what is really going on, mainstream political figures tell us, well, we just have to get a bit better at supervising the corporations through which government increasingly does the public's business. Confronted with evidence of the growing ability of corporations to call the tune rather than dance to it, and of most people's lack of trust in them or those corporations, the politicians sigh, shift to a different argument, and tell us it is too late to stop privatization, so we should stop fussing and get with the program—that we should see the corporations as our partners, not our rivals.

But surely it bears remembering that it wasn't We the People who decided to become the rivals of corporations for control of our democracy. We were there first, and we—especially those who long lacked democratic public rights and lives—do still care enough about the promise of democracy to stand up for it, no matter how large and powerful the opposition.

The Impact of Public Rights on Private Lives

According to legal scholar Patricia Williams:

> "Rights" feels new in the mouths of most black people. It is still deliciously empowering to say. It is the magic wand of visibility and invisibility, of inclusion and exclusion, of power and no power.[4]

When a government established to promote the public good is "shrunk," so is the possibility of acting for, preserving, and enjoying the rights conferred and backed up by that government. This is obviously reason to be deeply concerned about privatization. But to understand fully what we lose with the increase of privatization, more of us need to realize that whether we have or lack public rights has great effects on all aspects of our lives.

If we do not have the legal, political rights that protect free and equal public lives, we also do not have the rights that protect private lives. And without protected private lives, our personal lives are not safe, not free.

People who are enslaved have no public life, no rights. They cannot go where they will, do what they will, say what they will. Because as slaves they have no public standing, they also have no private life. They have no place of their own, no doors they have a right to shut that can protect their privacy. Slaves were raped and "bred" and their children taken from them. Not being public "persons," they also could not legally marry. They were vulnerable to intrusion at all times: no public life, no private life.

In ancient Greece, warriors captured in battle could be enslaved—turned from a citizen of the *polis* or city-state for which they had fought into a resource to be owned and used for someone else's profit. Some slave owners treated their slaves, their private property, better than others. But they did not have to. Those who have no public rights can only hope for mercy. They cannot demand justice.

When "free" women, from the poor to the more privileged, did not have the right to vote, the right to full and equal public citizenship, they also had no protected private life. They were privatized, their lives taken over, available for exploitation, domination, control by others who could and did use them for their own purposes.

There were good men who loved and cared for their wives, their daughters, who were respectful of other women. But there were others, far too many of them, who used their power as they chose. Wife beating used to be an everyday occurrence and the subject of jokes. The common expression *rule of thumb* then meant that men, who could and did beat their wives, should not do so with a stick thicker than their thumb. Whips were fine, and fists were not measured. A man who could not "control his woman" was scorned by other men.

When men and women married, the common thing for the official at the wedding to say was, "I now pronounce you man and wife." *He* stood there as a person, a man who had taken a wife; *she* had ceased being a person to be taken as his wife. His name became hers; she was publicly identified as his, but not he as hers. She bore his children; they bore his name.

Husband, what he was to her, is not parallel to *wife*. Husband is a term that applies also to animals and other resources for a man's life. There is *animal husbandry* and *husbanding your resources* to remind us of that. There is no *animal wifery*, no *wifing your resources*. A wife was a provision for a man, as animals and other resources were. She belonged to a household headed by a man. There was no such thing as marital rape. A husband had the right to plow his fields and his woman, to plant his seed in what was rightfully his.

For free men, the door of the home that was his castle swung both in and out. He had a private life to which he could retreat because he had a public life in which he had rights, rights that empowered him politically and economically. She had neither political nor economic rights, and so she was unequal in her personal life as well.

The man in the street is a phrase we use to mean an ordinary person. A *woman of the streets* is a prostitute. At home, a woman was vulnerable to the man to whose household she belonged. In public, a woman was vulnerable to men. No public life, no private life—a privatized life, vulnerable to intrusion, use and abuse.

People who do not live as heterosexuals are also privatized—closeted. If they *come out*, they refuse the secrecy that both limits and protects them. If they are *outed* they are at risk. *Gay bashing*: There is even a word for what can happen, because it does happen. But to remain closeted is not to have a private life; it is to be enclosed, hidden, kept from being public. Closeted people can be intruded on; there are still laws about sexual acts that allow their privacy to be violated. And if you are leading a secret life, there is always the threat of exposure. No public life, no private life.

People with disabilities were not long ago called *shut-ins*. Their struggle has been to have access: to be able to go out, to go where others go, do what others do. Their lives were privatized; they could not freely go in and out. They had to ask for favors where they did not yet have rights. They were expected to be grateful for things other people take for granted: public buses they can ride, private cars they are able to drive, public and private buildings they are able to enter, entertainment they are able to hear, to see, to participate in, schools they can learn and teach in.

Racialized groups—including South Asians, African Americans, Jews, Chinese, Native Americans, Japanese, Puerto Ricans, and all too many others—have been privatized. They have in different ways been denied public rights: the right to vote, equal schooling, freedom of movement, equal employment opportunities, equal health care, equal freedom to live where they choose, equal protection by—and from—the police. They have been privatized: In being denied public rights and freedoms, they have also been denied private lives. Those who did have public rights and freedoms could and did intrude on them, from shoving them off public sidewalks to forcing them into reservations and internment camps (yes, the United States has had them, too).

All these histories and stories are both different and overlapping. They are comparable, and they are strikingly different. But they should all teach us that to be privatized is to be unprotected, whether in public or in private, and everywhere to be disempowered and vulnerable to abuse and exploitation without recourse.

When we lessen the public sphere, with its government, laws, rights, and responsibilities, we leave more of us—as well as the earth on which we all depend—unprotected, available for exploitation and abuse.

When you are on someone else's private property, whether it is a home, a field, an office building, a mall, a factory, a corporate-owned theme park, or a corporate campus, you do not have as many rights as you do on public land, in public places. The owners have rights that supersede yours. When space is divided up, sold off, fenced in, it lessens the sphere of freedom and responsibility that we share.

So the effects of privatization take much more from us than it appears, and much more than the privatizers want us to know. When our government hands what was public over to the private sector, it is putting the license to seek private profits over protections for our liberty. We should know by now just how dangerous that is, and not willingly give up the governmental protections, the rights, that still feel so delicious to those who know what it is to lack them.

Privatizing Consciences

The moral equivalent of the realization that our private lives are related to our public rights is the Golden Rule: Do unto others as you would have them do unto you. Or as the philosopher Immanuel Kant advised, act only such that the maxim of your act could become a universal law. In plain English (although Kant wrote in German), what he meant was, Don't make an exception for yourself. If you steal, the maxim, or lesson, of that action is that stealing is okay—which means someone may think it just fine to steal from you what you took from someone else. Similarly, if you put your self-interest first, then you have no right to object when someone tramples you in pursuit of his self-interest.

Kant also taught that we should not treat other people only as means, as if they were no more than tools or resources that we can use for our own ends.

The Golden Rule and Kant's teaching are hardly alone in recognizing that morally, as well as politically and legally, we can choose to put limits on ourselves as part of an agreement, or covenant, with others that they will do the same. This does not mean that we are all then lessened, limited. On the contrary: It means that we are sharing our freedom so that no one—not even we ourselves—claims as her own the freedom to deny that precious gift to others. Do unto others as you would have them do unto you also means, Don't do what you don't want others to do. Or as Rabbi Hillel said over two thousand years ago, when a skeptical student asked him to explain the Torah while standing on one foot, "What is hateful to you, don't do to your neighbor. That is the whole Torah. All the rest is commentary. Now go and learn."

We define ourselves (from the Latin de finis: about boundaries) not in order to divide ourselves from all others but in order to connect with each other as equals who are free to be the same in some ways, different in others, and in order to share in cultures and traditions that are the same in some ways, different in others. We do so to renew the present as it creates the future through combinations and connections, not imposed sameness repeated as if it were all there is, all there can and should be. And so we also check and balance our powers in order to keep anyone, or any group or institution, from achieving a monopoly of power, of potential.

We are not free when life is nothing but a struggle to survive, or when life is nothing but a struggle against other people who invade, intrude, dominate. Nor are those who dominate free: They must constantly reinforce their dominance, constantly fight against others who also lust for dominance. Freedom, like power, like equality, like truth, like life itself, grows and renews itself only when it is spread and shared and renewed from the interrelating of our differences.

Monopoly of any kind is deadly.

Privatized Democracy?

Democracy is the opposite and opponent of monopoly. A democracy is strong when we recognize that the rights we have to protect our freedom to differ, and be different, depend on others having those same rights. It is strong when, through our elected representatives, we make laws and set rules that protect those rights, and keep them in balance, in harmonious relation with each other. A democracy becomes weak when laws and rules are turned to the protection and profit of some more than others. Then, democratic *power* is perverted into undemocratic *force*. The stronger impose their will on others through laws and governmental actions that no longer provide the equal voice and recourse that alone make rule of the people a reality. And democracy has failed when force escalates into *violence*—when fear turns into paralyzing terror.

When power is not widely and genuinely shared, constitutions are not worth the paper they are written on, elections are no more than play-acted democracy. Democratic power flows up, not down: from the people to the few who temporarily serve them as leaders. A democratic leader is neither an administrator nor a boss. She or he cannot fire the people. He or she is accountable to them, not the other way around.

Such an open society, served and protected by a responsive, accountable government in which significant decisions about the public good are made by We the People, is not what the privatizers want. Quite the contrary. Their imperatives are set by a corporation-dominated economy that just does not have the public good as its primary concern. So, privatizers of all stripes have had to work hard to convince us (and perhaps themselves) that what is in their self-interest is also in ours. What is good for them, is good for us. What profits them, profits the whole country. What profits the whole country, profits the whole world. They speak of competition, of free markets, but their drive is for monopoly—of their market, of all other sources of power, of all other ideologies, faiths, moralities.

Making their one way seem right and true for all has required the elaboration of an ideology—and, in some cases, the nullification of a theology: Jesus did say, after all, "For what is a man profited, if he shall gain the whole world, and lose his own soul?"

Destroying the balance between a government and an economy threatens the ability of both to do what, separated, mutually checked and balanced, each should do well in its own sphere.

Liberty for all must be protected from license for the few, whatever the form of that license—economic, political, personal, religious. And the methods we use to protect liberty make all the difference in the world.

A Word About Privatization and Organized Religion

Destroying the separation of government from economic powers is like destroying the separation of church and state. State, or government, and religion have different roles to play. Religion is threatened when it is reduced to serving worldly power. It cannot then remain true to its claimed transcendent and universal principles and beliefs. Government is threatened when it is reduced to serving one religion. It cannot then serve all the people, whatever their beliefs. Instead, it divides them dangerously into "true believers" against all others.

We have not focused on, although we have mentioned, the efforts of the privatizers to gain the collaboration of and share the spoils of power and money with some organized religious groups and establishments that are more than happy to join them. What makes religion wrong as a political power is another complex story. But it should not be forgotten as we analyze the threat to democracy that we face and take it on. Remember the collaboration of the Puritans with the Crown of England in creating the Massachusetts Bay Company. Religion gave the corporation the authority, the corporation gave religion the money, and the Crown gave both the right to use force to control peoples' lives. The combination of religious authority and secular political and economic power, we should know by now, can be a deadly one.

Freedom is suffocated by such an alliance.

These insights, once so familiar, are not lost, although they have become all too rare. Some lessons we who believe in democracy seem to have to learn over and over again.

CHAPTER 21

Resistant Strengths

Too often we pour the energy needed for recognizing and exploring differences into pretending those differences are insurmountable barriers, or that they do not exist at all. This results in a voluntary isolation or false and treacherous connections. Either way, we do not develop tools for using human differences as a springboard for creative change within our lives.

—AUDRE LORDE, *Sister Outsider*[1]

THUS FAR, the balanced, shared-power governance system in the United States has endured through a civil war, foreign wars against far more hierarchical and tightly organized states, economic crises, and significant struggles that challenged the system on its own principle of equal rights for all.

Unions, Independent Media, NGOs

Even after the concerted efforts of privatizers to take over our democratic government during the last quarter of a century, we've not lost it entirely. There is still dissent from the ideology of privatization, from among as well as within all our groupings. There are still movements of many kinds that are active on behalf of differing and overlapping causes. There are still unions, and they are reorganizing in order to do their essential work more effectively. There are significant independent media that are neither accountable to nor owned by the corporate media conglomerates, as well as evolving technologies that vastly differing people are using to go around the ever more corporate-controlled media. There are still some politicians, activists, artists, educators, reporters, publishers, and whistle-blowers speaking up and speaking out.

There are also growing numbers of NGOs—nongovernmental organizations—that work to do what neither multinational corporations nor governments will do, or do well, such as forge international agreements to save the environment and to stop violence against women and children at home and around the globe. There are grassroots community organizations representing geographical areas (neighborhoods, barrios, reservations, towns, cities, counties, states), constituencies (women, immigrants, students, people of color, senior citizens, lesbians and gays, disabled people), and issues (health care, workers' rights, the environment, prison reform, tax justice, corporate accountability, peace).

Countervailing Powers Abroad

At the same time, there are changes taking place at the international political, economic, and legal levels that are building the countervailing powers needed to keep the United States from monopolizing the world. Consider the European Union, which is surely economically motivated, but still holds some very basic beliefs about the importance of governments providing for the public good. There is growing worldwide support for international law even though there is no world government to stand behind it. The Nuremberg trials of Nazis after World War II set precedents we saw further developed in the South African Truth and Reconciliation Commission trial process and in the trials of leaders of states and factions that have carried out genocides and "ethnic cleansing."

Even as corporate powers are bending state and national laws, rules, and regulations to their own purposes, moving across international borders in order to avoid them, being given "free enterprise zones" in which usual laws and rules don't apply, the world is also trying to find ways to control these and other outlaws.

So the situation today is frightening, but it is by no means all bleak. And the most remarkable stories that indicate that the dream of democracy is a stubborn one are emerging from among some of the least powerful people of all. These stories are crucial: They call us to remember that people *do* have power when they stand together. Listen to one such story, which appeared in the *New York Times* in 2004:

> SHENZEN, CHINA The scene on the street did not look like much, just the comings and goings of small groups of women from their factory dormitory, with a few lingering here and there to discuss their situation.
>
> Since Friday, though, work has stopped inside the Uniden factory's walls here, where 12,000 workers, mostly young women from China's poor interior provinces, make wireless phones, which the Japanese manufacturer supplies in large number to the giant American retailer Wal-Mart.[2]

This is a remarkable thing. These young, poor women were standing up against China, which "proscribes public demonstrations" and has not enforced its usual requirement that unions be allowed "for fear of losing overseas investment": Wal-Mart, of course, doesn't allow unionization in the United States, let alone in the other countries to which it has gone precisely in order to find cheaper goods and cheaper labor. The young women in China were also standing up against the Japanese corporation that supplies Wal-Mart, which forced them to live and work in what amount to company towns for the same kind of too-long hours and low, low wages from which so many U.S. workers used to suffer—and from which some still do.

"The women say they must spend nearly half their wages"—earned in "11-hour days, including three hours of mandatory overtime," amounting to "a basic monthly salary of . . . about $58"—on the drab company dormitories where, as migrants, they must live. They must also pay the small clinic that is provided, although "'the medicines they give you,' said one woman, 'are much more expensive than outside.'"

"All the women interviewed seemed determined to press their demands, the most important of which, they said, were shorter work hours and enforcement of minimum-wage laws"—the same basic rights for which U.S. unions fought years ago, and are now having to defend again today.

One of the women said, "If we were men, there would have been a strike a long time ago. . . . Women are easier to bully, but we have hearts of steel."

Workers in the United States may take heart from the struggles of those young women so far away across the globe, as the Chinese women took heart both from their own traditions and belief in their rights and from the struggles of other women, and workers, including those in the United States.

Concerns Among Some Corporate Leaders

Some people in corporate circles know that something must be done, and are increasingly speaking out. Lester C. Thurow, professor of economics and former dean of the Sloan School of Management at MIT, is not alone in being clear that the principles and practices of capitalism, *however good or bad we judge them to be as economic drivers*, can be antithetical to the principles and practices of democracy. As Thurow put it, slavery is unacceptable to democracy but it is not unacceptable to the free market.

Here's another opinion from inside the corporate world: "Corporations need to become more trustworthy," says Sam Gibara, the former chairman and CEO of Goodyear Tire and Rubber Company. Why? Because "there has been a transfer of authority from the government . . . to the corporation, and the corporation needs to assume that responsibility . . . and needs to really behave as a corporate citizen of the world; needs to respect the communities in which it operates; and needs to assume the self-discipline that, in the past, governments required from it."[3] That's a fine sentiment in some ways, but also a chilling one. It accepts as settled and done that authority has been transferred from government to the corporation, and that public requirements for corporate responsibility are now in the past. And it says nothing about how to ensure that all corporations accept calls such as Gibara's to use both power and authority responsibly.

The problem with calls on conscience that are not backed by enforceable regulations and laws is, of course, that the pressures of the corporate marketplace work against acceptance of social responsibility. The good people who work in the corporate world in all roles, the true believers in democracy, in social responsibility, in all the rights and freedoms so hard-won here and elsewhere in the world—and their numbers do appear to be growing—need the help of countervailing powers, and of limit-setting rules that are genuinely enforced and enforceable, to stay true to their beliefs. Just as you and I do: that's why we have laws, and not just exhortations to be good people, please. Only government is large and powerful enough, and representative of enough, to make and enforce laws that stand a chance against corporations as large and powerful as those of today.

Social Movements

In an effort to retrieve such balancing powers, social movements have become increasingly sophisticated and effective at confronting the power of the privatizers. In the mid-1990s, global corporations and their political allies found themselves faced with mass demonstrations. Students, union members, environmentalists, and differing political groups came from near and far to show their opposition to the corporate privatization agenda. They successfully disrupted the efforts of global economic powers to meet and lay plans together, behind elegant and fiercely guarded doors, in the protected privacy to which they are accustomed.

As in the 1970s, though, such movements have apparently made the corporate privatizers only the more determined. Their efforts at global centralized economic planning now have more of an aggressively defensive, and secretive, aspect. And they're now used to managing us, the public. They have ratcheted up their efforts to sell themselves as the good guys.

Both the good corporate guys and the bad corporate guys now put even more effort into selling themselves as responsible, green, progressive. Their marketing, public relations, crisis management, and human resources offices are bustling. Money is being made by those who specialize in convincing you and me that the corporations are really dedicated to the public good, and if we will just let them alone, will do right by us.

Nonsense. We do not want favors—we need rights. We do not want public relations campaigns—we want openness, public responsibility, and strong referees to hold the players to the rules we make democratically. We do not need a privatized world, we need a strong and accountable public sector. We do not need government by corporations, we need government by the people. We do not need an unfettered private profit culture, we need the public good.

> Who owns the future, who owns the earth
> Who owns our labor, who says what it's worth
> Who owns our children, who owns our lives
> Who decides if we get jobs with justice
>
> Good union wages, the right to organize
> Safety conditions—we're fighting for our lives
> Health care and pensions, that's what we mean
> When we say that we want jobs with justice
>
> They want our labor—we want our rights
> They make the profits—we make a fight
> They take the money—we take a stand
> Let me hear you, raise your voice for justice
>
> Diga a los patrones que no pasarán
> En esta lucha no nos moverán
> Estamos unidos para luchar
> Vamos cantando para justice

Think of all the people out there on this earth
Hungry and homeless, looking for work
Young folks and old folks walking the streets
Don't they have the right to jobs with justice?[4]

State Governments, the Courts, and U.S. Law

In the 1990s, state governors from around the nation came together to pledge to invest in "improvements to the general economic climate" instead of "subsidies for individual projects and companies."[5] This was a clear effort to revitalize their role as public employees committed to the public good rather than to private profits for corporations. It is a beginning effort to retrieve the political, democratic control over the economic powers of corporations that was lost when, in the late 1800s, states began breaking ranks to attract corporations from other states.

The governors' efforts may well fail now that Republicans elected on George W. Bush's coattails in 2004 outnumber not only Democrats but those Republicans who, earlier, were open to the proposed effort. But clearly, some of our elected officials do know that nothing less than such a concerted political, governmental effort will work. Some mainstream political people also understand that it is necessary to retrieve public control over corporate charters.

If the governors can come together—if we elect and then press them to do so—we can then hold the line while we work to pass national legislation to hold corporations responsible, to undo the vast, antidemocratic power they now have. Republican President Teddy Roosevelt took them on; it can be done again.

But we need not wait. There are still laws and some courts that are able and willing to act to rebalance power. We can let it be known that we do want that to happen by whom we work and vote for in elections, by writing letters to the editor of our local newspaper, by contacting our elected representatives, by informing ourselves and our neighbors, by supporting organizations that take on corporate powers when they threaten to do harm.

Some courts are already acting. In the late nineties, the giant auto manufacturer Daimler-Chrysler used its muscle as one of the major employers in Toledo, Ohio, to get some very sweet deals from government. The city and the state succeeded in keeping the large Jeep factory from carrying out its threat to move away by offering "a ten-year exemption from all property taxes" and "hundreds of millions of dollars in tax credits." They also bought, with public tax dollars, "eighty-three homes and sixteen small businesses in order to give the company more land."[6] Note that this huge private corporation thus became ever more subsidized by public money. Note also that the supposedly precious property rights of home and small business owners were trumped by Daimler-Chrysler's threat to cut and run if it didn't get its way. The corporation made it more than clear to the people of Toledo that it was "my way or the highway."

No surprises there: We know the cycle is hard to break not just for governors but for corporations. Their corporate competitors, after all, will move just about anywhere to find cheaper labor, more perks, fewer regulations. Even if responsible corporate leaders would rather keep the jobs where they've been, where people and communities have given their lives to the corporation, they have to worry about their competition. However the CEOs may feel personally, if they don't make the decision to cut labor costs by moving from Toledo to, let's say, Thailand, they risk failing in their true purpose, serving the bottom line—and if they do that, it will be their job next on the corporate chopping block. They're probably not going to put their fabulous executive salary and perks on the line just because a couple thousand Jeep workers in Toledo are about to be thrown out of work. Big money first, conscience a distant second is the sad norm.

In this case, we did not find reports of well-paid executives of the multinational Daimler-Chrysler putting their consciences first (please do let us know if any did; those stories need a lot more publicity than they tend to get). The deal was made.

But then "the Sixth Circuit Court of Appeals, in Cincinnati, found that Daimler's tax credits in Toledo were unconstitutional. (The court ruled that the credits interfered with interstate commerce, which only Congress has the power to regulate.)"[7] The court thus reinforced the lesson that power must be returned to or strongly reinforced by government on the federal level if we are to deal effectively with national and international corporations— just as all legislative and executive power must remain balanced by an independent judiciary, and an actively involved electorate.

This is hardly the end of the Daimler-Chrysler matter. There will be appeals; corporations have staff lawyers and law firms on retainer. They're all set to fight. But it is a very big thing that what is widely called corporate welfare may finally be found to be broadly illegal. We still have our judicial branch of government; sometimes it still works, and nobly.

There is a stirring around the land and around the globe. It is not too late.

Afterword:
Returning Home, Remembering Meanings of Freedom

I read in the paper, I watched on the show
They said that it happened a long time ago
The years had gone by, I just didn't know
Working for freedom now
The songs that we sang still ring in my ears
The hope and the glory, the pain and the fears
I just can't believe it's been forty-five years
Working for freedom now

Sometimes we stumble, sometimes we fall
Sometimes we stand with our backs to the wall
This road will humble the proudest of all
Working for freedom now
Though the road up ahead may stretch out far and long
We must always remember the roads that we've gone
Memory will help us to keep keeping on
Working for freedom now

Those who have fallen and given their last
Have passed on to us what remains of their task
To fight for the future and pray for the past
Working for freedom now
The song of their laughter, the step of their feet
The voice of their pain that cries out in our sleep
Will be judged in the end by the faith that we keep
Working for freedom now

The wind in the winter is bitter and chill
The cries of the hunted are heard on the hill
I just can't believe there's such suffering still
    Working for freedom now
The wind blows the summer from fields far away
We stand in the dust in the heat of the day
Our hearts stopped so still that there's nothing to say
    Working for freedom now

Been a long time, but I keep on trying
For I know where I am bound
Been a hard road, but I don't mind dying
I have seen freedom[1]

W E CLOSE OUR BOOK by returning to the beginning, to the roots of our own political, moral commitments in the families, the places, the times that for us, as for you, remain interwoven with all that we have learned and experienced, thought and done. We don't tell these bits of our stories because we think who we are weighs much in the large scale of things. In public matters, actions have effects far beyond the individuals who suffer or benefit from them, far beyond what any of us intends when we take the risk of "going public."

But the small stories of our lives also matter. No big story, no grand narrative, no generalizations however sound, can take adequate account of how differently the Big Events are experienced by individuals, communities, groups. No one Big Story can show us how different are the meanings, the lessons, drawn from those events by those who lived through them and passed those lessons on to their friends and children. If we do not sometimes tell each other our own stories and those of our families, friends, and communities, we will not only continue to disagree, which is not at all a bad thing in a democracy, but to misunderstand what we are disagreeing about.

What *freedom* and *equality* and *democracy* mean can be argued endlessly and fruitlessly if we don't stop sometimes and say, But what do you mean when you use those words? Why do they matter to you? What is it that frightens, or inspires, or outrages you when you realize that others mean something very different than you do when they speak about equality, democracy, freedom? What strands of memory, of experience, of hope, of fear, of personal loyalties start vibrating?

Because we believe responses to those questions do matter, we asked ourselves how we would tell some of our stories in response to them. Here's where we came from, where we started, that put us on the road to where we are today.

Renewing Roots

Si grew up in State College, Pennsylvania. His father, Benjamin M. Kahn, was the rabbi at Penn State, where he worked with students at the Hillel Foundation and taught Hebrew and Jewish studies. His mother, Rosalind (Aronson) Kahn, was an artist, a homemaker, and an active partner in Ben Kahn's daily work with Hillel and the Jewish community it served.

As it is for so many minority groups, their life in rural, largely Christian central Pennsylvania gave them both the closeness of community supported by a rich cultural heritage and the daily challenge of negotiating their neighbors' mix of curiosity, unreliable superficial acceptance, ignorance, occasional overt hostility, self-congratulatory tolerance—and in no small measure, genuine respect and welcome. Si knew himself to be a "real American" at the same time as he knew he was "different," a small-town kid who studied Hebrew, the son of an admired and beloved couple central to their community, and one of the few Jewish children in his school.

Today, State College is a small city and Penn State a major university with some thirty thousand students on just that one campus. But when Si was growing up there, it was both a very small place and a complicated one: a largely homogeneous, white, Christian, rural community and a college town, set in the middle of one of the one hundred poorest counties in the country, an academic center surrounded by the Appalachian mountains, just on the edge of the anthracite coal fields.

Si recalls cornfields that started at the edge of his backyard, and going to school with a fishing rod strapped to the crosspiece of his bicycle. He remembers driving to Lewistown with his parents to take the Pennsylvania Railroad Pullman sleeper to Boston to visit relatives, passing the mined-out coal camps with ragged children staring from the porches of falling-down tarpaper shacks. After midnight, as the train pulled through Carbondale, Pennsylvania, his father would wake him so together they could watch the mine fires that had been burning underground for nearly one hundred years, the flames shooting high into the air through cracks in the earth's surface.

Elizabeth grew up in the Maryland suburbs of Washington, D.C., during the years when our nation's capital was changing from a sleepy, segregated southern town, with separate drinking fountains and bathrooms for "colored" and "white" within sight of the U.S. Capitol, to a modern, diverse, cosmopolitan city. Her father, Andrew M. Kamarck, an economist, went to work at the World Bank after his time at the U.S. Treasury Department, where, following military service in Italy and Germany during World War II, he participated in the effort to get Europe back on its economic feet. His cause then and throughout his life has been to find and, wherever possible, take action that addresses the worldwide causes of poverty.

Elizabeth's mother, Margaret (Goldenweiser) Kamarck, like Si's mother an artist, was active in local politics, civil rights, and organizing for fair housing. Their house was filled with a wide and fascinating array of thinkers and activists from across the street and around the world—public officials who believed government could and should be dedicated to social and economic justice, emerging political leaders from newly liberated countries, dissidents from apartheid South Africa, suburban women who were determined to open their neighborhood to anyone who wanted to live there, who worked at the polls on election day, carried around petitions, organized political campaigns for candidates they believed in.

There were similarities in our early years and family backgrounds that were more important than the differences, similarities that we rediscovered with interest as we wrote this book together.

Among our grandparents, of whom we've written earlier, all but one were immigrants who came to this country to escape both poverty and discrimination. All of them knew what a narrow escape they'd had. Of the six out of nine grandparents who were Jewish, every one lost sisters, brothers, mothers, fathers, aunts, uncles, cousins, murdered by the Nazis during the Holocaust. They remembered, although they were careful to protect their children and grandchildren from confronting them too early, too starkly, the unbearable realities that not even escape and years of safety can erase. They worked hard to give their children safety, security, and belief in the possibilities of a better life. But because they did also remember, somehow we also knew that there were horrors in the world.

Years ago, in his song "Children of Poland," Si wrote:

Had my grandparents stayed in that dark, bloody land
My own children, too, would have marched hand in hand
To the beat of the soldiers, the jackbooted stamp
That would measure their lives 'til they died in those camps

The cries of my children at night take me back
To those pale, hollow faces in stark white and black
Only the blood of the children remains
It runs in the streets—and it runs in our veins[2]

Elizabeth, whose Russian Jewish grandfather never told her his stories, took one of her first graduate school courses with Hannah Arendt, author of *Origins of Totalitarianism* and *Eichmann in Jerusalem: A Study of The Banality of Evil*, among other works.[3] The course was titled Political Experiences of the Twentieth Century. Elizabeth wrote her paper on the 1938 purge trials in the Soviet Union. As she did her research for the paper, she realized she had to reflect on the question of how people can, and do, remain loyal to an ideology that has turned murderous, even when it is turned against them. She became Hannah Arendt's teaching assistant after that course, and continued, with her, to study political philosophy in an effort to comprehend both the achievements and the horrors of political history.

The America to which our grandparents fled from some of the worst of those horrors offered them freedom and safety, and real economic opportunity. They took advantage of its promise. This too they remembered, and we remember. In Europe, they had been more or less locked into their particular class and caste level. Here, although there was still discrimination, there was opportunity. Even those grandparents who were Jews were, by that point in U.S. history, able to find some openings they could take to better themselves. And while Elizabeth's other grandfather was a Polish Catholic, and largely Protestant America did have its issues with both Poles and Catholics, he declared himself and his children "American," and was able, as some people of color were not, to help them sustain their belief that what he claimed could become true.

In the course of one generation, making full and determined use of public education, scholarships, and fellowships to private as well as public colleges, universities, and graduate schools, our immigrant families were able to move up economically and in society, to change classes. They had started out in North America as laborers, hod carriers, paper mill workers, window glaziers, students. They became gas station and clothing store owners, economists, government officials. Their children, our parents, aunts and uncles, became economists, college professors, physicians, rabbis, dentists, artists, small business owners, Hebrew high school principals, civil rights workers, psychiatrists, writers, salespeople, artists, homemakers, engineers.

So, looking back on where they had come from, what they had escaped, what they and their children had accomplished, our grandparents were grateful to this country that had taken them in, that had given them the chance to move up the economic and social ladder, to give their children a good start in life. They had good reason to believe that, even with its flaws, which they surely recognized, the United States offered opportunity, if not for all, for some—and they went to work to get their country to live up to its promise for all.

They remembered, we remember. Success, in all its different forms, is—but is never only—an individual matter. Had there been no free schools, no teachers to encourage and challenge and help find scholarships, no unions, no health clinics, no GI bill, no affordable decent housing open to anyone, no freedom of religion, their stories and ours and our children's would be entirely different.

Our parents all came of age during the Great Depression of the 1930s. They knew how bad it could get, even in America. They had seen the unemployment lines, the breadlines, the desperate poverty, the unending hunger, the hobo jungles, the great migrations of people looking for work, any work, anywhere. Elizabeth remembers her father, from whom she inherited both her love of music and her inability to reliably carry a tune, energetically singing "The Soup Song" that we included earlier: "Soo-oup, soo-oup, they give me a bowl of soo-ooo-oup."

During the Depression our parents experienced what was, when you think about it, a true ownership society. The problem was that if you didn't own anything, or if you lost what you owned when the economy collapsed, you had nothing. It would actually be more accurate to describe this, as well as what George W. Bush is proposing today, as an on-your-own society. If you didn't work, you didn't eat, no matter how hard you tried to find a job. If you couldn't afford fuel, you shivered in the cold. If you couldn't pay the rent, you and your family slept in the street, in an abandoned car, under a river bridge, in a hobo jungle. If you got sick, you were just plain out of luck.

Of course, there was private charity; among the most wrenching photographs from the Great Depression are those of the soup lines, ragged, starving families waiting their turn for that bowl of soup. It is wonderful that, in times of human tragedy, community and religious organizations come forward to help those in desperate need. But voluntary charity is equipped to help small numbers of people who fall into occasional adversity, not to address the systemic ills of an entire economy that is the cause of people being out of work, homeless, hungry.

What our parents, and this country, learned from the Great Depression is that only government action can deal with that level of economic and societal dislocation. The genius of President Franklin Delano Roosevelt and his "brain-trusters," who included Elizabeth's grandfather Emmanuel Goldenweiser, is that they not only understood this but acted with speed commensurate to the crisis. The laws establishing Social Security, workers' compensation, unemployment insurance, the right of employees to unionize and bargain over their wages and working conditions—we owe these all to the Great Depression, to the courageous people in unions and community organizations who created movements for change rather than submit passively to economic injustice, and to the New Deal that Roosevelt and his advisers and allies helped them establish to pull the nation out of its hard times.

Because of this dramatic action, Roosevelt is either praised or blamed, depending on your political point of view, for helping create a modern welfare state in the United States. But Roosevelt did something else that is of comparable importance: He helped save capitalism in the United States from its own worst excesses. In the American tradition of checks and balances, he established systems that allowed the leading corporations in this country, some of which had nearly gone bankrupt during the Great Depression, to reestablish themselves. Some of them took such advantage of what was done for them that they prepared the way for the multinational conglomerates of today.

But Roosevelt also tried to make sure that the price paid by these corporations' employees and consumers would not be unsustainably, unethically high. The corporations would have a safety net to ensure their continued survival and productivity. They would not go hungry, they would not be lacking for work. But neither would you and I. All of us, corporate "persons" and individual human beings, would be protected and our lives enhanced. Whether it was the Social Security check Si's great-aunt Nellie Israel drew after working in shoe factories for some fifty years, the degree in dentistry his uncle David "Dubby" Kahn received on the GI bill after serving in the U.S. Army in World War II and his public sector job in a Veterans' Administration hospital, or the disability pay from the military that allowed Elizabeth's uncle Larry to work as a writer when he was unable to stand or walk, the experiences of their own lives let our family members understand how important it is to have a strong government and a healthy public sector for democracy itself to work.

Now, as much as we love to watch the Olympics on TV, neither of us is particularly a fan of the other varieties of international competition among nations. Both economic and military domination are particularly low on our list of things we think countries should do to each other. So we're not exactly wild about the idea of there being a "greatest country on earth." Arrogance and imperialism are not the drives of healthy people or countries. If you really know who you are, you do not need to be a bully.

We do, however, think that the United States actually has the opportunity, at this moment and in our lifetimes, to become—in concert with an increasingly interdependent world—a great community, a great society, a truly great country.

It is up to us whether or not this is the legacy we leave to future generations.

> We are not the first and we won't be the last
> For the thread's wound too tight to unravel
> If we stare in our mirrors and never look back
> We won't see the roads we have traveled
>
> The sound of the blood running fast through our veins
> Is louder than any word spoken
> The ties that now bind us to those who are gone
> Have grown far too strong to be broken

Our grandmothers' stories will still keep the faith
When grandchildren gather together
The songs of our mothers that rocked us to sleep
Will sing to our daughters forever

> *Generations*
> *Like a rock beneath the waters*
> *Generations*
> *More and more*
> *Generations*
> *From mothers to our daughters*
> *Break and blend like the waves on the shore*[4]

Envisioning Possibilities

We have said a lot about the public good, about democracy and equality and freedom, about a balanced, healthy society in which power is spread around, rather than being monopolized in just a few hands. That's what we are struggling for. If we fully bent our hearts and hands to it, what could our society and country look like?

We could become the first country in human history in which no one ever, ever goes to bed hungry.

We could find cures for old and new diseases—those that affect millions, but also those that affect hundreds and dozens. We could make sure that, in the very near future, there is a mechanical heart for the smallest infant, even if there's no profit in developing one, and medicines that we can afford.

We could make sure that every person has work that is respected, that is recognized for its contributions to others, whether it pays a decent living wage or a large professional salary.

We could be the first society ever in which all have a home of their own, a room of their own, a place of their own, and where all have the public rights that ensure they can go in and come out freely, and safely.

We could make education of every sort central to our national life, so that every person can feed that part of us that is hungry to learn and grow throughout a lifetime.

We could have as many public libraries as there are video stores, as many public health clinics as there are shopping malls, as many assisted living centers as there are hotels.

We could nourish and sustain the artists, the activists, the dreamers, the visionaries, the scholars among us, so that all of our public and private lives are made more meaningful, imaginative, and informed by the empathy that comes with openness to the vision of others.

We could preserve the extraordinary physical gifts this country has been given, the mountains, rivers, valleys, plains, deserts, prairies, lakes, forests, so that our great-grandchildren will be able to explore them freely, their hearts stopped by the sheer beauty and wonder of it all.

We could protect the earth, give it the space and time to heal itself from the damage we have ignorantly and greedily done to it and to the animals and plants that depend on it just as we do.

We could take away some of the fear and retrieve the dignity of growing old by ensuring that we all have security, care, respect, company, and sustenance in our last years.

We could help make the world safe, not just for U.S. citizens but for everyone, so that children, women, and all those who are preyed upon, all those who are at risk because they have been kept powerless for so long, can be safe at home, at school, at work, in public and private places everywhere.

We could make sure that "one person, one vote" means that every one of us can vote and have that vote count, and that big money cannot buy elections, or governments.

We could make sure that independent and differing views have a chance to be heard not just through alternative media but through all the media, and in free, open public spaces.

We could keep our economy strong and growing by enforcing the rules of fair competition and by controlling would-be monopolizers, so small businesses can keep springing up and large corporations can do well without having to do harm.

We might then bring back a time when, all around the world, people looked to the United States as a beacon of democracy and hope.

And you know what else? We could do all that and still have millionaires. We could do all that and still have corporations. A country in which as many people as possible are educated, respected, healthy, self-confident, self-determining individuals with equal rights and responsibilities is a country that can be productive without the need for distorting motivators like force, greed, fear, desperate need, or dirty competitive practices.

That's the opportunity, the vision of what a public good culture supported by a good, strong public sector and a democratic government could look like for all of us—not in some mythic faraway future, but in a time not far from now.

We do not lack the resources. We lack the political will, the moral determination, and the systems that put them into action. It is not just a cliché to say, "If we can put people on the moon, we can do other 'impossible' things too." The lesson of history is that democratic government really can work, and that it can be saved when, once again, things get out of balance.

We have the basic constitutional framework that a healthy democracy requires. The checks and balances established by the Constitution allow this country to make haste slowly and wisely. Our system of elected representative government, from the local to the national levels, although not perfect, creates a potentially responsive set of links from the grassiest roots to the highest office in the land.

Si was once asked, "What is it that you people [here meaning progressives] want anyway?" He replied, "Well, for a start, how about the Constitution with a good grievance procedure and binding arbitration?"

We not only have democratic institutions and systems of governance, but national wealth the likes of which the world has never seen or known. That wealth was not created by a few supranational corporations with no loyalty to this country, or to its economy. Our brew of people and talents and our natural resources are extraordinary. We have both the people and the money to solve almost any problem, if we can get our priorities straight and decide as a country and as a society to do so.

But the other side of great potential for good is an equal potential for tragedy. Instead of choosing to come together to serve the public good and its healthy Siamese twin, a fair and strong market economy, we could decide to be an ever more privatized, private-profit culture, with a government that is bought and sold to the most powerful bidder. Here's what that might look like.

We could dismember the system of checks and balances that has served us well for so long and replace it with an antidemocratic corporate model, with a commander-in-chief CEO, a board-of-directors Congress whose seats are handed them by monied interests, and a judiciary that is as independent as the accounting firm Arthur Anderson was from Enron.

We could continue and reinforce the current race to the moral and economic bottom, where the corporations' goal is to get their employees to work harder for less money, with the fewest benefits, with minimal job security—wherever in the world they move our jobs to do so.

We could measure our national worth by the amount of money corporations make by mining, drilling, damming, stripping, clear-cutting—the water, the air, the soil, the future be damned.

We could eliminate government employees at every level, so that every service any of us ever receives comes at a price and at a profit to some corporation, with no protection and no recourse for us.

We could "get government off our backs"—and end up lying flat on our backs in front of corporations that can then run over us at will.

We could define ourselves as a nation of individuals, and mean that each of us must be out for her or himself, and devil take the hindmost.

We could use our military might to intervene unilaterally anywhere in the world where there are, or could be, corporate economic interests—and then wonder why our country is so hated around the globe.

We live in a country founded on the sovereignty of its people. The choices we make today, and over the next few years, as individuals, as a society, as We the People, are as critical as any we have ever made.

Notes

Preface

1. Si Kahn, "What Will I Leave," *I'll Be There* (Chicago: Flying Fish Records, 1989).

2. For more information, see the Grassroots Leadership website: www.grassrootsleadership.org.

3. Participants included current Grassroots Leadership staff members Kamau Marcharia, Alfreda Barringer, and Naomi Swinton; former staff members James Williams and Margaret Chambers; former board member Sally Thomas; and South Carolina United Action staff member Corry Stevenson.

Introduction

1. John McKinnon and Christopher Cooper, "President Provides New Detail of Plan for Private Accounts," *Wall Street Journal*, Feb. 3, 2005, 1.

2. We wrote this description. It is a distillation of the key points, using typical language.

3. Esther Kingston-Mann, "The Return of Pierre Proudhon: Privatization, Crime, and Rule of Law" (unpublished paper, 2005). The "more developed nations" refers to countries belonging to the Organization for Economic Cooperation and Development.

4. Kingston-Mann, "The Return of Pierre Proudhon."

5. In September 2003, Yegor Gaidar said that the Americans "want to figure out how to minimize the risks and privatize the [Iraqi] economy as quickly as possible." Given the shocking effects of the fast privatization of Russian industry, we surely should be asking *whose* risks Americans so want to minimize. As Kingston-Mann writes: "Reformers"—which is to say, people following the international agenda of privatization—"instituted no meaningful safeguards to prevent [former Soviet officials and enterprise directors] from insider trading or asset stripping of state enterprises in the auctioning process. . . . Former Minister of Gas Viktor Chernomyrdin . . . became head of Gazprom, and one of the wealthiest men in the world. . . . Corrupt and dishonest collaborations flourished in the giant shadow of a Russian Mafia that controlled some 70 percent of private business and freely assassinated the journalists who exposed their activities" (Kingston-Mann, "The Return of Pierre Proudhon").

6. Dinesh D'Souza, in an interview with Jeffrey Brown, *The NewsHour with Jim Lehrer*, Feb. 16, 2005; see www.pbs.org/newshour/bb/social_security/jan-juno5/ss_2-1b.html.

Part I

1. Lieutenant Colonel Ralph Peters, in an interview with Gwen Ifill, *The News-Hour with Jim Lehrer*, Dec. 23, 2004; see www.pbs.org/newshour/bb/middle_east/july-deco4/insurgents/12-22.html.

Chapter 1

1. Alicia Guard and Peter Fimrite, "Army Reserve Irked by Soldiers' Fundraiser," *San Francisco Chronicle*, Dec. 22, 2004; see http://sfgate.com/eqi.bin/article.cqi?file=/c/a/2004/12/22/mnguiaflpl.dtl.

2. Si Kahn, "When the War Is Done," *We're Still Here* (Hoofdorp, The Netherlands: Strictly Country Records, 2004).

3. P. W. Singer, *Corporate Warriors: The Rise of the Privatized Military Industry* (Ithaca, N.Y.: Cornell University Press, 2003).

4. Scott Ainslee, "Letter to the Editor," *The Reformer* (response to Associated Press story "CIA Contractor Charged in Death of Afghan Detainee"), June 18, 2004.

Chapter 2

1. Joel Bakan, *The Corporation: The Pathological Pursuit of Power* (New York: Free Press, 2004), 112.

2. Bakan, *The Corporation*, 112.

3. Tim Weiner, "Lockheed and the Future of Warfare," *New York Times*, Nov. 28, 2004, B1.

4. Weiner, "Lockheed and the Future of Warfare," B1.

5. Weiner, "Lockheed and the Future of Warfare," B1.

6. See, for example, Polly Ross Hughes, "Texas Blazing Welfare Trail: Stakes Are High as State Rushes to Privatize System," *Houston Chronicle*, Nov. 19, 1996, 1.

7. James Madison, "Monopolies, Perpetuities, Corporations, Ecclesiastical Endowments" (unpublished essay), cited in Charles Derber, *Regime Change Begins at Home: Freeing America from Corporate Rule* (San Francisco: Berrett-Koehler, 2004), 6.

8. Jim Yong Kim, Joyce V. Millen, Alec Irwin, and John Gershman (eds.), *Dying for Growth: Global Inequality and the Health of the Poor* (Monroe, Maine: Common Courage Press, 2000), 36.

9. Barnaby J. Feder, "Wal-Mart's Expansion Aided by Many Taxpayer Subsidies," *New York Times*, May 24, 2004.

10. Reed Abelson, "States Are Battling Against Wal-Mart Over Health Care," *New York Times*, Nov. 1, 2004, 2.

11. Abelson, "States Are Battling," 3.

12. Abelson, "States Are Battling," 5.

13. Abelson, "States Are Battling," 2.

14. Singer, *Corporate Warriors*.

Chapter 3

1. Paul Krugman, "For Richer: How the Permissive Capitalism of the Boom Destroyed American Equality," *New York Times Magazine*, Nov. 20, 2005, 62.

2. See, for example, Ted Nace, *Gangs of America: The Rise of Corporate Power and the Disabling of Democracy* (San Francisco: Berrett-Koehler, 2003), chapters 1 and 14.

3. Bakan, *The Corporation*, 36.

4. Milton Friedman, *Capitalism and Freedom*, 40th anniversary ed. (Chicago: University of Chicago Press, 2002), 133.

5. Kahn, "We're Still Here," *We're Still Here*.

6. Si Kahn, Jane Sapp, and Pete Seeger, "The Soup Song," *Carry It On* (Chicago: Flying Fish Records, 1987). Words by Maurice Sugar.

Chapter 4

1. M. Bryna Sanger, *The Welfare Marketplace: Privatization and Welfare Reform* (Washington, D.C.: Brookings Institution Press, 2003), 98.

2. See, for example, Martha Minow, *Partners, Not Rivals: Privatization and the Public Good* (Boston: Beacon Press, 2002), 21.

3. Maureen Dowd, "W's Stiletto Democracy," *New York Times*, Feb. 27, 2005, op-ed page.

4. Frank Rich, "The White House Stages Its 'Daily Show,'" *New York Times*, Feb. 20, 2005, 1.

5. James A. Krauskopf, "Privatization of Human Services in New York City: Some Examples and Lessons," presentation to the Annual Research Conference of the Association for Public Policy Analysis and Management, Oct. 1995; quoted in Sanger, *The Welfare Marketplace*, 106.

6. Robert J. Samuelson, "The Trouble with Fannie," *Newsweek*, Jan. 10, 2005, 49.

7. Matt Kranitz, "Ousted Fannie Executives Could Still Collect Millions," *USA Today*, Dec. 28, 2005, B1.

8. Si Kahn, *The Forest Service and Appalachia* (New York: John Hay Whitney Foundation, 1974).

9. See again Minow, *Partners, Not Rivals*.

10. Paul Kivel, *You Call This a Democracy? Who Benefits, Who Pays, and Who Really Decides* (New York: Apex, 2004), 84.

11. Minow, *Partners, Not Rivals*; see chapter 4.

12. Kingston-Mann, "The Return of Pierre Proudhon."

13. See, for example, Margaret Kohn, *Brave New Neighborhoods: The Privatization of Public Space* (New York: Routledge, 2004).

14. Patrick Hosking, "The Business: Patrick Hosking Junks General Motors," *New Statesman*, Jan. 31, 2005; see www.newstatesman.com/Economy/ 200501310021.

15. For a thorough, technical discussion of how costs and savings can be studied, see Elliott D. Sclar, *You Don't Always Get What You Pay For: The Economics of Privatization* (Ithaca, N.Y.: Cornell University Press, 2000), 160–161.

16. See, for example, David Macarov, *What the Market Does to People: Privatization, Globalization, and Poverty* (Atlanta: Clarity Press and London: Zed Books, 2003), 33. Macarov cites the United States Census Department report of "the officially poor," in which "children or armed forces" make up 32 percent of this group, the second largest category, with "not in labor force" the only one larger at 41 percent.

17. Grover Norquist is president of Americans for Tax Reform, and the Leave-Us-Alone Coalition. He was a key Republican planner of the 1994 elections that installed Newt Gingrich as leader of the U.S. House of Representatives. George W. Bush and Dick Cheney always had their personal representatives present for Norquist's weekly meetings of the Leave-Us-Alone conservative strategy meetings. See Pablo Pardo, "The World According to Grover Norquist," Vancouver Indymedia [Vancouver.indymedia.org], Sept. 12, 2004.

Part II
1. Paul Von Zielbauer, "When 10 Hard Days in a County Jail Cell Is a Death Sentence," *New York Times*, Feb. 27, 2005, 1.

Chapter 5
1. Portions of this section originally appeared in Si Kahn, "Cells for Sale," in "Captive Lives" [special issue], *Southern Changes*, Fall 2000, 22(3). Si wishes to express his appreciation to the Southern Regional Council [www. southerncouncil.org] for the use of these excerpts.

2. Alex Friedmann, "Private Prisons—What's Really Going On," *Grassroots Leader*, Summer 2003. Friedmann was incarcerated for six years in Corrections Corporation of America's South Central Correctional Center in Clifton, Tennessee.

3. Si Kahn, "Vann Plantation," *Blood From Stones* (Charlotte, N.C.: Joe Hill Music, 2005).

4. See David Oshinsky, *Worse Than Slavery: Parchman Farm and the Ordeal of Jim Crow Justice* (New York: Free Press, 1996).

5. Oshinsky, *Worse Than Slavery*, 46.

6. Oshinsky, *Worse Than Slavery*, 62.

7. Oshinsky, *Worse Than Slavery*, 80.

8. See Oshinksy, *Worse Than Slavery*.

9. Martha Minow points out that deals between government and religious organizations have been widespread for years now. What is striking is that President Bush is not only encouraging more of them but making these blurrings of the separation of church and state an open, fully claimed agenda. See Minow, *Partners, Not Rivals*.

10. Si Kahn, "There But For," *Blood From Stones*.

11. *Education Not Incarceration: A Mississippi Case Study* (Charlotte, N.C.: Grassroots Leadership, 2002); see www.grassrootsleadership.org.

Chapter 6

1. The three companies were Correctional Medical Services (CMS), Prison Health Services (PHS), and Wexford.

2. See the Grassroots Leadership website: www.grassrootsleadership.org.

3. Marguerite G. Rosenthal, letter to the editor, *New York Times*, June 27, 2004.

4. "Prescription for Recovery Presents Plans for Improving Prison Health Care Delivery," press release by South Carolina Fair Share and Grassroots Leadership, June 10, 2004, 2.

5. *The State*, July 5, 2004; see www.thestate.com/mld/state/news/opinion/908255.htm.

6. James Shannon, "Profits & Prisons—South Carolina Has a Bad Idea—Again," *MetroBeat*, Apr. 21, 2004.

7. Shannon, "Profits & Prisons."

Chapter 7

1. Si Kahn, "Talking Politician," *New Wood* (Cambridge, Mass.: Rounder Records, 1994).

2. Ed Bender, *A Contributing Influence: The Private-Prison Industry and Political Giving in the South* (Helena, Mont.: Institute on Money in State Politics, 2001), 1.

Chapter 8

1. Bakan, *The Corporation*, 114.

2. Sanger, *The Welfare Marketplace*, 86.

3. Kim, Millen, Irwin, and Gershman, *Dying for Growth*, 146.

4. Kim, Millen, Irwin, and Gershman, *Dying for Growth*, 146.

5. Kim, Millen, Irwin, and Gershman, *Dying for Growth*, 146.

6. Kim, Millen, Irwin, and Gershman, *Dying for Growth*, 127.

7. Paul Farmer, *Pathologies of Power: Health, Human Rights, and the New War on the Poor* (Berkeley: University of California Press, 2005), 186.

8. Farmer, *Pathologies of Power*, 186.

9. Farmer, *Pathologies of Power*, 186.

10. Farmer, *Pathologies of Power*, 186.

Chapter 9

1. Si Kahn, "Cotton Mill Blues," *Threads* (Wolfenschiessen, Switzerland: Double Time Music, 2002).

2. This is one of many song parodies Si wrote while working with the Amalgamated Clothing and Textile Workers Union (ACTWU) on the J. P. Stevens campaign during the 1975 to 1980 period. He calls this one the "Song of the Northern Industrialist." Words by Si Kahn to the tune of "Dixie."

3. Aunt Molly Jackson, "Hunger," *Aunt Molly Jackson: Songs and Stories* (Washington, D.C.: Library of Congress Recordings, 1972). Transcription by Si Kahn.

4. Several people have tried to find the film, but it's apparently disappeared without a trace. If you happen to know where a copy is, please let us know.

5. From the film *Red, White, and Blue for Uncle Charlie* (Washington, D.C.: Public Citizen).

6. Kohn, *Brave New Neighborhoods*, 71.

7. Lewis F. Powell's memo, "Attack on American Free Enterprise System," written to the U.S. Chamber of Commerce in August 1971, laid out an agenda for business to pursue to influence "the campus," "graduate schools of business," "secondary education," "the media," "scholarly journals," "books," the "political arena," "the courts," "stockholder power." This was two months before Powell's successful nomination to the U.S. Supreme Court. See the Media Transparency website: www.mediatransparency.org/stories/powellmanifesto. htm.

8. Kohn, *Brave New Neighborhoods*, 72.

9. There are an estimated twenty-thousand gated communities in the United States, with some 8.4 million people living in them; see www.pbs. org/peoplelikeus/resources/stats.htm. There are two kinds of gated communities in which people who can afford them may choose to live: lifestyle (including leisure and retirement communities as well as suburban "new towns") and elite (for the very rich and the famous).

10. Edward J. Drew and Jeffrey McGuigan, "Prevention of Crime: An Overview of Gated Communities and Neighborhood Watch," copyright 1996–2005, International Foundation for Protection Officers [www.ifpo.org/articlebank/gatedcommunity.htm].

11. Kohn, *Brave New Neighborhoods*.

Chapter 10

1. Si Kahn, "Mississippi Summer," *In My Heart* (Hoofdorp, The Netherlands: Strictly Country Records, 1994).

2. The Black Commentator, "Vouchers: The Right's Final Answer to Brown," Susan O'Hanion.org [www.susanohanian.org/show_commentary.php?id=254], Jan. 6, 2004.

3. The quotations in this paragraph and the following are from Sam Dillon, "Charter Schools Alter Map of Public Education in Dayton," *New York Times*, Mar. 27, 2005, 15.

4. Si Kahn, "What Did You Learn" (Charlotte, N.C.: Joe Hill Music, 2005).

Chapter 11

1. David L. Kirp, *Shakespeare, Einstein, and the Bottom Line: The Marketing of Higher Education* (Cambridge, Mass.: Harvard University Press, 2003), 7.

2. Kirp, *Shakespeare, Einstein, and the Bottom Line*, 240.

3. Stephen Burd, "Lawmakers Are Urged to 'Go Slowly' on Loosening Rules for For-Profit Colleges," *Chronicle of Higher Education*, Mar. 11, 2005, A24; see http://chronicle.com/daily/2005/03/2005030201n.htm.

4. Silla Brush, "Report Blames Federal Student Aid for Rising Tuition and Urges Elimination of Aid Programs," *Chronicle of Higher Education*, Jan. 26. 2005; see http://chronicle.com/daily/2005/01/2005012602n.htm. For the full text see www.cato.org/pub_display.Php?pub_ld=3344. Also, for a report from the Futures Project on the market versus higher education ideals, see "The Ideals of Public Higher Education," *Chronicle of Higher Education*, Feb. 25, 2005, A23.

5. Governor Mark Sanford of South Carolina has proposed exactly that: privatization of *all* public colleges and universities. See Peter Schmidt, "Accept More State Control or Go Private," *Chronicle of Higher Education*, Dec. 19, 2003, A24.

6. Eyal Press and Jennifer Washburn, "The Kept University," *Atlantic Monthly*, Mar. 2000; see http://theatlantic.com/issues/backissues.htm. See also Jennifer Washburn, *University Inc.: The Corporate Corruption of High Education* (New York: Basic Books, 2005).

7. Jennifer Washburn, *University Inc.*, 9.

8. Denise Grady, "Tubes, Pump and Fragile Hope Keep a Baby's Heart Beating," *New York Times*, Aug. 22, 2004, 1.

9. Peter Rost, "Lives Matter More Than Drug Company Profits," *Charlotte Observer*, Dec. 30, 2004, 9A.

10. Rost, "Lives Matter More," 9A.

11. Association for the Advancement of Science Newsletter, Summer 1998, 1(3).

Chapter 12

1. Ruth Rosen, "Old Woman Out in the Cold," *The Nation*. Posted on AlterNet [www.alternet.org], Apr. 1, 2005.

2. Rick Henderson and Steven Hayward, "Happy Warrior" (interview with Grover Norquist), *Reason Online* [http://reason.com/9702/fe.int.norquist.shtml], 1996.

3. Karen Tumulty and Eric Roston, "Social Security: Is There Really a Crisis?" *Time Magazine*, Jan. 24, 2005, 23.

4. Erik Elkholm, "Auditors Testify About Waste in Iraq Contract," *New York Times*, June 16, 2004, A49.

5. Si Kahn, "Hard Times," *We're Still Here*.

Part III

1. Jose Latour, "More Outsourcing: Governor Jeb Predicts an Employee-less Florida," usvisanews, Jan. 14, 2003; see www.usvisanews.com/ articles/memo1987.shtml.

2. Mike Pope, "Governor's Philosophy 'Too Deep' for Tallahassee," *Tallahassee Democrat*, Jan. 19, 2003.

Chapter 13

1. Vandana Shiva, *Water Wars: Privatization, Pollution, and Profit* (Cambridge, Mass.: South End, 2002), ix–x.

2. This quote from Amartya Sen's *Development as Freedom* is in Farmer, *Pathologies of Power*.

3. This quote from Wendell Berry is in Farmer, *Pathologies of Power*.

4. Shiva, *Water Wars*, 40.

5. Elie Wiesel was objecting to President Reagan's trip to lay a memorial wreath at Bitburg, the German cemetery where Nazi SS men are buried; see www.worldnetdaily.com/news'article.asp?ARTICLE_ID=27344.

6. Andrew M. Kamarck, *Economics for the Twenty-First Century* (Aldershot, England: Ashgate, 2001), 83.

7. Kamarck, *Economics for the Twenty-First Century*, 83.

8. Kamarck, *Economics for the Twenty-First Century*, 84.

9. Singer, *Corporate Warriors*, 80.

10. Singer, *Corporate Warriors*, 181.

11. Singer, *Corporate Warriors*, 15.

12. Kamarck, *Economics for the Twenty-First Century*, 89.

Chapter 14
1. Friedman, *Capitalism and Freedom*, 27–28.

2. Friedman, *Capitalism and Freedom*, 30.

3. Si Kahn, "Freedom Is a Funny Thing," *Blood From Stones.*

4. Friedman, *Capitalism and Freedom*, 30.

5. Friedman, *Capitalism and Freedom*, 33.

6. Sanger, *The Welfare Marketplace*, 91.

7. Russell Bourne, *Gods of War, Gods of Peace* (Orlando: Harcourt Brace, 2002), 91.

8. George Orwell, *Animal Farm* (New York: New American Library, 1996), 133.

Chapter 15
1. Si Kahn, "Going Going Gone," *I Have Seen Freedom* (Chicago: Flying Fish Records, 1991).

2. Gretchen Morgenson, "Envelopes, Please: The Melmotte Awards," *New York Times*, Jan. 2, 2005, B4.

3. Morgenson, "Envelopes, Please," B4

4. Morgenson, "Envelopes, Please," B4.

5. See Nace, *Gangs of America.*

Chapter 16
1. Lester C. Thurow, *The Future of Capitalism: How Today's Economic Forces Shape Tomorrow's World* (New York: Penguin Books, 1997), 242.

2. Nace, *Gangs of America*, 141.

3. Nace, *Gangs of America*, 191.

4. Kohn, *Brave New Neighborhoods*, 1.

5. Kohn, *Brave New Neighborhoods*, 69.

6. John Carson-Parker, "Commentary: The Options Ahead for the Debt Economy," *Business Week*, Oct. 12, 1974, 120.

7. Nace, *Gangs of America*, 192.

8. See chapter 9, note 7.

9. Mark Lilla, "The Closing of the Straussian Mind," *New York Review of Books*, Nov. 4, 2004, 59.

Part IV

1. Langston Hughes, "Freedom's Plow," *Selected Poems of Langston Hughes* (New York: Random House/Vintage Books, 1974), 293–294.

Chapter 17

1. See Federal News Service, "There Is No Justice Without Freedom," *Washington Post*, Jan. 21, 2005, A24.

2. See, for example, Thomas Jefferson, "To James Madison" (Dec. 20, 1787), in Bernard E. Brown (ed.), *Great American Political Thinkers: Vol. I* (New York: Avon Books, 1983), 333–334.

3. Esther Kingston-Mann, "The Romance of Privatization: Historical Case Studies from England, Russia, and Kenya," paper prepared for presentation at the Changing Properties of Property Conference, Max Planck Institute for Social Anthropology, Halle, Germany, July 2–4, 2003, 2.

4. Kingston-Mann, "The Romance of Privatization," 4.

5. Kingston-Mann, "The Romance of Privatization," 1–2.

6. Si Kahn, "Silk and Satin," *We're Still Here*.

7. Irene Macauley, "Corporate Governance: Crown Charters to Dotcoms," Museum of American Financial History, Dec. 2004; see www.financialhistory.org/fh/2003/77-1.htm.

8. Macauley, "Corporate Governance."

9. Irene Macauley, Museum of American Financial History [www.financialhistory.org], Dec. 2004.

10. John Winthrop, "On Religion and Government," in Brown, *Great American Political Thinkers*, 15.

11. Winthrop, "On Religion and Government," 15.

12. Winthrop, "On Religion and Government," 16–17.

13. Thomas Paine, "Rights of Man, Part I," in Brown, *Great American Political Thinkers*, 142–143.

14. James Madison, "Federalist Papers, No. 51," in Brown, *Great American Political Thinkers*, 250–251.

15. Lee Drutman and Charlie Cray, *The People's Business* (San Francisco: Berrett-Koehler, 2004), 20–27.

Chapter 18
1. Si Kahn, "Abe Lincoln Walks Tonight" (Charlotte, N.C.: Joe Hill Music, 2005).

2. Abraham Lincoln, "The Gettysburg Address" (Nov. 19, 1863), in William A. McGeveran (ed. dir.), *World Almanac and Book of Facts* (New York: World Almanac Books, 2002), 538.

Chapter 19
1. Si Kahn, "Government on Horseback," *Signs of the Times* (Cambridge, Mass.: Rounder Records, 1994).

2. George Gilder, *Wealth and Poverty* (New York: Basic Books, 1981).

3. Gilder, *Wealth and Poverty*, 304–305.

4. Gilder, *Wealth and Poverty*, 304.

5. Gilder, *Wealth and Poverty*, 304.

6. Gilder, *Wealth and Poverty*, 304–305.

7. John Blake, "Dollar and the Gospel," *The Atlanta Journal/The Atlanta Constitution*, Mar. 5, 2000, G1.

8. See Ben Brandzel, Eli Pariser, and the MoveOn PAC team, www.moveon.org and www.moveonpac.org, Mar. 9, 2005.

9. David Frum, *What's Right: The New Conservative Majority and the Remaking of America* (New York: Basic Books, 1996), 99.

10. See Leslie Wayne, "Air Force at Unease in the Capital: Questions About the Boeing Scandal Just Won't Go Away," *New York Times*, Dec. 16, 2004, C1.

Chapter 20
1. "Survival Plan," *The NewsHour with Jim Lehrer*, July 15, 2003; posted on "Online Newsletter," http://pbs.org/newshour/bb/healthy/july-dec03/brazil_7-15.html.

2. Derber, *Regime Change Begins at Home*, 66–67.

3. David Sirota, "Debunking 'Centrism,'" *The Nation*, Jan. 3, 2005; see www.truthout.org/docs_05/printer_010305L.shtml.

4. Patricia Williams, *The Alchemy of Race and Rights* (Cambridge, Mass.: Harvard University Press, 1991), 164.

Chapter 21

1. From Audre Lorde, *Sister Outsider* (Trumansburg, N.Y.: Crossings Press, 1984), quoted in Johnetta Cole (ed.), *All American Women: Lines That Divide, Ties That Bind* (New York: Free Press, 1986), 28.

2. Howard W. French, "Workers Demand Union at Wal-Mart Supplier in China," *New York Times*, Dec. 15, 2004, A4.

3. Bakan, *The Corporation*, 27.

4. Si Kahn, "Jobs with Justice," *I'll Be There*.

5. James Surowiecki, "It Pays to Stay," *The New Yorker*, Dec. 13, 2004, 40.

6. Surowiecki, "It Pays to Stay," 40.

7. Surowiecki, "It Pays to Stay," 40.

Afterword

1. Si Kahn, "I Have Seen Freedom," *I Have Seen Freedom*.

2. Si Kahn, "Children of Poland," *In My Heart* (Hoofdorp, The Netherlands: Strictly Country Records, 1994).

3. Hannah Arendt, *The Origins of Totalitarianism* (New York: Meridian Books/World Publishing Co., 1958). Hannah Arendt, *Eichmann in Jerusalem: A Report on the Banality of Evil*, rev. ed. (New York: Penguin Books, 1994).

4. Si Kahn, "Generations," *I'll Be There*.

Bibliography

Anton, Anatole, Fisk, Milton, and Holmstrom, Nancy (eds.). *Not for Sale: In Defense of Public Goods.* Boulder, Colo.: Westview, 2000.

Arendt, Hannah. *On Revolution.* New York: Viking, 1965.

Bakan, Joel. *The Corporation: The Pathological Pursuit of Profit and Power.* New York: Free Press, 2004.

Bender, Ed. *A Contributing Influence: The Private-Prison Industry and Political Giving in the South.* Helena, Mont.: Institute on Money in State Politics, 2001.

Brown, Bernard E. (ed.). *Great American Political Thinkers. Vol. 1: Creating America: From Settlement to Mass Democracy.* New York: Avon Books, 1983.

"Captive Lives" [special issue], *Southern Changes,* Fall 2000, 22(3).

Coyle, Andrew, Campbell, Allison, and Neufeld, Rodney (eds.). *Capitalist Punishment: Prison Privatization and Human Rights.* Atlanta: Clarity, 2003.

Dahl, Robert A. *On Democracy.* New Haven, Conn.: Yale University Press, 2000.

Derber, Charles. *Regime Change Begins at Home: Freeing America from Corporate Rule.* San Francisco: Berrett-Koehler, 2004.

Drutman, Lee, and Cray, Charlie. *The People's Business: Controlling Corporations and Restoring Democracy.* San Francisco: Berrett-Koehler, 2004.

Farmer, Paul. *Pathologies of Power: Health, Human Rights, and the New War on the Poor.* Berkeley: University of California Press, 2005.

Faux, Jeff. *The Party's Not Over: A New Vision for the Democrats.* New York: Basic Books, 1996.

Friedman, Milton. *Capitalism and Freedom* (40th anniversary ed.). Chicago: University of Chicago Press, 2002.

Frum, David. *What's Right: The New Conservative Majority and the Remaking of America.* New York: Basic Books, 1996.

Gilder, George. *Wealth and Poverty.* New York: Basic Books, 1981.

Goodman, Amy, with Goodman, David. *The Exception to the Rulers: Exposing Oily Politicians, War Profiteers, and the Media That Love Them.* New York: Hyperion, 2004.

Hayek, F. A. *The Road to Serfdom.* Chicago: University of Chicago Press, 1994.

Hughes, Langston. *Selected Poems*. New York: Vintage, 1959.

Kahn, Si. *The Forest Service and Appalachia*. New York: John Hay Whitney Foundation, 1974.

Kahn, Si. *The Si Kahn Songbook*. Milwaukee, Wis.: Hal Leonard, 1990. Available at www.sikahn.com.

Kahn, Si. *Organizing: A Guide for Grassroots Leaders* (rev. ed.). Washington, D.C.: National Association of Social Workers Press, 1991.

Kahn, Si. *How People Get Power* (rev. ed.). Washington, D.C.: National Association of Social Workers Press, 1994.

Kamarck, Andrew M.. *Economics for the Twenty-First Century: The Economics of the Economist-Fox*. Aldershot, England: Ashgate, 2001.

Kamarck, Andrew M. *Economics As a Social Science: An Approach to Nonautistic Theory*. Ann Arbor: University of Michigan Press, 2003.

Kaye-Kantrowitz, Melanie. *The Issue Is Power: Essays on Women, Jews, Violence, and Resistance*. San Francisco: Aunt Lute Press, 1997.

Keillor, Garrison. *Homegrown Democrat: A Few Plain Thoughts from the Heart of America*. New York: Viking, 2004.

Kim, Jim Yong, Millen, Joyce V., Irwin, Alec, and Gershman, John (eds.). *Dying for Growth: Global Inequality and the Health of the Poor*. Monroe, Maine: Common Courage Press, 2000.

Kirp, David L. *Shakespeare, Einstein, and the Bottom Line: The Marketing of Higher Education*. Cambridge, Mass.: Harvard University Press, 2003.

Kivel, Paul. *You Call This a Democracy? Who Benefits, Who Pays, and Who Really Decides*. New York: Apex, 2004.

Kohn, Margaret. *Brave New Neighborhoods: The Privatization of Public Space*. New York: Routledge, 2004.

Korten, David C. *When Corporations Rule the World: Life After Capitalism* (2nd ed.). San Francisco: Berrett-Koehler and Bloomfield, Conn: Kumarian Press, 2001.

LeRoy, Greg. *The Great American Job Scam: Corporate Tax Dodging and the Myth of Job Creation*. San Francisco: Berrett-Koehler, 2005.

Macarov, David. *What the Market Does to People: Privatization, Globalization, and Poverty*. Atlanta: Clarity, 2003.

Mattera, Philip, and Khan, Mafruza, with LeRoy, Greg, and Davis, Kate. *Jail Breaks: Economic Development Subsidies Given to Private Prisons*. Washington, D.C.: Good Jobs First, 2001.

Mattera, Philip, Khan, Mafruza, and Nathan, Stephen. *Corrections Corporation of America: A Critical Look at Its First Twenty Years*. Charlotte, N.C.: Grassroots Leadership, 2003.

Minnich, Elizabeth. *Transforming Knowledge* (2nd ed.). Philadelphia: Temple, 2004.

Minow, Martha. *Partners, Not Rivals: Privatization and the Public Good*. Boston: Beacon, 2002.

Moyers, Bill. *Moyers on America: A Journalist and His Times*. New York: Free Press, 2004.

Nace, Ted. *Gangs of America: The Rise of Corporate Power and the Disabling of Democracy*. San Francisco: Berrett-Koehler, 2003.

O'Farrell, Sheila, Diehl, Kim, and Ellis, Robin. *Privatization Versus the Public Interest*. Charlotte, N.C.: Grassroots Leadership, 1997.

Oshinsky, David. *Worse Than Slavery: Parchman Farm and the Ordeal of Jim Crow Justice*. New York: Free Press, 1996.

"The Prison Issue." *Feminist Studies*, Summer 2004, 20(2).

Rawls, Tonyia, Brown, Natalie Bullock, and Glover, Danny. *The Private Prison Problem: Not Here, Not Anywhere* (DVD). Charlotte, N.C.: Grassroots Leadership, 2005.

Reiser, Bob, and Seeger, Pete. *Carry It On*. New York: Simon & Schuster, 1985.

Rosenthal, Marguerite G. *Prescription for Disaster: Commercializing Prison Health Care in South Carolina*. Charlotte, N.C.: Grassroots Leadership and South Carolina Fair Share, 2004.

Rosenthal, Marguerite G. *Prescription for Recovery: Keeping South Carolina's Prison Health Care Public and Making It Better*. Charlotte, N.C.: Grassroots Leadership and South Carolina Fair Share, 2004.

Sanger, M. Bryna. *The Welfare Marketplace: Privatization and Welfare Reform*. Washington, D.C.: Brookings Institution, 2003.

Sclar, Elliott D. *You Don't Always Get What You Pay For: The Economics of Privatization*. Ithaca, N.Y.: Cornell University Press, 2001.

Sclar, Elliott D. *Amtrak Privatization: The Route to Failure*. Washington, D.C.: Economic Policy Institute, 2003.

Shiva, Vandana. *Water Wars: Privatization, Pollution, and Profit*. Cambridge, Mass.: South End, 2002.

Singer, P. W. *Corporate Warriors: The Rise of the Privatized Military Industry*. Ithaca, N.Y.: Cornell University Press, 2003.

Soros, George. *The Crisis of Global Capitalism: Open Society Endangered.* New York: PublicAffairs, 1998.

Stelzter, Irwin. (ed.). *The Neocon Reader.* New York: Grove, 2004.

Sunstein, Cass R. *The Partial Constitution.* Cambridge, Mass.: Harvard University Press, 1993.

Tabarrok, Alexander. *Changing the Guard: Private Prisons and the Control of Crime.* Oakland, Calif.: The Independent Institute, 2003.

Thurow, Lester C. *The Future of Capitalism: How Today's Economic Forces Shape Tomorrow's World.* New York: Penguin, 1997.

Wills, Garry. *A Necessary Evil: A History of American Distrust of Government.* New York: Touchstone, 2002.

Wu, Chin-Tao. *Privatising Culture: Corporate Art Intervention Since the 1980s.* London: Verson, 2002.

Zinn, Howard. *A People's History of the United States.* New York: HarperCollins, 2003.

Index

Resources

Web Sites of Interest

Elizabeth Minnich: www.elizabethminnich.com. Elizabeth's book *Transforming Knowledge* can be ordered from this site.

Si Kahn: www.sikahn.com. Si's CDs and books can be ordered from this site, which also has a number of his songs available for free downloading.

Real People's Music: www.realpeoplesmusic.com. For Si Kahn concert and festival bookings, lectures, and residencies, as well as information about other progressive musicians and speakers.

Grassroots Leadership: www.grasssrootsleadership.org. Resources for people and organizations working on privatization, prison and criminal justice issues, plus a secure way to make tax-deductible contributions online to support the work of this progressive non-profit founded and directed by Si Kahn.

Si Kahn's Music

Most of the songs that appear in *The Fox in the Henhouse* are available on Si's CDs. The following CDs are currently available for purchase at www.sikahn.com and can also be ordered through your local independent bookstores and music stores. The songs shown in italics following each album description are included in this book.

BLOOD FROM STONES (Joe Hill Music 018, 2005**):** Si's newest CD, specially released to accompany *The Fox in the Henhouse*. Songs about the campaign to end private prisons and related issues, from the so-called "war on drugs" and the death penalty to immigration and violence against women. *Vann Plantation, There But For, Freedom Is a Funny Thing*.

WE'RE STILL HERE (Strictly Country SCR57, 2004**):** A tribute to the courage and persistence of working people everywhere. Recorded live in the Netherlands and released in 2004 on Si's sixtieth birthday. *When the War Is Done, We're Still Here, Hard Times, Silk and Satin*.

THREADS (double time music 010, 2002**):** A history of the mills, of the threads that link South and North, cotton field and cotton mill, field hand and mill hand, black and white, slave and free, immigrant and native-born. The story starts in 1846, when a young woman leaves her family farm in New Hampshire to go to work in the cotton mills of Lowell, Massachusetts (Si's father's hometown), and ends in a Moose Lodge somewhere in the South 110 years later, at the close of the Korean War. *Cotton Mill Blues*.

BEEN A LONG TIME (Sliced Bread 71202, 2000**):** Si's bluegrass album, with all-time great artists Pete Wernick, Charles Sawtelle, Laurie Lewis, Tom Rozum, Todd Philips, and Sally Van Meter.

COMPANION (Appleseed 1020, 1997**):** Love songs for Si's family, friends, and co-workers. Produced by and recorded with Si's longtime musical and personal friends, Grammy winners Cathy Fink and Marcy Marxer.

NEW WOOD (Philo 1168, 1994**):** Si's classic first CD (well, it was an LP back in 1975), remastered and rereleased. *Talking Politician*.

SIGNS OF THE TIMES (Rounder 4017, 1994**):** Si and the great John McCutcheon (also president of Si's American Federation of Musicians local) on tour together. Check out the wonderful harmony singing on *Here Is My Home*—it's the audience at Myers Park High School in Si's hometown of Charlotte. *Government on Horseback.*

IN MY HEART (Strictly Country SCR 33, 1993**):** Folk artists don't really have "hits" as the music industry understands them. But if they did, these would be Si's greatest hits. With twenty-four songs, the lowest price per song of any CD! *Children of Poland, Mississippi Summer, What Will I Leave.*

GOOD TIMES AND BEDTIMES (Rounder, 1993**):** Si is aware that, despite being a longtime union activist, when it comes to his children, he's management. Still, this CD takes the side of the kids when it comes to bedtime.

I HAVE SEEN FREEDOM (Flying Fish 578, 1991**):** Songs of family, community, work, hope, and freedom, recorded live with an audience of friends and family. *I Have Seen Freedom.*

I'LL BE THERE (Flying Fish 509, 1989**):** Labor music you can dance to—well, up to a point. With harmony singing from Ysaye Maria Barnwell of Sweet Honey in the Rock and Mary Chapin Carpenter. *Jobs with Justice, What Will I Leave, Generations.*

CARRY IT ON (Flying Fish 70104, 1987**):** Si joins Pete Seeger and Jane Sapp on twenty-one songs of the civil rights, labor, and women's movements, taken from the book of the same name by Pete Seeger and Bob Reiser. The songs you want to pass on to the next generations. A great gift for children, grandchildren, and great-grandchildren. *The Soup Song.*

About the Authors

S I KAHN has been organizing against privatization for the past ten years. The nonprofit organization he founded and directs, Grassroots Leadership, works to abolish for-profit private prisons, jails, and detention centers as a step toward establishing a system of justice that is truly just and humane.

Si began his social justice career forty years ago with the Student Nonviolent Coordinating Committee (SNCC), the student wing of the southern civil rights movement. In the 1970s he worked with the United Mine Workers of America on the Brookside strike in Harlan County, Kentucky, and with the Amalgamated Clothing and Textile Workers Union on the J. P. Stevens campaign.

A songwriter and performing artist as well as an organizer, Si has recorded fourteen albums of his original songs, plus a collection of traditional labor, civil rights, and women's songs with Pete Seeger and Jane Sapp. He has written two organizing handbooks, *How People Get Power and Organizing: A Guide for Grassroots Leaders*. He is the official poet laureate of the North Carolina AFL-CIO by unanimous vote of the convention in 1986, a member of the American Federation of Musicians and the National Writers Union.

E LIZABETH MINNICH has been thinking, speaking, and writing about privatization, inclusiveness, and excellence in education true to the values of democracy for more than thirty years. She has spoken and consulted at colleges, universities, philanthropic foundations, and academic professional associations throughout the United States and abroad.

Elizabeth has served as chair of the North Carolina Humanities Council and has held both faculty and administrative positions at institutions including Hollins College, Sarah Lawrence College, Barnard College, and the Union Institute and University's Graduate College of Interdisciplinary Arts and Sciences. She has participated in national projects on curriculum transformation, liberal arts education, diversity, democracy, and public life. She has been a Visiting Scholar at the Getty Research Institute for the History of Art and the Humanities, the Hartley Burr Alexander Chair for Public Philosophy at Scripps College, and the Whichard Visiting Distinguished Professor in the Humanities and Women's Studies at East Carolina University.

The first edition of her book *Transforming Knowledge* won the Frederic W. Ness Award for the best book on liberal learning from the AAC&U in 1990. The second edition, significantly updated and revised, with a major new introduction, was published in 2005. She is currently at work on a book, *Thinking Friends: A Propos Hannah Arendt, Thinking, Political, and Moral Considerations.* She has been called "one of the most insightful and compassionate feminist philosophers writing today" (Chandra Talpade Mohanty). Elizabeth is a member of the National Writers Union.

About Berrett-Koehler Publishers

BERRETT-KOEHLER is an independent publisher dedicated to an ambitious mission: Creating a World that Works for All.

We believe that to truly create a better world, action is needed at all levels—individual, organizational, and societal. At the individual level, our publications help people align their lives and work with their deepest values. At the organizational level, our publications promote progressive leadership and management practices, socially responsible approaches to business, and humane and effective organizations. At the societal level, our publications advance social and economic justice, shared prosperity, sustainable development, and new solutions to national and global issues.

We publish groundbreaking books focused on each of these levels. To further advance our commitment to positive change at the societal level, we have recently expanded our line of books in this area and are calling this expanded line "BK Currents."

A major theme of our publications is "Opening Up New Space." They challenge conventional thinking, introduce new points of view, and offer new alternatives for change. Their common quest is changing the underlying beliefs, mindsets, institutions, and structures that keep generating the same cycles of problems, no matter who our leaders are or what improvement programs we adopt.

We strive to practice what we preach—to operate our publishing company in line with the ideas in our books. At the core of our approach is *stewardship*, which we define as a deep sense of responsibility to administer the company for the benefit of all of our "stakeholder" groups: authors, customers, employees, investors, service providers, and the communities and environment around us. We seek to establish a partnering relationship with each stakeholder that is open, equitable, and collaborative.

We are gratified that thousands of readers, authors, and other friends of the company consider themselves to be part of the "BK Community." We hope that you, too, will join our community and connect with us through the ways described on our website at www.bkconnection.com.

This book is part of our BK Currents series. BK Currents titles advance social and economic justice by exploring the critical intersections between business and society. Offering a unique combination of thoughtful analysis and progressive alternatives, BK Currents titles promote positive change at the national and global levels. To find out more, visit www.bkcurrents.com.

Be Connected

Visit Our Website

Go to www.bkconnection.com to read exclusive previews and excerpts of new books, find detailed information on all Berrett-Koehler titles and authors, browse subject-area libraries of books, and get special discounts.

Subscribe to Our Free E-Newsletter

Be the first to hear about new publications, special discount offers, exclusive articles, news about bestsellers, and more! Get on the list for our free e-newsletter by going to www.bkconnection.com.

Participate in the Discussion

To see what others are saying about our books and post your own thoughts, check out our blogs at www.bkblogs.com.

Get Quantity Discounts

Berrett-Koehler books are available at quantity discounts for orders of ten or more copies. Please call us toll-free at (800) 929-2929 or email us at bkp.orders@aidcvt.com.

Host a Reading Group

For tips on how to form and carry on a book reading group in your workplace or community, see our website at www.bkconnection.com.

Join the BK Community

Thousands of readers of our books have become part of the "BK Community" by participating in events featuring our authors, reviewing draft manuscripts of forthcoming books, spreading the word about their favorite books, and supporting our publishing program in other ways. If you would like to join the BK Community, please contact us at bkcommunity@bkpub.com.